MILES & MILES

Miles W. Hewitt

Published by Limelight Classic Productions Ltd

MILES & MILES

A special thank you to a cast of individuals who assisted the author on his creative journey:

Irma Benitez-Llamas
Ann Bower
Sandy Chatwin
Brian Copeland
Elaine Cusack
Alan Dobson
Stephen Hetherington
Richard Hills
Teresa Magnowska
Patrick McCaughey
Paul Aiden Richardson
Jane Roberts-Morpeth
Mike Rogerson
Walter Ross
Calum Sherlock
Angie Stanger-Leathes
Ian Thomas
Humphrey Weightman
Erika Zaragoza

First published in Great Britain in 2018 by
Limelight Classic Productions Ltd
The Book House, 6 Beresford Road,
Whitley Bay, NE26 4RQ

ISBN 978-1-9999375-2-2

© Miles W. Hewitt 2018

All rights reserved. The moral rights of the author have been asserted. Some names and identifying details have been changed to protect the privacy of individuals. No part of this book may be reproduced or transmitted in any form or any means without written permission from the copyright holder, except by a reviewer who may quote brief passages in connection with review for an insertion in a newspaper, magazine, website or broadcast.

A catalogue record for this book is available from the British Library.

Set in 10.5/13 Melior
Design by www.simprimstudio.com

www.limelightclassics.com

Limelight

Author's Note

Miles & Miles is written from the heart, of the experiences and observations I hold dear and wish to share with you, my brothers and sisters of all nationalities. Throughout our voyage together you may unearth something in your subconscious which inspires you to step out, catch the scent and explore.

A fascination of travel began in the summer of my childhood. Our family of three motored in a Morris Minor from Morpeth in the North East of England to Saltdean on the South Coast to visit grandparents. It was a drive time of twelve hours down the A1 and in those days routed by way of every village and town. For the duration I slid around on the smooth bench seat in silence, enthralled by the ever-changing scenery. When we eventually clambered out of the car, a disparity in ambience was distinctly evident.

What stuck in my mind was the polarity of sound between the two locations. At the seaside on the English Channel, the rippling waves rolled ashore over the smooth round pebbles, poppling, purling and babbling. In contrast to the Northumberland coastline, where rolling breakers trimmed by frothy foam flopped onto the sandy shoreline with a ruffle, a splosh and a splash.

In fact everyday acoustics played a major part in my craving to uncover more from this exciting world. In class at school, I could hear the captivating boom of foghorns shrouded in mist on the River Tyne, evoking a desire to become a stowaway aboard a cargo ship and sail to exotic lands. At night in bed I would listen to the metallic pounding of locomotives on the East Coast Railway – spellbound by their lonesome whistle – as they thundered through the station *en route* to London or Edinburgh. I dreamt of being a hobo while scaling these monstrous metal structures and freighthopping to faraway cities.

My first recollection of an adventure was aboard a tricycle aged five. I furiously pedalled down the street and across the common to a holding pen for farm animals, climbed the gate and released a herd of pigs to freedom. They scattered into the market town. From the age of seven I camped in all weathers. At nine, hitchhiked hundreds of miles and by my early teen's wanderlust had taken me all over the country and into Europe. Sometimes accompanied by friends but frequently alone. At midnight on my 15th birthday I left home forever. With a student grant and part-time job I shared a bedsit in the attic of a terraced house in Jesmond, Newcastle upon Tyne, fifteen miles away from my parents.

Miles & Miles is a lifetime of travel split into two eras. *On the Road* represents the globetrotting years of 1973 to 1981 as a wide-eyed, curious young man with an open mind, hungry for new experiences. It began with an overland journey from England to Australia. After the return trip from Perth to London, a pause in travel was followed by a spell as an expedition driver in the Near East; thereafter my roaming moved on through the Soviet Union to the Far East.

In-between the two eras, I pursued a career in commerce which evolved into running my own company. Once this activity took me overseas, I reconnected with the world at large and the second era, *On Assignment* was underway.

Although cushioned by an executive lifestyle, the real soul and spirit of a now seasoned traveller remained as I journeyed into Latin America, China and Asia from 1998 to 2006, the events of which shaped the remainder of my life.

Travel rewards us with such largesse — the cobwebs of outdated dogma are blown away — our minds adopt a veritable understanding of culture and we develop an overriding appreciation of simplicity.

'Wherever you go, go with all your heart.' Confucius

Contents

ON THE ROAD

01	**Singapore Sling** ~ Singapore, 1974	1
02	**Feast of the East** ~ Turkey, Iran, 1973	12
03	**Land of the Pashtuns** ~ Afghanistan, Pakistan, 1973	31
04	**Wisdom of India** ~ India, Malay Peninsula, 1973	51
05	**Western Australia** ~ Perth, the Outback, Adelaide, 1974	67
06	**Indian Summer** ~ Tamil Nadu, Karnataka, Goa, Bombay and Germany, 1975	84
07	**Turkish Delight** ~ Istanbul, 1980	105
08	**Through the Iron Curtain** ~ Poland, Russia, 1981	114
09	**Quezon City** ~ The Philippines, Thailand, 1981	127

ON ASSIGNMENT

10	**El D.F. – Federal District of México** ~ Mexico City, 1998	145
11	**Pearls of the Orient** ~ Jakarta, Indonesia. Bangkok, Thailand. Taipei, Taiwan, 2000	158
12	**Shanghai** ~ Shanghai City, 2002	174
13	**City of Pandas** ~ Chengdu, Hainan Island, China, 2003	192
14	**State of Jalisco** ~ Guadalajara, Tlaquepaque and Ajijic, El Escálon, Mexico, 2004	208
15	**Neon Cities** ~ Tokyo, Hokkaido, Japan, Seoul, South Korea, 2005	230
16	**Viva Mexico** ~ Puerto Vallarta, Puebla, The Silver Cities and Michoacán, Guadalajara, 2005	243
17	**Pura Vida** ~ New York, Costa Rica, 2006	262

MILES & MILES

On The Road

01 Singapore Sling

'To move, to breathe, to fly, to float, to gain all while you give, to roam the roads of lands remote, to travel is to live.'
HANS CHRISTIAN ANDERSON

Singapore 1974

THE DOOR BURST OPEN WITH A FLURRY OF STACCATO ORIENTAL voices as I stirred from my dreams, both arms gripped by strong silent men dragging me naked from my cosy bed. They held me firm as their dapper superior quietly strode into the room brandishing a wicked smirk. In a brisk, authoritative, flawless English accent he introduced himself as 'Fan' slowly approaching my person – standing too close for comfort – invading my personal space while discharging a rancid stench of fermented fish.

'Good evening sir, where is she?' He enquired politely.

'Who?' I blurted.

I could feel the colour drain from my face and a panic descend in its place.

'Who?' He questioned, breathing that horrid smell into my face.

His henchmen tightened their grip.

'The lady you are sleeping with English man!'

'Yukari, my girlfriend?' I spluttered.

He backed away from my inner zone gently stroking his chin and pondering his next move before sharply swivelling his head to meet my eyes with his piercing gaze.

'Where is she now, my friend?'

'At work and not home until late.' I gasped.

His narrow intelligent eyes glanced towards the window and slowly retraced their path.

'Please, what is the problem Fan? She is a gentle soul.'

His glacial stare evaporated. 'Enjoy your time in Singapore English man, we will return.' He signalled to the silent men to release me.

They left quietly as if gliding on air. I stood motionless in my naked state, listening to the late evening chatter from the night market below fused with the high-pitch whine of a moped whizzing past. I tried to understand my position and grab hold of reason. My girlfriend was a mix of Malay and Japanese whom I had met three months earlier. Our home was a compact first floor room above Ma's dumpling cafe in the heart of Chinatown. Yukari worked downtown Singapore as a nightclub hostess in a notorious area of the dockside. Her primary role was to serve cocktails and chat to the clients. Yukari was a pretty girl with a wide smile and sharp wit characterised by an outstanding mane of black-blue shiny flowing hair half the length of her demure stature and sometimes elegantly pleated.

I rushed into my clothes, grabbed our passports and money before flying out of the door and hailing a bright yellow city cab. I sat back panting and flushed as we weaved our way through the narrow streets to the Paddle Club. Nodding at the dark-suited security men dotted around the dazzling neon entrance, in recognition as always, they waved me through the heavy crimson curtains into the bar area. Yukari was talking with some English sailors at the far end of the room, serving brightly coloured cocktails in tall stemmed glasses which I remembered as being her favourite tipple, Singapore Sling. A national drink created in 1915 at the renowned Raffles Hotel by bartender – Ngiam Tong Boon. Made from a gin base with pineapple juice, grenadine, a dash of lime and Dom Benedictine. It glows with a pretty pink hue and was designed with the ladies in mind.

The Chinese barman, Hon Sang, caught my eye and smiled, promptly pouring me a much-needed cold beer. Clutching the frosted glass and holding it to my temple as a brief respite from the humidity of the night, I gulped the chilled liquid refreshing my parched throat and steadying my nerve. Yukari glanced in my direction and our eyes met. Her expression was one of concern as she rushed over and held my head in her warm silky hands.

'What's the problem my darling?' she spoke rapidly noting my worried look. I related the earlier incident in finite detail, detecting a hint of recognition in her countenance when I mentioned the name, 'Fan.'

'I finish in an hour my darling, we cannot go to our place tonight. We'll travel to Malacca and stay with my family which will give us time to think.'

Feeling more relaxed, I ordered another cold beer. My mind drifted back to the first day I met Yukari when she flashed past in a taxi waving frantically from the cab window as I walked along Orchard Road. It screeched to a halt and I ran over thinking it was someone I must have known. The traffic bunched up behind the stationary vehicle and I jumped into the car as it drove off towards the Indian Quarter. She thought I was someone else, making the three of us, including the driver laugh all the way to the picturesque Sakya Muni Buddha Gaya Temple. We had coffee nearby and talked non-stop throughout the day and most of the night to the soundtrack of *Born Free* by Matt Monro, a popular song in the Far East at the time.

I had been on the road for nearly two years and my appearance was bedraggled. A few days after meeting Yukari she wanted to smarten me up and insisted upon paying for a new outfit. We went on a shopping spree and I felt obliged and thankful to accept her clothing choice as she converted my image to a modern day colonial with cream flannels, a Hawaiian shirt and a straw Panama hat.

The original plan after leaving Australia, where I worked for eight months to replenish my travel funds, had been to spend one week in Singapore. I would then take a train through Malaysia up to the island of Penang and catch a boat to South India but this unexpected romance had anchored me to Singapore.

My daydreaming abruptly switched to reality when Yukari returned to the bar area having changed from her work attire looking radiant as always and ready to leave the club. She appeared emotionally in control and pensive in her thoughts. Yukari smiled her beautiful sunshine smile while wrapping her elegant fingers around my hand and looking into my eyes in that meaningful way.

'My love, together we will fight them,' she said.

'Fight them?' I responded shakily.

In my confused state the panic returned.

'Who are they my darling, what's it all about?' I stuttered.

'I will explain on the way, let's go,' she said, walking towards the exit.

I began to suspect that Fan misunderstood the nature of our relationship and was of the opinion I hired her as a working girl. Operating as an independent sex worker would be considered a violation within the rules of a controlling Triad syndicate. My mind imagined the worst scenario as to the punishment for such a breach. We left the club quickly and took our regular cab whose driver, Sang, was a friend. We gushed out an explanation relating to the night's events but no sooner had we pulled away onto Victoria Street when Sang spotted a black Mercedes following close behind.

'Get your heads down now we are being tailed,' he shrieked, slamming his foot down hard on the accelerator while zipping in and out of the late night traffic. He knew the area inside out but it still took him an eternal fifteen minutes to lose them. As we glided into a side street to reappraise our earlier decision, I turned to Yukari.

'What do we do now? Who are they? What do they want? Are they organised crime? Is it the Triad? What connection do you have with them? Do they think you are working for yourself?' I asked impatiently.

'One moment Miles.' She smiled warmly and lightly caressed my cheek.

Yukari spoke to Sang at length in her native Malay before we drove out of the street and onto the bypass at a more gentle speed as he talked hurriedly on the radio. Soon after, we stopped again in a pretty avenue lined by mature plane trees and swapped to a different cab driven by Han who had been good enough to pick up some hot food for our onward journey.

Yukari relaxed while gracefully stripping meat from a chicken leg and began to expound how the problem may have originated. As I suspected it was the Triad, transnational organised crime who were in charge of all things illegal in Singapore. Yukari had been approached in the recent past by a gang member and turned down their seedy offers. She was also aware of others who had experienced problems with the Triad and the high price they paid for stepping out of line, in some cases with their lives. She was not afraid and felt angry they should disrupt our day-to-day lives.

I pointed out, 'We alone cannot fight this huge violent animal my love. We are guilty until proven innocent in their eyes.'

'We will see,' she said.

We travelled throughout the night, across the Malay border and into the southern state of Malacca to the sound of Matt Monro singing *Born Free* on the radio as Yukari slept in my arms.

At daybreak we rolled to a stop at a jungle clearing alongside a blue-green lagoon bordered by stilted wooded houses. As we stepped out of the car, I stared up in silent wonderment at the golden orange sky peppered with the pinks, yellows and reds of tumbling cockatoos and gliding parrots. The air was still, warm and humid with a light smell of smouldering brushwood. We thanked Han before quietly walking to the end of the village and climbing some creaking wooden steps into a traditional single storey Malay dwelling, coloured green and mauve. We crept into the bedroom, lay down on the lumpy mattress and fell into a deep sleep.

A few hours later Yukari's mum, Aisha, tapped gently on the door and brought in two terracotta pots of sweet milky tea on a carved wooden tray, giving us both a welcome hug. I had met Aisha several times during her visits to Yukari in Singapore but it was my first time at the family home. We tried to go back to sleep but the persistent shrill call of a cockerel kept us awake. Yukari leapt out of bed and I remained stretched out thinking what was best for this lovely family given the circumstances.

'How did I find myself in this position?' I pondered and my thoughts wandered back to the day I left Newcastle upon Tyne in England. My father had dropped me outside the city at Birtley roundabout to travel overland to Australia with £400 in my pocket and a small bag containing one change of clothing. I had intended to make this trip with friends as travel companions but during the planning process they peeled away one by one, so I decided to travel solo. I distinctly recall that Tuesday morning in late March when heavy rain fell from the slate-grey sky and made everyone miserable. I began hitchhiking on the south side of the A1 as the downpour plinked into puddles and the roofs of cars danced with spray. Within 30 minutes, a welcome Mercedes pulled alongside driven by a stylish elderly lady. I jumped into the warm luxurious car with a rich smell from the red leather and we cruised in comfort down to Stamford in Lincolnshire.

Sunlight pierced the white cumulus as we slowed to a stop outside the Lady Ann Hotel at the top of the town. I gave Mary an energetic wave as she sped away. My accommodation that night was a hay barn next to Wing Hall in the village of Wing. The kindness of Mrs Page, the farmer's wife who invited me into the farmhouse at first light and cooked four fried eggs with a tin mug of hot tea was very much appreciated. She gave me a tearful goodbye as I climbed aboard the tractor and Mr Page dropped me at the nearest junction. Mrs Page's kindness reminded me of Aisha and my thoughts flowed back to Malaysia as I crawled out of the bed and lingered under a cool shower.

Aisha allocated some household chores to both of us. Yukari would make breakfast while I assisted her arthritic grandfather, Samad, with his daily routine. Aisha handed me a clay pipe, two small leather pouches and a box of matches to prepare the tobacco and hashish mix for his morning smoke. It had been a long time since I handled a clay pipe so it took me a while to get it operational. Once it was smouldering, I placed it gently into Samad's mouth and as it curled down his chin he lifted his bony hand to hold the stem and began puffing away happily, inhaling the smoke and hissing it out through his hairy nostrils. I liked the old man, he seldom spoke but always smiled and had a warm sincere aura about him. For the next few days I became his personal assistant and my ability to create a good smoke became evident as his eyes twinkled whenever I walked into the living room.

Yukari and Aisha were chattering next to the blackened stove while preparing nasi lemak; Malaysia's national dish of basmati rice cooked in coconut milk with a pandan leaf torn into strips and tied in a knot. This leaf added a vanilla flavour and the fragrant rice was served with a boiled egg, dried anchovies and peanuts fried in oil. There was no mention of why we were there, no discussion or reason, it was an everyday family gathering within the confines of their own wooden home.

In the back garden, golden spangled and blue breasted hens fluffed out their feathers as they strutted and squawked among the black spotted and ginger haired pigs. These charismatic beasts made me laugh. Koko, the heaviest hog was the stubborn one, always in pole position with Tami and Miki following his every move. They loitered in front of the kitchen making the odd grunt from their muddy snouts held high to catch the essence of bubbling nasi lemak. Their curious eyes and wiggling snouts could only be understood as, 'Give me food.' After eating, they scratched their backs up and down the palm trees before slumbering in the shade next to a white tethered goat. The hens followed suit by assembling their pecking order to roost on top of the sleeping sows and creating a stereotypical image of a picturesque farmstead.

In this rural family environment, I felt so relaxed and happy but the turmoil was never far from my mind and the more I thought about the situation, the more it made sense for me to leave Singapore. It was a quick and easy solution to the problem but Yukari and I were in love and the family cared for me as one of their own. Although it was three months since my arrival in Singapore from Western Australia, in emotional terms it was far longer.

Little did I know of my prolonged stay when I boarded the MV Eastern Queen for the 2,400 miles sailing from the port city of Fremantle. The journey took one week in the rusty vessel of character chugging over the Indian Ocean and across the equator without air conditioning. A tasteless diet of mushed vegetables à *la diesel* was included in the price of £75 for a one way ticket in a four berth cabin.

I had made friends among the crew from an earlier sailing during the previous year and they invited me to the crow's nest to sample their homemade hooch. The metal ladder up to the platform at the top of the masthead swayed from side to side with the movement of the ship as we slowly ascended to this lofty position. Once in the crow's nest, the viewpoint below made the sixty ton vessel seem like a toy. It took me until 4 a.m. to pluck up the courage to climb down the ladder. When I made it onto the main deck two security guards took me to an office and demanded an explanation. Not wanting to get the crew in trouble I invented a silly story. As a result, on arrival in Singapore, I was escorted by two Singaporean officials to a windowless room for further questioning followed by a strip search. Soon after I was given the all clear but before they allowed me entry I had to endure an enforced haircut by a military barber who took the easy route and shaved it bald. It was a mandatory requirement to have short hair in Singapore, if it grew over the collar, the traveller was banned from entry. A city state which was a great deal more disciplined than its neighbours, Indonesia and Malaysia.

A coconut aroma filled the room and my thoughts quickly returned to the present as Aisha proceeded to serve up the piping hot nasi lemak. We enjoyed her beautiful food accompanied by laughter and banter from the family unit. Once the melee had died down, Aisha, Yukari and I moved to the balcony to discuss the Triad situation while we sipped our teh tarik, hot milky tea. To my surprise, Aisha who was smaller again than Yukari and bordering on the feeble, held my hand gently but made a firm statement.

'We will fight them together,' nodding her head with certainty.

The terror returned and I had a vision of us all hanging upside down in a lifeless state from the nearest cheesewood tree.

As Yukari and Aisha continued to speak to each other in Malay at length, my mind strayed back to Wing Hall and my onward journey to Dover. I took a late night ferry over the English Channel to Calais and hitchhiked from the dockside to Ostend where I caught a train to Paris and boarded the Orient Express to Istanbul. Something was tugging at my shirt and I realised it was Yukari waking me from my dreamy state. Preparing the pipe for the old man had sent me into a trance-like stupor.

'Well,' I slurred, 'What have you decided? Please don't say, let's fight! They will kill us all,' I begged.

Despite my viewpoint, both of them were determined to stand up to the Triad. They possessed an irrefutable mindset that a principled stance would be morally correct.

'I'm going to remove the problem from our lives by leaving the country. It's my duty to protect the family.' I stated.

Yukari burst into tears and Aisha's frail hands clenched mine - her pleading eyes spoke volumes - she wanted me to be her son-in-law. I was stubborn but clear in my mind this was a quick and easy solution. I had no choice. Yukari would be safe as long as she remained in Malacca. I would travel up through Malaysia to the island of Penang and take a boat to Madras (Chennai), India, as previously planned, prior to our unexpected romance. I would return to Singapore on my way to Australia the following year.

Three days later, Aisha hired a minibus to take the whole family of eighteen and accompany me to the nearest railway station in Tampin, thirty miles from the village. The entire journey was in complete silence except for a repetitive squeak from the windscreen wipers and the pitter-patter of raindrops on the roof. As we motored into the town Yukari held me tight, kissed me softly and whispered, 'Malaysia cry for you today because you leave.'

The porter blew his whistle and the train slowly creaked out of the station. Clutching my still warm prepared food, lucky charms and goodwill cards I wept silently as their solemn outlines disappeared from view. My mind retained a vivid memory of the whole family standing motionless on the platform with their heads bowed in the pouring rain. I wandered, feeling lost and lonely into the second class coach to be met with noisy catcalls from some of the passengers, 'Go home Yankee!' They shouted. As I reached the far end of the carriage next to the freight car the verbal abuse became a chorus. I span round to address the rowdy crowd and shrieked, 'I'm not a Yankee! I'm British.' On the advice of the train guard I slept in the locked cargo section on top of boxes of tiny squeaking new born chicks.

The reaction of the local people was understandable given the fact that the Vietnam War was going through its final stages during 1974 and tensions were running high. I remember the gravelly voice and fuzzy images of Richard Nixon on the black and white TV sets in the communal areas and cafés throughout the villages and towns.

The train gently trundled through the jungle into the darkness of that night. I lay awake thinking of Yukari. Why did I not take her with me? Did I want to break up the family unit? Was I too young? Singapore had a future, could I live there? In 1974, Benjamin Henry Sheaves was the second president after the country had achieved independence from Great Britain in 1966 which had given the nation a fresh confidence and a new dawn.

After one week and before I boarded the ferry to Madras, I could not bear it any longer and made a call from Georgetown in Penang to Malacca and Aisha answered the phone. Yukari had stayed with her family and would not be going back to Singapore. She had secured a job running an art gallery in Klebang, a town close the village, while the owner took a six month break to have her baby. I felt a great deal more relaxed knowing Yukari was safe and secure. To this day whenever I hear Matt Monro sing *Born Free*, my heart and soul return to Singapore.

02 Feast of the East

'Travel is fatal to prejudice, bigotry and narrow-mindedness..."
MARK TWAIN

Turkey 1973

THE FABLED ORIENT EXPRESS EVOLVED FROM ITS FORMER GLORY AND storybook characteristic to an everyday rail service by the 1970s but towards the end of the decade this route would be terminated. I was about to embark on an overland journey through Europe and Asia to Western Australia. At the Gare de l'Est, I boarded the Orient Express for the three day journey from Paris to Istanbul covering 1,700 miles.

The concept of visiting the Mystic East became popular when The Beatles visited India in 1968 and the number of young people hitting the road from Western Europe increased dramatically. We had many reasons for going to the East – spiritual enlightenment – escaping a conventional lifestyle or simply to see the world. Together we shared a sense of adventure and the largest contingent by far were the pot smoking hippies.

Although I opted to travel by public transport, a popular mode of transit was the legendary Magic Bus. A generic term used for independent people driving a variety of vehicles from pickups to London double-deckers who advertised their low-cost tickets in the underground press. A great number of these vehicles never completed the journey there or back. It was, after all, a distance of over 6,000 miles in each direction on mostly rough roads over high mountain passes and through scorching deserts.

The two-tone cream and green carriages rolled to a stop at the platform from which the first Orient Express departed on October 4th 1883. Within twenty minutes it was rattling through the suburbs of Paris. I shared a cramped couchette with two Englishmen whose destination was Erzurum, a city on the eastern side of Turkey and close to the Iranian border.

Andrew was a tall, sturdily-built hippy in his late twenties with swept back shoulder length hair and a black beard crowned by his trademark bobble-less hat. A confident and experienced traveller having toured Africa. This was his first trip to Asia. He acquired his travel funds working as a labourer for a road-building company and no doubt where his penchant for practical jokes must have originated. He was far from being a rough diamond, born into a middle-class family from Caterham in Surrey with a career in medicine, however, his wanderlust took precedence.

Martin, his companion and apprentice traveller was adjusting to life on the road and who was the subject of Andrew's wisecracks. A young man of small stature with pasty skin heavily mottled by acne. Corkscrew-shaped curls of ginger hair squiggled ringlets and obscured his bulging eyes like an Old English sheepdog. A quiet and reserved type from Lincoln who preferred to follow rather than lead. He had spent one year as a forklift driver in a sauce factory to finance his quest to see the world.

The following morning the train arrived in Munich but the departure time was not until 10 p.m. As the delay was broadcast, Andrew's eyes sparkled, 'Let's go to the world-famous Hofbräuhaus. I went there for my brother's stag night. It's a gigantic brewery which hosts the Munich Beer Festival every October. It opened way back in 1589 and nothing has changed.' Martin and I grinned and nodded our heads.

The beer hall at lunchtime was packed with over 1000 raucous Germans and a further 400 in the beer garden. The mob sat bunched together, side by side, on long wooden tables drinking cloudy wheat beer from two litre steins.

Black, pink and white sausages on wooden platters, bowls of sauerkraut and mild mustard were scattered over the tables. In the centre of this melee played a German oompah band in traditional costume blasting out nationalistic tunes to the delight of their supportive audience. Lots of laughter in the big party as overflowing earthenware jugs were deftly positioned in front of us to swig with foamy mouths as we sang the chorus. After my fourth visit to the bathroom, I returned to find Martin standing on the table among red-faced Germans stomping their feet and swinging their dripping flagons as they bellowed out their favourite songs.

'Get up here you wimps,' Martin shouted down at us with swashbuckling bravado.

Andrew managed to drench two sausage eating Australians as he scaled the table and I followed by standing in their food. They gave a bleary-eyed smile. When a man fell of the table, I briefly sobered up and noticed it was 9.30 p.m. The Orient Express was due to leave at 10 p.m. and the walk from the station had taken twenty-five minutes.

'Let's go!' I screamed over the racket frantically pointing at my wrist.

We staggered out into the cold night air and proceeded to walk in the wrong direction.

'Wo ist der Bahnhof,' mumbled Andrew to several German pedestrians who avoided eye contact and steered clear of his unsteady demeanour.

Our passports, tickets and rucksacks were on-board and we now had fifteen minutes. Martin hailed a passing taxi which sped to the station. We ran through the gate over the bridge and just as they blew the whistle we clambered aboard the now moving train.

'That was a close call,' said Andrew with an embarrassed smile as we puffed and panted to catch our breath.

The next prolonged stop was Sofia, the capital of Bulgaria, which was part of the Soviet Union. We wandered into the sombre city on a drab drizzly Monday morning stalked by the grey dreary buildings among droves of cheerless people in dark winter clothing staring vacantly at the glistening pockmarked pavements. We were told of a beautiful side to this ancient metropolis but on this particular day it was grim.

When the Orient Express finally hissed to a stop in Istanbul, the pervading Asian aura was a completely new experience. We set foot amongst the hustle and bustle of Haydarpasa, the busiest railway station in the Middle East. A splendid building of textured sandstone flanked by circular turrets with conical shaped roofs. Haydarpasa is perched on an embankment overlooking the Bosphorus – the waterway that connects the Black Sea to the Sea of Marmara – it separates European Turkey from Asian Turkey. On the ferry, an English speaking Turk enthused about a new bridge being constructed called the Bosphorus, to be completed in six months. It would have the fourth-longest suspension span in the world and connect the East to the West.

From the dockside we criss-crossed the lively city, dodging the wide and gaudy 1950s American cars which crammed into the narrow streets. They honked their horns and jostled for position with the trams, trucks, handcarts, bicycles and mopeds. The congested pavements spilled people into the road filling the gaps in the traffic. It made for an eclectic hullabaloo. Andrew's self-confidence was a guiding light in this strange environment for Martin and I so we followed his every move and mimicked his style. He strode through the vibrant city with his head held high and slapped the bonnets of slow moving cars as we manoeuvred our way over the busy avenues. In the bazaar, he bargained ferociously for our leather money belts to a tenth of the initial price and even managed a three for two deal with glasses of tea. Our dependence on Andrew was gradually replaced by our own conviction. By the end of the first week the three amigos had bonded and I decided to travel with them to Erzurum.

Up a cobbled cul-de-sac on Divan Yolu Street, which formed part of the Imperial Road from Rome to Constantinople, we found lodgings in a quirky pension. Our room was cheap, clean, centrally located and close to the Blue Mosque. There was a tiny communal washbasin at the end of a dark corridor where we stood in line and waited to perform our morning ablutions. The famous Pudding Shop was close by in a district called Sultanahmet. It sold sweets and yoghurt but its main role was a venue where travellers acquired vital information from those returning from India and Afghanistan.

After the second day touring the city we arrived at the pension to collect the room key. It was attached to a piece of wood the size and shape of a tennis ball engraved with number twenty-three. They were stored together in one box. After scratching around inside the container, we failed to locate our key. The elderly night porter sleepily looked up from his desk, 'All key open all door.'

A quirky teahouse with no name at the top of a narrow alley became our local hostelry and we connected with the owner, Kaleb, who sold bottled beers and kebabs. Andrew wanted to acquire a sheepskin coat of Afghan origin which was popular with hippies. He made a deal with Kaleb's uncle for a striking version of the garment, embroidered with gold zigzags, from Kandahar in Afghanistan. However, there were several problems with the tailoring. The sleeves were too short and the coat too long. The lengthy tassels acted in the same way as a truck's wheel fringe and sprayed water up his back. It also exuded a horrendous pong of dead animal.

Kaleb suggested we visit the Sultan Ahmed Mosque, 'The breathtaking symmetry and kaleidoscope of colour is an experience you will never forget.'

The Blue Mosque was built in 1609 and known as such due to the 20,000 blue ceramic tiles which adorn the ceiling. Entry for non-Muslims was free but we had to avoid prayer time, use the entrance to the west and take our shoes off at the door. The divine element of this fine Mosque was a meaningful introduction to both Islam and Islamic architecture. There is one main dome, eight secondary domes, six minarets and over 200 stained glass windows.

Before leaving Istanbul for Ankara we visited one of the oldest public Turkish baths in the city, Hammam Cemberlitas, built in 1584. The main chamber was capped by a high domed ceiling with ventilation holes directly above a hot marble platform known as the 'belly stone.' Shafts of sunlight streaked through these vents and illuminated the hot steamy atmosphere. People rested or took massages from attendants who exfoliated the skin with an abrasive mitt. As a treatment for his acne Martin elected to have a rub down but as the pummelling got underway he writhed in agony. The potbellied masseur tossed him around like a butcher handling a pig carcass and the exfoliation which followed reminded me of a fishmonger descaling a fish. The process produced an array of squeals, grunts and strange cracking sounds. Andrew and I sat in the corner in silent amusement. Feeling pristine and relaxed, apart from Martin whose deportment seemed a little shaky, we left this ancient building and poured into the early evening rush hour.

On Galata Bridge, a floating structure built on connecting pontoons, we walked between rows of fishermen and ate white fish sandwiches from a street cart. We stood quietly as the sun set over the Golden Horn, a trading harbour from the Byzantine period and our final image of Istanbul.

The following day, it took the overcrowded bus seventeen laborious hours to complete the 300 miles from Istanbul to Ankara. The rickety vehicle broke down twice, once in Istanbul and again on the open road. The driver managed to patch up the faults with help from two of the passengers and a roll of masking tape. Martin and I would constantly bicker as to who sat next to Andrew and his insufferably smelly coat.

In the toilets at the central bus station in Ankara I forgot to put a coin in the dish and as a result, a greasy lump of phlegm landed on my neck as retribution from the attendant.

We changed to an almost empty overnight coach from Ankara to Samsun, a port on the Black Sea.

As soon as we stepped into the crisp, clear and sunny morning I found myself the subject of intense scrutiny by the locals. Everywhere I walked I was surrounded by an assemblage who would occasionally stretch out a hand and touch me to see if I was real. I assumed they were curious because unlike my fellow travellers I had fair hair and blue eyes.

No tourism existed in Samsun and few foreigners visited the town. Martin and Andrew found it amusing while they roamed free of inquisitive spectators. It was March, below freezing and children were running around the streets in bare feet. I huddled next to the potbelly stoves in cafés drinking hot tea to stay warm but always encircled by a gaggle of onlookers.

Samsun was a twenty-four hour stopover on our way to Trabzon, 200 miles to the east, also located on the Black Sea and part of the Silk Road close to the borders with Georgia, Armenia and Iran. We found Trabzon a more relaxing place after the industrious melee of Ankara and the unwarranted attention in Samsun. We stayed downtown in a squalid room behind Uzun Sokak Street and close to Ataturk Square where the local population were outnumbered by students. Trabzon had one of the largest universities in Turkey.

This area was famous throughout the country for its anchovies, little silvery fish from the Black Sea referred to as hamsi. The entire cuisine of Northern Turkey, especially in winter, is devoted to hamsi and it formed part of our regular diet during our stay in this province.

One morning I wandered into Ataturk Alani Square to find a hot stove by which to warm my frozen hands, take some tea and observe the local people. In a side street café, I met an older Armenian gentleman by the name of Naak, born in Los Angeles to Armenian parents. His mother and father had emigrated to the USA during a period of political instability.

Naak told me, 'Historically, Trabzon is known as having been the place where thousands of innocent people died during the Armenian genocide of 1915.'

He pointed to a recent Turkish newspaper article he was reading which headlined, 'Turkey has recalled its ambassador to France in protest over the new Genocide Monument erected in Marseille.'

The plaque had read, 'To the memory of the 1.5 million Armenian victims of the genocide.'

'The Turkish government refuse to accept the term, genocide,' he said.

Andrew, Martin and I left the city for a walking weekend near Lake Uzungol in the district of Cay Kara. Situated on an elevated plain 1,000 metres above sea level where they grow hazelnuts, tobacco and tea. A local family accommodated us in their bungalow made of blood-red timbers with a pink pantile roof. One of many that were dotted around an undulating green countryside similar to the Lake District in Northern England. For breakfast we ate muhlama, a type of porridge in which cornmeal is mixed with homemade butter and sheep's cheese.

There were roe deer grazing in the pastures below as we trekked up the mountains and birds of prey followed us through the green valleys. On the second day, crossing a field, we heard a thunder of hooves as three angry goats charged our way. We sprinted to the nearest dry stone wall with these horned beasts in close pursuit and scrambled over to make our escape. Andrew fell and slid head first through a cow pat down a grassy knoll and into more animal faeces. By the time we arrived at the cottage, he reeked, and had to throw away some of his clothing before he was allowed into the kitchen. The landlady served a hearty concoction of black cabbage, carrots and potatoes accompanied by the ubiquitous hamsi.

After our visit into the countryside, we travelled back into Trabzon at first light and boarded a vintage bus for the full day's journey up and over the dark green mountain peaks to Erzurum. A city located on a plateau 2,000 metres above sea level. As we ascended the massif, we began to shiver in our seats and arrived at the windy bus station into a freezing -7 ºC, with a wind chill factor that made it feel a lot colder. The skies were grey, a white mist lurked and the air felt damp as we walked into the centre looking for accommodation. Martin and I were perishing as opposed to Andrew who was snug and comfy in his Afghan coat.

We hired a first floor room in the market square next to a teahouse which served cag kebab – marinated chunks of lamb – impaled on a horizontal rotating spit over glowing charcoal. In the café, sipping glasses of hot tea in the aromatic smoky warmth from the sizzling fire, we met Zorro. A lively character from Eritrea who dealt in black amber, referred to as oltu, and regarded as semi-precious. According to Zorro, there were two places in the world where oltu is found, Turkey and Russia, and Erzurum produced the best grade. He was a tiny guy with a big personality who in a previous life had been the captain of a merchant vessel sailing all over the world. His intense hazel eyes blinked owlishly from under a shock of jet-black hair which resembled a bearskin hat. When in Erzurum he stayed with Sayet, a friend who lived in a traditional Anatolian house on the edge of town. Sayet used his home as a venue to host local folk bands and Zorro would take us there later to listen to an Armenian folk group.

As Zorro pointed out, 'It's mild for the time of year as it can drop to -30ºC during the winter months. Last year, a cat froze to death in mid-air when it jumped from one roof to another.'

I wore most of my clothing before we ventured outside into the frosty night air and travelled by local bus to the entertainment venue. The external structure of Sayet's house was constructed of elaborately decorated willow and pine and designed with a pleasing arrangement of courtyards, balconies and open spaces. Inside, wide sumptuous timber panelled rooms with low ceilings were carpeted by deep crimson rugs and plump wine red cushions were scattered next to stubby wooden tables.

Sayet was a small, charismatic, elderly Armenian with bright beady eyes buried into a dark brown leathery skin. His frame was slightly stooped and he walked with a distinctive limp. In this area of Turkey we had been told alcohol was difficult to obtain so we had adopted a mindset of abstention. I was due in Iran and Afghanistan soon so it made sense to make the necessary adjustment. As we gathered in the main chamber and sat amongst the scatter cushions, close as possible to the potbellied stove, Sayet hobbled into the room wearing a mischievous grin and lugging a metal bucket full of beer bottles. We cheered at this unexpected luxury. He produced a wooden chillum, wrapped at the base with a wet handkerchief, which he fired up with a blow torch. (A chillum is a short ice cream cone shaped pipe used for smoking cannabis). Plumes of blue smoke and a pungent aroma of burning hashish pervaded the room. Andrew was in his element. When Martin coughed, the contents of the chillum singed his ringlets much to the amusement of Zorro who dampened the smouldering thatch by throwing a sopping wet rag over his head.

The Armenian folk band consisted of eight men with an assortment of stringed instruments, a small drum and a type of flute, none of which I had ever seen before. For the next few hours we were mesmerized by their extraordinary Arabic sound. The ale continued to flow as did the chillum well after the folk band had stopped playing. We slept where we sat and awakened at 6 a.m. by the cockerel crowing. Sayet made some tea and took us back into town on his horse and cart.

A few days later, Zorro and I accompanied Andrew and Martin to the bus station to begin the first leg of their return journey of 550 miles to Mersin on the Turkish Mediterranean coast. It would take four days. The three amigos had become brothers in arms having travelled overland from Paris to Erzurum. We had experienced so much together and it was a wrench to see them go. As their happy faces melted into the chaotic traffic, I felt isolated and alone. Zorro sensed my despair and threw his arm around my shoulder. That night, before I drifted off to sleep, my mind focused on the next stage. I would take a bus to the Iranian border, followed by a further 250 miles to Tabriz, the first city stop in Iran. It was going to be a long day.

Zorro came with me to the depot on a bitterly cold morning. After swapping contact details, he gave me a set of rosary beads made from black Oltu and pointed out that the more use they had, the shinier the stones would become. There would always be an open invitation to his home in Asmara, Eritrea which at the time was part of Ethiopia. The aging bus groaned under the weight of a full load. Zorro's bearskin blurred into a sea of furry hats as we roared out from the bus station onto the main highway in the direction of the Iranian border.

In my notebook, I wrote Sayet's assertion through Zorro's translation of an ancient Persian proverb.

'Arabic is a language, Persian is a sweetmeat; Turkish is an art, and the rest is for donkeys.'

I had discovered the Turkish culture to be multifaceted, characterised by its cuisine, social traditions and warmth towards foreigners. I promised myself to learn some basic conversation in one of mankind's oldest living languages for my next visit to this remarkable country.

Iran 1973

Leaving the Turkish border, I walked through No Man's land towards a gigantic poster of the Shah dwarfing the 'Welcome to Iran' sign. A bored immigration official sat alone in the passport control hut. He stamped an exit visa upside down and I crossed the frontier into Persia. An ancient civilisation dating back four thousand years. The Shah, Mohammed Reza Pahlavi, was in power and the Pahlavi dynasty had been the ruling house since 1925.

However, this monarchy would be overthrown by an Islamic Revolution six years later in 1979 when Ayatollah Khomeini became the Supreme Leader of the Theocratic Republic of Iran.

I boarded a modern coach for the seven hour journey to the city of Tabriz, 1,500 metres above sea level in the northwest corner of Iran. A geologically unstable area. Tabriz had been the epicentre of a severe earthquake in 1727 which took an estimated 77,000 lives. Five years after my visit, another quake would claim a further 25,000 lives. The city is situated on the Quru River with a population of 1.5 million people, most of whom were Iranian Azerbaijanis who spoke the Azerbaijani language. The saltwater Lake Urmia is nearby and considered a summer resort by the populace of Iran, referred to as 'The turquoise solitaire of Azerbaijan.'

The terminal in Tabriz was utter mayhem. Droves of chattering travellers and pilgrims crammed around rickety vehicles humping oversized bedroll bundles, dragging wooden trunks and struggling with packing cases. I fought my way through the milling crowds to a dilapidated guest house in a grubby back street behind the Grand Bazaar.

The call to prayer woke me at day break and I set off in the direction of the bazaar in search of breakfast. In a corner café, I cosied up to a cast-iron wood-burner. Hamid the chef, waiter and owner poured hot, sweet, honey-coloured tea with a light fragrance of rose petal into a narrow-waisted glass. Tabrizi, an oval-shaped pitta bread was stacked in bite-sized pieces around bowls of quince jam, feta cheese and walnuts. The smell in the air and the sound of Persian chit-chat made for a different ambience to that of Turkey, Iran felt more eastern. One more glass of that delightful tea and I was ready to tackle the world's largest covered bazaar. When I paid the bill, Hamid shook his head. I placed the rial note on the counter but he smiled and failed to pick it up. On the third occasion I waved it in front of his nose and he eventually put it in his purse. Strange behaviour, I thought to myself.

The Grand Bazaar is spread over twenty-six hectares to include four miles of retail stores and is one of the oldest markets in the Middle East. Their golden age was during the sixteenth century when it formed part of the Silk Road; however, it had continued to retain its status as the commercial heart of Tabriz and of northwest Iran. There were smaller souks within the Grand Bazaar specialising in specific categories: shoes, jewellery, gold, spices and carpets in addition to pottery, ceramics and leather. Swarms of street sellers, tradesmen and visitors thronged the alleyways and courtyards under brick vaulted ceilings which echoed their raucous chattering and intense bargaining. Rows of handcarts heaped with produce squeezed through tight gaps while an aroma of camel dung wafted from the caravanserais – open spaces for pack animals and camel trains.

At sundown, I stumbled upon a scruffy teahouse exuding a heavenly smell of mutton stew called abgoosht, daisy or dizi. Essentially, it was a hearty meat soup thickened with chick peas, white beans and potatoes. I watched as the Iranians strained the liquid from an aluminium jug into a soup bowl which they consumed with lavash, a round piece of thin, flaky pitta bread. They mashed the remaining contents into a gruel with a long mortar. I followed their lead. It was both filling and homely and formed part of my staple diet while in Iran.

At the pension, Saad, a Tehrani who had studied medicine in Scotland, talked enthusiastically about his three years in Edinburgh. Fiona, his girlfriend at the time had lived in a first floor period apartment on Leith Walk and together they enjoyed the art galleries. He had a fond memory of the many beautiful buildings in the city and in particular the abundance of red ashlar stone. A feature which had stayed in his mind. He gave me an address in Tehran to post him a haggis. The conversation gave me the opportunity to ask him about the custom of men holding hands and other affectionate gestures between males I had witnessed since arriving in Iran.

'In Islamic culture, because the sexes are segregated, emotions are channelled towards the same sex. Kissing cheeks, holding hands and long handshakes reflect both equality and a genuine affection for your fellow man. In fact, if you choose not to exchange a greeting in this way it can be interpreted as a sign of disrespect.'

I scribbled these points into my notebook. At the end of the week, I boarded the early morning bus to Tehran, about 400 miles to the east. During the many stops, the roadside stalls serviced travellers with chelo kebabs, lamb meat on skewers served with yellow basmati rice. A poor trader refused to accept payment for the food in the same way as Hamid in Tabriz. On the fourth attempt he accepted the money. I was bemused. Finally, we made it to the terminal in the heart of the capital after ten long hours. Tehran was an immense, ugly and chaotic city and arriving late at midnight added to my woes. A hippy directed me to Amir Kabir Street where I found a room in a traveller's hostel. It was home to a few million bed bugs and the following morning I woke up scratching.

After visiting a bank on a busy thoroughfare, I stopped to tighten my money belt and slipped backwards into an empty monsoon drain much to the amusement of passing Iranians. A portly black-bearded Tehrani helped me out of the pit and gave me a big wet kiss on the cheek. As he did so, I took two steps back and quickly regained my composure. The conversation with Saad in Tabriz came to mind and mitigated the actions of the man but to my surprise he was accompanied by a Caucasian. While I thanked him for his help, I asked the fair-skinned man if he spoke French or English.

'Wey aye man!' He replied.

'A Geordie in Tehran and I was positive you were a Frenchman,' I laughed.

The Gallic connotation derived from his silver aristocratic goatee and retro pompadour hairstyle. His name was Patrick from the North of England. In reality, his accent was ever so slight but he could not resist the effect of a broad Geordie opening line to tease a fellow Brit.

Patrick was at the end of his second year as an English language presenter for Iranian TV. He had graduated from Newcastle University in English Literature and acquired his TV and radio presentation skills in London. After he introduced Fahim, his Iranian work colleague from Esfahan, they invited me to join them for lunch.

'What on earth is this Patrick? Certainly looks interesting.' There was a rich burgundy sauce poured over meat.

'It's a regular dish called fesenjan. They soak chicken pieces in pomegranate molasses overnight and cook them with heaps of ground walnuts to make the thick gravy.'

'It's so different and delicious, I ate abgoosht for the first time in Tabriz.'

'It's their national dish and best with mutton.'

'It tasted of an Irish stew.'

'Have you tried the koofteh tabrizi?'

'What's that?'

'A jumbo Azerbaijan meatball simmered in broth and resembles a scotch egg.'

'No, I didn't see those.'

'Well you must sample one, they are divine.'

Fahim pointed out of the window, 'Café on Amir Kabir street make good.'

While Fahim went to pay, I asked Patrick a cultural question. 'Twice, I've had to insist on paying the bill. It's unsettling. Why is that?'

'It's the Persian art of etiquette referred to as taarof, a courteous custom and complex system of saving face; it dictates that a gift is offered even if the person can't afford it.'

'I was on the verge of thanking the owner and leaving.'

'One must deny the gift three times to give the donor ample time to back out. This helps to make the generosity seem truly genuine.'

'I've learned a great deal about their culture today.'

We left the café in the late afternoon and I thanked them for lunch, their advice and for Fahim's help in pulling me out of the monsoon drain. Patrick and I promised to meet again in England and Fahim and I embraced followed by a long handshake.

My next destination was Mashhad, 550 miles to the East. Clutching the steaming koofteh tabrizi, I boarded the bus in darkness. As it nudged through the Tehran traffic I nibbled at the stuffed meatball. At roadside stopping points I topped up my food supply with bags of pomegranates and handfuls of chaghale badoom, unripe almonds sprinkled with salt. The journey took, to include a breakdown, nearly twenty hours to reach Mashhad. The city is in the far north-east of Iran close to the borders with Turkmenistan and Afghanistan.

Mashhad is Iran's second largest city and also Islam's second holiest place with more than twenty million pilgrims visiting the Imam Reza Holy Shrine annually. Imam Reza is a descendant of the Prophet Mohammad and the eighth Shia Imam. The shrine complex contains the biggest mosque in the world with a capacity of 500,000. Although the vast majority of Mashhadis were ethnic Persians who spoke Farsi, the national language, they talked with a Mashhadi accent reminiscent of an ancient dialect.

Walking from the bus depot to a pension, I found Mashhad to have a cooler climate and a friendlier aura to it than Tehran. I asked a soldier for directions. Although he was helpful, passers-by pushed him away as if to stop him talking to a foreigner. I suspected this incident may have been symbolic of the Shah's repressive regime. Under the Shah, a western lifestyle was apparent but only connected to the elite whose young wore seventies hairstyles and trendy clothes. Girls wearing mini-skirts and boys in flares would cause tension between traditional and modern influences. The upper class lived an American way of life but the majority were confined to poverty. However, the populous as a whole were subject to the Savak, the Shah's secret police – a brutal and repressive tool of the state – no-one would even think to criticise the system publicly because of the Savak. The Shah's own military courts tried anyone brave enough to protest against his regime and were noted for deciding their verdict beforehand.

For the first time, I began to differentiate between the disparate nationalities found in this part of Iran including Kurds, Turkmen, Uzbeks and Afghans. Their anthropological identity could be determined not only by their physical characteristics but also their clothing. Kurdish women wore long silk dresses and striped trousers with their hair tucked away under light scarves; the men in colourful baggy pants, narrowed at the ankles with a sash tied round the waist. In the teahouse, I identified the diner opposite as being a Turkman with a notably large stature, oblong shaped head, high forehead and swarthy complexion. He wore a black shaggy goatskin hat which resembled an afro hairstyle and a full length quilted robe coloured crimson. Lamb abgoosht was served with sangak; a flatbread baked on small round stones and shaped into crispy triangles. The dark eyes of the Turkman flashed at me repeatedly between spoonfuls of the stew. Eventually, in broken English he introduced himself as Mergen from Merv in Turkmenistan. Mergen's English was self-taught and indecipherable but we communicated effectively through body language, pencil drawings and laughter.

Mergen was brought up in Turkmenbashi, a port on the Caspian Sea. His visit to Iran was relevant to his job in the cotton industry and a recent discovery of natural gas near his home town had changed the environment for the worse. He indicated that a non-Muslim would have difficulty visiting the Imam Reza Holy Shrine without a guide who in turn would fear a negative reaction from the Savak.

The bedbug itch began to subside as I prepared to leave Mashhad for the four hour trek to the Afghan border at

Islam Qala and the onward journey to Herat, the first city in Afghanistan. The Afghan visa was a separate document as opposed to a stamp in the passport and as it was easily lost, I sealed it into my money belt before catching the bus.

One of my greatest memories of Iran would be the Persian cuisine which had evolved through the influence of a myriad of cultures from the ancient Babylonians, Assyrians and Greeks, to the Romans, Indians and Turks. The personality of the Iranian people is something to be admired. Their system of taarof made it impolite to express themselves in a direct way and to use kind words in their place. A learned and talented people.

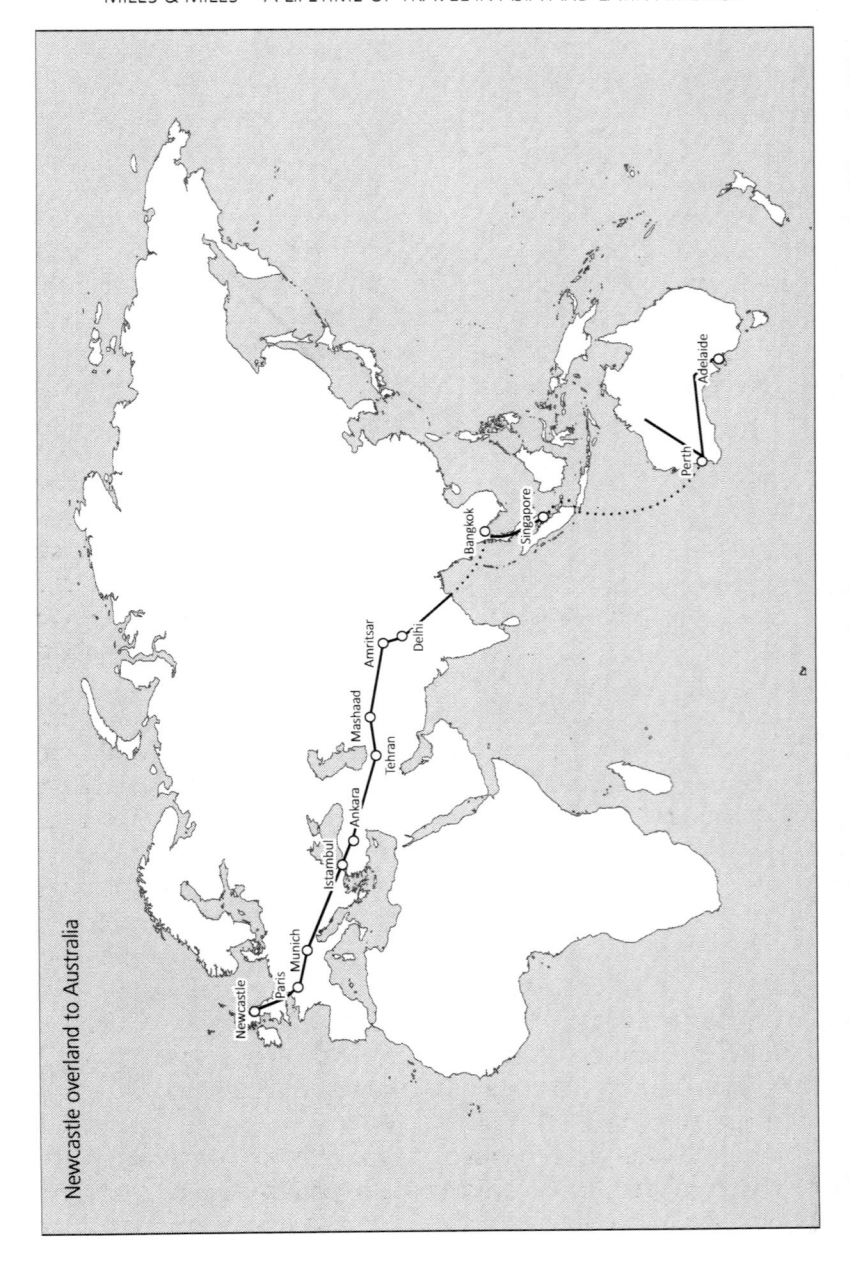

MILES & MILES ~ A LIFETIME OF TRAVEL IN ASIA AND LATIN AMERICA

Newcastle overland to Australia

03 Land of the Pashtuns

'Travel brings power and love back into your life.'
JALALUDDIN RUMI

Afghanistan 1973

THE IRANIAN BORDER CONTROL OFFICE WAS A SHIPPING CONTAINER with a flimsy wooden door and inside the metal box were two decorated officials who stood behind an office desk. One stamped an exit visa into the passport and the other initialled it. I strolled under a sign which spanned the narrow road with a message in Pashto and assumed it translated as, welcome to Afghanistan.

A lone Afghan immigration officer sat on a bench in-between his turban and rifle in a rickety wooden hut painted in stripes of black, green and red, the colours of the Afghan flag. 'Salaam,' he greeted me with genial hospitality, 'Salaam,' I responded and handed over my passport. When I failed to understand his persistent requests his expression became agitated. It suddenly dawned on me that he was asking for my Afghan visa. I promptly undid my trousers to access the money belt and he instantly reached for his gun. I threw my hands in the air and my pants fell down. The three Afghans queuing behind chuckled and the official embossed my visa. 'Kha safer walare,' have a safe journey he grinned and I was allowed entry into the country.

My first stopover in Afghanistan would be Herat, the fourth largest city in the country with a population of 100,000, almost a rural town in comparison to the populous cities of

Iran. At the Afghan border, I had expected feedback from other western travellers returning from India which could be crucial especially travelling into Afghanistan for the first time but it was not to be the case. There were only Afghans waiting for the connecting bus and nobody spoke English.

After three hours, a decrepit two-tone red and cream 1950s American school bus appeared from nowhere enveloping the waiting passengers in plumes of black diesel fumes and swirls of brown dust. The overladen vehicle was jammed with Afghans both inside and on the roof. I had to run for cover when it emptied of people with their bulging hessian sacks, crates secured by rope and caged chickens.

Surprisingly, we departed half-full with everyone inside and no-one in the roof rack for the four hour ride into Herat. Within a few miles the road vanished into a desert scrub and the driver weaved between sporadically placed yellow or red oil drums which marked out the route like buoys at sea.

As the bus clattered over this barren wilderness the passengers stared at me without expression. An older, leathery-faced Afghan dressed in a scarlet robe and an ivory pakol, a round woollen cap, shook my hand as he nodded his head and placed the other on his heart. I mimicked the actions in response. His grip was strong and his palm felt hardened, no doubt from a great deal of physical work. He behaved as if he was welcoming me to Afghanistan and perhaps his name might have been Jabar. All of a sudden, I felt like an outsider in an alien land – there was nothing familiar to relate to – I had been transported back in time to another world.

The bus rattled and rolled over the scrub. Occasionally we passed small villages comprising of single story dwellings built with tawny-coloured mud. They blended into the ochre landscape becoming almost invisible to the naked eye. Jabar was talking to the driver and waving at me at the same time. I was becoming concerned as to what he wanted. 'Are they going to throw me out into the desert?' The British had done some hideous things in Afghanistan during the wars and it would be understandable if they sought revenge.

An Uzbek with a sequinned pork pie hat embroidered with miniature arches, pushed me gently on the shoulder, indicating I should go and see Jabar. I gingerly made my way down the aisle stepping over cages of clucking hens when Jabar grabbed me by the arm. He pointed at settlements of wide, dark brown tents, shaped in the same way as Mongolian yurts with small herds of camels tethered nearby. I understood from him they were a nomadic tribe called the Kuchi.

As we continued to communicate by hand gestures and mannerisms, the driver was rolling a cone-shaped joint from a soft sticky lump of black cannabis while wrestling with the steering wheel. He fired it up and the powerful aroma of Afghan hashish filled the bus. After he had taken a long drag, he passed it to me. Jabar was spurring me on so I took a few draws and handed it to him. He positioned it upright between his fingers whilst gripping his hands together and sucked the smoke through the two thumbs in his clenched fist. He demonstrated in visual terms this method avoids mouth contact with the joint. It was then circulated to some of the passengers before the driver finished it and threw the stub out of the window. I had intended to try the cannabis in Afghanistan given the fact that it was part of their culture and originated from the Hindu Kush but I didn't expect to have it so soon. Alcohol was prohibited for Afghanis and only available to foreigners through private sources.

The bus stopped in the middle of nowhere, a few hundred metres from the Kuchi tents. The passengers silently filtered out carrying small mats and I realised it was prayer time. When they were kneeling I walked towards the Kuchi settlement and observed from a distance. Bright blue and red striped blankets were draped over the camels and donkeys which stood out against the beige background. I made a mental note to find out more about these nomadic people. The sound of a car horn made me jump to find the bus ready and waiting.

I ran over to clamber aboard and was greeted with a chorus of laughter.

The clattering continued along with their good-natured banter during which time they taught me some basic Afghani, 'Salaam alaikum,' (hello, peace be with you), and 'Koor wadaan' (thank you very much). A communal wicker basket filled with nogi (sugared almonds) was handed round. The bus eventually mounted a road and stopped shuddering. The scenery changed to a more fertile green and soon after we entered the Afghan city of Herat.

Jabar was met at the bus terminal by Gorbat, a tall, striking Afghan tribesman in a black lungee, a turban with extra material to protect the face, and a gold waistcoat over his white shirt. Gorbat had the most incredibly dense black beard and moustache, a strong Roman nose and huge candid green eyes. There was an odd car here and there but the main form of transport was either a horse and cart, donkey or bicycle. To my surprise Gorbat spoke a little English from his time in Mashhad.

'What you do?' Gorbat growled.

I stared up into his dark gaping nostrils. 'I want a cheap hotel or pension.'

'Here Herat, three hotel. Bazaar, good bazaar, very good bazaar.' He stood with his legs apart and his arms folded.

'What you think Gorbat?'

'Very good bazaar.'

'Koor wadaan,' I said proudly.

He chortled and whistled in the direction of a row of horses and buggies. One came trotting over. He lifted me up like a child onto the bench seat and piled in next to me as Jabar climbed in the other side. The driver manoeuvred the horse and buggy through the dusty streets into a spot outside the very good bazaar hotel. The owner was fast asleep when we strode into the passageway. He roused from his siesta and looked up at Gorbat then down at me, shook our hands with a 'Salaam alaikum' and introduced himself as Tolwak. He slowly turned the grimy pages of an antique guest register while continually raking his greasy tassel sideways over his shiny bald head. Gorbat and Jabar negotiated a rate per night at less than the price of a coffee in Europe.

Gorbat, Jabar and I followed Tolwak to the first floor bedroom, positioned on a street corner with views up the main avenue towards a golden dome flanked by statuesque minarets from a mosque in the square. An orange tree had grown through the window and permanently wedged the shutters open. The toilet was a communal squat a few metres down a darkened corridor.

Gorbat helped Tolwak translate, 'Eurpeen England of hotel.'

'An English person once slept here?' I asked with intrigue.

'Womanland,' said Tolwark.

Our goodbyes took some time. I believed 'Eurpeen England' referred to a British person who may have stayed there in the distant past or it was a mistranslation. After they left, Tolwak brought up a bowl of nogi, some fresh tea and tried to sell me some cannabis. As he closed the door, I stretched myself out on the wafer thin mattress to absorb the events of the day. I could hear the clip clop of passing horses, a distant wail from a call to prayer and the rustling of leaves from the orange tree. The combination of these soporific sounds made me doze and I was soon asleep.

During the hours of darkness I was awakened by a light tapping on the door. As I rallied from my slumber I could feel the warm air flowing through the open window wafting an aroma of horse dung blended into the fragrance of burning cannabis.

'Salaam alaikum,' I whispered cautiously through the flimsy door.

'Hello, my name is Joan, I'm English.'

I opened the door and to my complete surprise, standing in front of me was a little old lady in a pretty pink dress.

'Well I'm in shock! Am I dreaming?'

'I'm for real,' she laughed, 'I'm from Whitstable in Kent.'

'Thank God, I thought I was hallucinating. Pleased to meet you Joan. Come in. I expected to meet hippies in Afghanistan but certainly not an older person, especially a woman on her own.'

'I'm on my way overland to Australia to see my daughter and granddaughter in Perth.'

She had travelled by public transport all the way from England to Herat with one piece of hand luggage containing a change of clothes and a sandwich box. We were both in need of sustenance so we decided to go out and find a teahouse.

'Maybe we should act publicly as if we are mother and son,' Joan said.

She plucked a roll of purple material from her handbag and carefully wrapped a hijab scarf around her head and neck. We walked side by side along the dimly lit streets in the mellow night air filled with a delicious smell of chickens crackling on a spit-roast. We manoeuvred our way through clusters of market stalls illuminated by barbeques of glowing charcoal and hanging oil lamps. She had discovered a local haunt known for its kabuli palaw, steamed rice with boiled mutton, lentils, carrots and raisins.

At the small café we removed our shoes and sat cross-legged on cushions in the semi-darkness. Flickering paraffin lamps shadowed the other diners. A vinyl tablecloth was spread out on the floor between us with a jug of water to wash our hands. The cook placed one bowl of hot kabuli in the centre of the tablecloth and brought a rolled up naan, the size and shape of a tea towel.

'Watch me Miles,' she said. 'Use your right hand and scoop the food up with a piece of naan. Never use your left hand.'

I told Joan of my eventful bus trip from the Iranian border and while I was talking she dipped into her purse and pulled out a lump of black cannabis resin the size of a plum. I was dumbfounded.

'Do you have any other surprises for me today?'

'No, I promise, no more,' she laughed, 'I've always wanted

to try it, especially in Afghanistan. I experience as many cultural things as I can when I travel and since you've already had some, let's get high together and I will feel more secure.'

'OK, perhaps in a day or two. Where did you buy it from?'

'Tolwak.'

'Do you know anything of the Kuchi tribe?'

'Yes, I have read several books about them. Kuchi means 'nomad' in Dari.'

'What is Dari?'

'Dari and Pashto are the two main languages spoken in Afghanistan. Dari is a form of Persian and is spoken widely but the national language is Pashto.' she continued. 'The Kuchi are a nomadic tribe formed along patrilineal lines. The head of the family is responsible for the general well-being of the community. They have no fixed abode and are dependent on animals for their livelihood. Life is tough for Kuchi women. The male and female roles are rigidly adhered to as in other segments of traditional Afghan society. The men tend to the livestock while the women are responsible for the children, the provision of food, water and weaving clothes and tents.'

'Are they receptive to visitors?'

'No, they don't warm to strangers. I met some German travellers who approached their tents and were pelted with stones.'

'I viewed them from a distance but didn't get close enough to be noticed.'

'While I'm in Herat, I want to visit the Musallah Complex. Would you like to join me?'

'What's its significance, Joan?'

'Well, I have studied the life of Gower Shad, the wife of Shah Rukh and she was one of the most remarkable women in Afghan history. She commissioned some of Islam's finest buildings. The one that stand out is the Musallah Complex which is a masterpiece of Islamic architecture and includes a mosque, madrassa, mausoleum and around twenty minarets. However, it suffered badly during the wars. In the nineteenth century, it was dynamited by the British for a clear view of the invading Russians who apparently never arrived,' she grimaced.

'Are they the minarets I can see from my room?'

'Yes. She was also responsible for the Great Mosque which forms part of the Imam Reza Holy Shrine in Mashhad.'

After the kabali I suggested, 'Shall we retire now and continue our conversation over lunch tomorrow?'

'That will be fun and we can buy a chillum from the market to smoke the hashish.'

'OK,' I said with a certain amount of trepidation.

The next day I woke up during the early morning rush hour to the sound of horses and carts thundering up and down the dusty street. I washed myself in a ceramic bowl with water from an aluminium jug. The bustling streetscape from my window was so interesting I ran downstairs to take some hot tea back to my room and sat for hours observing the local Afghans going about their daily business. The Heratis were respectful of each other, they radiated a proud aura and I felt humbled in their presence. Little did we know that within a short time the tide would turn and the people of Afghanistan would endure twenty years or more of pitiless war, attrition and conflict.

Joan knocked at my door, walked straight in and joined me on the window seat as we chatted. In a few days, she would be taking the bus directly to Kabul whereas I had chosen a more circuitous route through Lashkar Gah and Kandahar in Helmand Province. She gave me the address of Jake, her American friend who lived in the capital and suggested I pay him a visit. At midday, we wandered through the chattering markets to the same café and took lunch of zamarod pulao, a wonderful emerald green vegetarian rice dish made with spinach.

Buying the chillum involved lengthy negotiations with the seller and copious refills of tea before we agreed the purchase of a medium sized marble version, a box of matches, loose tobacco and a handkerchief. Joan wanted to smoke it in my room. I heated the pliable resin, crumbled it into the tobacco and pushed the mix into the cone-shaped chillum. Once the wet handkerchief was wrapped around the base, I positioned it between my fingers in the same way Jabar had smoked the joint on the bus and used several matches bunched together to light it. After multiple attempts the room filled with plumes of strong hashish smoke. Both Joan and I lay sprawled out on the floor gibbering inanely for hours. I did become paranoid at one point when her uncontrollable high-pitched laugh drowned out the call to prayer. Tolwak had told Joan that Afghans often smoke hashish and eat melon at the same time to increase the high. She continued to talk about food, especially sweets. After slowly regaining our self-control we made our way to the market and munched our way through handfuls of malida balls, a sweet bread mixed with dried fruit. Between us, we managed to chomp the seller's entire display.

The following day we left by buggy for the Musallah Complex but due to an unexpected security incident we were turned back by fierce looking warriors on horses. Prior her departure, Joan gave Tolwak the remaining hashish and chillum as a parting gift. I suggested we say our goodbyes in the hotel in case we offended anyone at the bus station. She was old enough to be my grandmother but sharp enough to be my friend. I lifted her up, twirled her around and gave her a big hug. We promised to meet up in England the following year. She intended to visit Jake, her contact in Kabul after the arduous twenty-four hour bus journey from Herat. I walked with her to the bus station to see her safely aboard. At the glassless window, she returned my wave as she dabbed her eyes with the stained handkerchief we had bought at the market and within minutes the old rickety bus had disappeared into a cloud of yellow dust.

As I strolled through the alleyways of Herat, I worried about her travelling alone, especially from Kabul and through the

Khyber Pass. At the hotel, Tolwak ran towards me waving a brown package in the air. 'Mees Johnso,' he said with a smile. I tore open the brown paper and inside was a red and gold waistcoat with a note pinned to the lapel. 'To my friend Miles xx.'

I set about discovering Herat by walking all over the central area and taking horse-drawn buggies to various outlying districts. There was much more to this city than met the eye, something meaningful in those dusty streets, crowded by a strong, dignified and independent people. In a crossways up a narrow alley there were four donkeys covered by vibrant hand woven blankets and tethered to a post outside a tea shop. Inside they cooked yakhni pulao, boiled mutton with cashew nuts and spicy basmati rice. I sat cross-legged among the brightly attired Afghan tribesmen who smoked hashish from a communal hookah pipe. They referred to me as an Inglistani and roared with laughter at my attempt to draw smoke through the bubbles. I stumbled out of the café, made a fuss of the donkeys before heading to the market where I bought some Afghan clothing to go with my new waistcoat. The seller also topped up my Afghan currency as the exchange on the street was more favourable and much faster than through the bank.

When the time came to leave Herat, its charm and distinctive personality had retained an everlasting presence in my soul. During the onward journey, I blended into the crowds by wearing Joan's waistcoat with a white Afghan shirt and a brown pakol. The effect worked well, especially when I jostled to the front of the queue and secured a decent seat on the decrepit bus to Lashkar Gah. It vibrated and groaned through the desolate countryside of Helmand Province, similar to the Wild West. Habib, an Afghan farmer who spoke some English told me that King Zahir Shah had outlawed cannabis following a financial donation from the USA and the army was rampaging through the countryside burning crops and killing farmers.

After an uncomfortable night's sleep in a sleazy hostel up a back alley in Lashkar Gah, I travelled onto Kandahar, the second largest city in Afghanistan. It was relatively small, laid out in a grid system over an arid plain and circled by distant mountain peaks. I took a room in a scruffy but friendly hotel within walking distance from the bus station. On the main street, there were rows of small stores selling cannabis. I began to wonder if Habib had been ill-informed. The hashish came in many different grades and shades of greenish black. One Afghan seller boasted his premium version stamped with a square gold seal was the best in the Middle East. I decided to keep away from hashish now that it was illegal and avoid being locked up in an Afghan prison. In the extreme heat of that late afternoon, I would have traded all my traveller's cheques for an ice cold beer. At nightfall I ate maash palaw, a tasty and light dish of mung beans, dried apricots and bulgur wheat.

Within three days of leaving Kandahar I arrived in Kabul and took a room at the Jamil Hotel overlooking a main square and opposite the gold market. The city was surrounded by snowy mountain peaks stretching up into the Hindu Kush. The room had a loudspeaker outside the window, centimetres away from my pillow. At day break, the call to prayer produced a piercing squeal which cackled from the tinny speaker and jumpstarted my day. I leapt out of bed, opened the window, pulled out the cables and the screeching stopped. I hoped it would not result in my arrest by the religious police. The broadcast was normally hypnotic but this particular PA system must have been defective in some way.

Chicken Street was a well-known shopping location where travellers met to swap information. Mahboob, an Afghan retailer whose English was exceptional took time out to give me elaborate directions to the home of Joan's American friend, Jake. He lived in the suburbs but close to the centre of Kabul. After some hours walking the avenues I eventually located Jake's home – a large detached residence enclosed by high walls – accessed through towering red metal doors. The building was locked and deserted. There was no answer to my banging so I pushed a note through a slit in the door. Later at the Jamil, I received a message from Jake suggesting we meet tomorrow afternoon at his house. The next day, I retraced my steps and thumped hard on the metal door. After ten minutes, it slowly creaked open to reveal Jake, a young American with brown curly hair, a tapered goatee and a wide smile.

'You must be Miles from England?'

We shook hands. 'Hello Jake. We meet at last.'

'Come on in, Joan told me all about you.' He locked the door from the inside and dropped two heavy cross bars into their respective slots.

'Are they for additional security?'

'They certainly are, it can be dangerous after dark. By the way, have you heard the news?'

'No, nothing at all. I have been on the road for so long, I am out of touch. What's going on?'

'The US administration gave the Afghan government a bucket load of dollars to ban the sale of cannabis. King Zahir Shah reacted by murdering loads of dope farmers before he took off to Europe on a holiday. While he's away, a guy called Daoud Khan took advantage of the backlash and with the support of the People's Democratic Party has taken control of the country. Worse still, they are pro-Soviet.'

'Yes, I had heard of a change in policy by word of mouth. Are we safe?'

'Yes, for the moment there's no change but I'm not sure how it will all pan out.'

'What are you doing here?'

'My father works in the American Embassy. Joan told me she had a hoot of a time with you in Herat and I am under strict instruction to give you a cold beer,' he grinned, heading to the kitchen.

He handed me a chilled bottle of Busch. 'Wonderful, thank you, what a treat. How on earth did you manage to buy beer?'

'My father brings several cases in his diplomatic bag.'

'Now that's what I call diplomacy!' He threw me another.

We talked throughout the afternoon and into the early evening when his friends arrived in the form of twin brothers, Bruce and Curtis from Chicago. Their father was writing a publication on the political history of Afghanistan. During our conversation, Curtis brought up the subject of the Afghan proverb which are used colloquially in everyday Pashto.

'These proverbs are a poetic element of the Afghan language. It makes communication more expressive and graceful. For instance, in an ant colony, dew is a flood, meaning, a little misfortune is a great deal to one in need.'

'Enchanting, I want to learn more Pashto. Language reflects the personality of the people,' I said.

'My father understands the two major dialects spoken here in Kabul and in Northwest Pakistan,' said Curtis.

'How did the extensive use of proverbs originate into modern day Pashto?' I asked.

'The language has a heritage of the written word and a culture of poetry traditionally composed by women. There are thousands of two and four line folk poems which reflect their views,' said Curtis.

'The Afghan women have a voice through their poetry,' said Bruce.

Look into My World

'They made me invisible, shrouded and non-being
A shadow, no existence, made silent and unseeing
Denied of freedom, confined to my cage
Tell me how to handle my anger and my rage?'
ZIEBA SHORISH-SHAMLEY

Published on the 50th anniversary of the
United Nations Universal Declaration of Human Rights

As his parents were in New York, Jake invited us all to stay for dinner. Their Afghan chef, Piruz, normally prepared western food but the twins asked if he would cook mantu, their favourite Afghan dish. He was delighted by the request. After a few hours, Piruz brought a huge platter of lamb dumplings with pots of garlic yoghurt, sour cream and chickpeas. He had also baked obi non, a thick dense bread which Jake understood to be from an Uzbek recipe. It felt strange to sit at a table once again and the mantu reminded me of Lancashire hotpot. When I thanked Piruz for his fine fare using my hand in the same way as in the greeting from Jabar on the bus to Herat, his face lit up with a sunny smile which stretched from ear to ear.

During dinner the three boys discussed the game of buzkashi which they were going to attend the next day.

'Come and join us,' they suggested in unison.

'What is it?' I asked.

'Buzkashi is a sort of Afghan polo free-for-all played on horseback with the carcass of a headless goat,' said Bruce.

'It's a brutal sport and anything goes,' added Jake. 'Sometimes, dog fights follow on after the game but they don't fight to the death.'

'I don't want to see dogs bite each other, it's horrendous. We'll have to go as soon as the polo match is over,' said Curtis who continued, 'I know they say, a bad wound heals but a bad word doesn't; meaning a cruel tongue does more harm than a sharp sword. But dogs attacking dogs is sickening.'

Having made our arrangement to meet in the square the following morning, the twins and I left the walled house together and shared a horse-drawn carriage into the city centre. At 8 a.m. I stood in the square dressed in my Afghan attire but neither the twins nor Jake recognised me until I spoke. Throughout the day, my outfit would be a constant source of amusement which they referred to as a 'chapandaz.' An Afghan on horseback who plays buzkashi.

We drove out of the city through a stark landscape and arrived at a desolate valley where rows of pickups, trucks and cars were parked. There must have been 800 people surrounding a natural dip in the landscape, encircled by the brilliantly white snowy peaks of the Hindu Kush. The spectators sat in neat rows on a stony incline, some of whom brought a padded prayer mat for comfort. We made our way through the crowds, down the slope to the base for a good view of the game. Two teams of ten tribal horsemen rode into focus dragging a headless goat through clouds of dust amid roars from the crowd.

Curtis shouted over the hullaballoo, 'Better to be a poor rider on a good horse than a good rider on a poor horse; the horse is more important than the rider.'

I could see what he meant when the horses joined in the scrap which followed by biting and kicking each other, while the riders used any means whatsoever to take ownership of the carcass. Twenty horsemen fused together in a violent struggle with their fellow riders on a pitch that had no apparent boundaries. All of a sudden, I felt a painful stinging sensation on my shoulders and realised the crowd controllers were thrashing the front line with a horse-whip to force us away from the players. The stinging continued until we scrambled up the loose scree to a higher point.

After the game of buzkashi, earless muscular dogs were set against each other with an unpleasant growling, biting and bloodied muzzles. At this point we left and drove into Kabul. On Chicken Street we ate chalao, which translates to jewel. A basmati rice with fried eggs, butter and spinach. Bruce and Curtis discussed their plans to drive to Jalalabad, known as the most beautiful city in Afghanistan, about 100 miles to the east and close to the Khyber Pass. I was unable to travel with them as my visa for Pakistan had expired. I spent the next few days in their embassy and had it reinstated with the correct dates. I would leave Kabul in the morning and join Bruce and Curtis in Jalalabad. When I returned to the hotel, Jake was sitting in the dark passageway with a grim expression on his face.

'What's wrong Jake?'

'Curtis is dead and Bruce is wounded.'

I sat next to him. 'Did they have an accident in the car? What happened?' I was in shock and anxiety knotted my stomach.

'Their vehicle broke down and some tribesmen tried to rob them.' He spoke with anger in his voice. 'It's their own fault. Curtis would insist on carrying a handgun.'

'Where's Bruce now?'

'He's been airlifted to a military hospital near Bagram but he will be fine. They think it's a flesh wound. Curtis's body will be flown home in a few days.' He added, 'It's the most dangerous road in Afghanistan.'

That night, we sat quietly at Jake's house waiting for news of Bruce. A late call confirmed the bullet had passed through his thigh and there was no lasting damage. Since leaving England it was the saddest night of my trip. A few days later I took the same route by bus to Jalalabad passing the spot where Curtis had been killed. During the journey, a small Afghan boy pulled at my sleeve and in broken English asked if the big silver bird, (he was referring to an aircraft), folded its wings back into the body once it flew into the clouds. Using my arms, I demonstrated the motions of an aeroplane during flight and his laughter brought me out of my sadness.

In Jalalabad an event had filled up all the hotels, guest houses and hostels. After an exhaustive search I managed to find a place to sleep in the corner of a cramped room above a fruit merchant. The beds were made of rope netting and I had to share with seven other Afghanis. I found Jalalabad to be a lovely green city as I made my way to a popular area downtown by the name of Mokhaberat Chowk. I drank a litre of pomegranate juice with a dish of bonjan-e-roomi; meat from a sheep's head served with red rice and tomatoes. All that was left on my plate were two eyeballs and a nostril.

After what happened to Curtis I was sensitive about travelling through the lawless no-man's-land of the Khyber Pass with its violent history. The Pass was not under the control of any nation state and tribes existed by their own rule of law, the AK-47. The Pass threads through the Spin

Ghar Mountains and is in the region of thirty miles long. I did not sleep a wink in the crowded lodgings from the snoring and rustling which were continuous throughout the night mixed with an assortment of foul odours. I found myself in the bus station at day break.

The distance from Jalalabad to Peshawar, my first stopover in Pakistan, was close to 100 miles but due to the border controls, slow mountain roads and the Pass itself, it would take more than twelve hours. The journey would involve taking four successive buses: Jalalabad to Torkham on the Afghan border where the Pass began, a local bus from Torkham through to Landi Kotal, the highest point in the Khyber Pass and from there to the Pakistani border before the final leg to Peshawar.

The first available bus was full and I had to stand in the centre aisle for three hours. The straddling mountain village of Torkham was packed with travellers and pilgrims. I waited in line to obtain my Afghan visa exit stamp next to a huge ominous sign in many languages – warning travellers of impending danger in the Khyber Pass – and to never cross during the hours of darkness. When the doors of the bus opened for boarding, I was pushed out of the way by aggressive crowds and ended up in the last space available, on the roof. The top heavy vehicle thundered along the narrow winding roads which clung to the mountainside. On each twist and turn, all of us on the roof were propelled from one side to the other over the shiny surface; thin wooden planks held together with string took the strain of thirty people in motion. Sporadic gunfire could be heard echoing around the ravine and when we pulled into Landi Kotal I breathed a sigh of relief.

The link bus to the Pakistani frontier was supposed to leave in three hours but no one seemed to know for sure and I was concerned with being trapped in the Pass at night. The tiny ragged village was buzzing. The market stalls sold heroin piled high in kilo blocks or displayed weaponry and ammunition from a single shot fountain pen gun to AK-47's, hand grenades and ornate daggers. Sitting next to a tethered donkey, I ate quoroot, a ball of hard goat's cheese with sapati bread, the tribal name for a chapatti, and watched intrigued as the clans bartered their wares. When the bus spluttered through the crowds, a noisy scrum formed and jostled to board. Not everyone was successful and I felt fortunate to have secured a place on the roof. It was dusk when it arrived in Jamrud on the Pakistani border.

Occasionally, I experience something special. An encounter which gives a spiritual tug of the heart. This inner and abstract feeling is difficult to articulate but it remains there for life. Afghanistan is one of those exceptional places in my world.

Pakistan 1973

Handing over the passport to Pakistan immigration, an arrogant official flicked through the pages and stopped at the photo. He stared into my eyes and screwed up his face, 'Why you look so stupid?' Cleared his throat, spat in the dirt and threw the documents on the ground. His attention moved up the queue to the person behind. I picked up the paperwork, wiped away the dust and walked into Pakistan with a scowl.

Rows of neatly parked buses were ready to leave for Peshawar and by midnight I had checked into a smart hostel on a busy thoroughfare downtown. Peshawar was the ninth largest city in Pakistan with around two million inhabitants, much bigger than any city in Afghanistan. In fact Pakistan's population was seven times greater than Afghanistan although the land mass of each country was not dissimilar.

In the morning I caught an orange tuk-tuk to the old town formed in part by mud brick structures with separate wooden buildings built internally to allow for movement during earthquakes. In Sethi Mohallah, an area in the heart of the walled city, intricate wooden trelliswork balconies overhung the crowded streets below. I had not seen this many people since Tehran. Their national language is Urdu but many people spoke English. In a long dark narrow teahouse I wolfed down a vegetable biryani with some lentil dhal and a glass of almond milk.

From Peshawar, the distance to Lahore and the border with India was a journey of 400 miles. I stopped half-way in Rawalpindi, referred to locally as Pindi, twinned with the capital, Islamabad a few miles away. For some odd reason, I visited a cinema, which was a bizarre experience considering the film dialogue was in Urdu but the visuals told the story and I sensed a strong camaraderie amongst the audience. On my way to the pension, the driver of the cycle rickshaw and I argued over the price of the fare which escalated into a shouting match and attracted a crowd. Pakistani rupees were formatted into little booklets with perforations in the same way as bingo tickets and three of these notes were equivalent to a small coin. I realised the disparity amounted to a few pence so I tore bunches of rupees from the book and gave them to the now speechless trishaw owner.

Pakistan was founded in 1947 but it was during the Presidency of Zulfiqar Bhutto that the parliament approved a more centralised constitution which became the supreme law of the country in this year, 1973. It was a landmark stage in the development of this embryonic nation state and provided an independent judiciary which guaranteed the right for each citizen to be protected by law.

At a kiosk, I bought a copy of *Dawn*, an English language newspaper printed daily. It was my first glimpse into the events occurring back home and it made for uncomfortable reading. In the early 70s, Great Britain entered what many regarded as an optimistic new era as a member of the common market; the term used for free or low trade tariffs linking European countries, known today as the EU. Soon after, the Yom Kippur war between the Arab States and Israel quadrupled the cost of oil and food prices soared. A European butter mountain was sold to Russia at a huge discount and as a result British pensioners were allocated butter vouchers. Marlon Brando and Maria Schneider discovered an alternative use for it in the film, *Last Tango In Paris*.

Industrial strife and the banking crisis created sheer turmoil in Edward Heath's Conservative Britain resulting in galloping inflation where interest rates exceeded seventeen per cent. The miner's strike combined with the oil crisis resulted in a three day week with power cuts all over the country and a state of emergency was declared. It was a time when trade unionists appeared on the TV news as often as politicians. Meanwhile violence in Northern Ireland spread to the mainland with bomb attacks in Central London.

All of these activities were happening to the sound of American pop, *Tie A Yellow Ribbon Round The Ole Oak Tree* by Tony Orlando and Dawn, *Me And Mrs Jones*, Billy Paul and *You Are The Sunshine of My Life*, Stevie Wonder.

A few days later I arrived in Lahore, Pakistan's second city and regarded as the cultural heart of the country with an impressive skyline of golden domes and minarets. In the old town, wooden buildings coloured: pink, ochre, blue, orange and green with carved latticed windows were clustered around small squares. Swarms of Lahorites percolated through the rickshaw traffic jams and donkey trains. Roh, sugarcane juice hand-pressed on the street, washed away the dust clogging my throat and reinvigorated the energy.

From Lahore, it was an hour to Wagah on the Pakistan-Indian border where soldiers from both sides performed their daily ceremonial parade. They wore bright-red or jet-black turbans with what looked like an open, hand-held fan perched on top of their turbans like a rooster's comb standing to attention. Although Pakistan and India share a history riddled with conflict there was no tension in the air and the process of entering India was welcoming. I caught the early evening coach to Amritsar. All my life I had dreamt of visiting India and here I was travelling through the Punjab. I could not contain my excitement.

04 Wisdom of India

'Speak like a parrot; meditate like a swan; chew like a goat; and bathe like an elephant.' INDIAN PROVERB

India 1973

AMRITSAR IS IN THE STATE OF PUNJAB AND HOME TO THE GOLDEN Temple, the spiritual shrine of the Sikh religion. It is surrounded by the Amrit sarovar, a sacred pool fed by the River Ravi. There are entrances to the north, east, south and west to indicate that people from all four corners of the world are welcome. Before entering, protocol dictated I remove my shoes and cover my head. A young Sikh standing in line told me, 'The temple has over 100,000 visitors each day, more than the Taj Mahal, and we feed thousands for free.'

The Golden Temple has a devout presence cocooned by an ambience of serenity and is festooned with deep warm colours. Golden domes are hewn from white marble and plated with real gold. Brilliant saris and rich turbans circulate through the marble corridors. Yellow, red and green foodstuffs are ladled onto shimmering silver platters between long neat rows of pilgrims who face each other while sitting cross-legged on the floor.

Sikhism was founded more than five hundred years ago and is followed by millions of people worldwide. It represents a way of life and a philosophy based upon the principles of truthful living, the equality of mankind and social justice. In Sikhism, a place of worship is referred to as a Gurdwara, meaning the gateway through which the Guru can be reached.

The Gurdwara is open to all people of all religions and can be any size or at any location but their holiest Gurdwara is the Golden Temple.

After experiencing such a stunning introduction to India, I caught an early morning tuk-tuk to Amritsar railway station to catch the flying mail for the full day's journey to New Delhi. My first train ride since Europe. Indian railways at the time were the biggest employer in the world. Buying a ticket involved queuing at four different booths for a variety of documents which then required rubber-stamped approval at several desks. At one ticket window it took two hours to reach the counter as the blind was promptly pulled down in front of my eyes. An hour later it popped open. Each segment of the entire process was meticulously logged into a king-sized ledger book by fountain pen; using the same system as the Victorians employed one hundred years earlier.

Travelling third class, I secured a portion of the luggage rack above a Sikh family crammed onto the bench seat below. My head rested next to the metal bars of an open window cooled by a dusty breeze. As the locomotive shunted to a stop at each station, a chorus of wailing street sellers would greet us with hot, sweet, milky teas (chai), in conical-shaped terracotta pots which they fed through the open bars. Beggars, young and old, extended their spindly arms with open palms and pleading eyes repeating the word, 'Baksheesh.' When the train came to rest in New Delhi at dusk, a dark red encrustation had solidified in my eyes, nostrils and corners of the mouth.

Connaught Circus was the colonial heart of New Delhi and the former headquarters of the British Raj. If it was not for droves of Indian people and plum-red splashes of disgorged betel nut juice staining the pavements, these whitewashed cloisters reminded me of Cheltenham. A Sikh showed me to a shared room above the arched colonnades but I found myself sleeping on the balcony where it was cooler. At dawn I gazed down at a continuous stream of saffron tops of the ubiquitous two-tone black and yellow ambassador taxis. They rumbled through the avenues, tooting their horns as a superior species to the rickshaws, handcarts, mopeds and bicycles. Flocks of Delhiites in their brilliantly white kurtas, sherwanis and dhotis daubed by the vibrant iridescence of flowing saris flowed either side and through the moving traffic.

Launched into this anarchic hurly-burly in a dog-eared rickshaw, one of thousands of yellow and green tuk-tuks which raced around the city, I sped to the Chandni Chowk in Old Delhi. Perhaps one of the oldest markets in all of India. Built in 1650, it was designed by Jahanaraa, the daughter of Shah Jahan, a Mughal emperor. She had lived next to the market in the Red Fort – the main residence for emperors of the Mughal dynasty – who ruled most of northern India for two hundred years until the mid-eighteenth century.

The overhead electricity cables of Chandni Chowk criss-crossed the streets and alleyways like spider's webs leading to bare wires bunched together as birds' nests. They hung precariously above the chattering crowds and tumultuous traffic. The beauty of these markets, other than the experience of having a sensory overload, was the assortment of skills available. My leather boots, clothes and rucksack were all in need of repair and I sat and watched with interest as the craftsman delicately rejuvenated my sad and tired travelling kit. Next door, a barber choreographed the movements of his shimmering cut throat razor as it slid through the creamy foam while reflecting the afternoon sun. On the other side of the alleyway there were heaps of conical-shaped bundles of cigars similar to golf tees in length and shape. Indians referred to them as 'bidis.' An auburn shade of tobacco leaf rolled into a thin cigarette and tied in place with a piece of thread.

In a back street Tibetan café, I sat next to a huge triple-deck steamer packed with dough balls wafting a warm breeze of ginger and garlic. These irresistible and delicate dumplings were filled with tofu, red sesame seed paste and mushrooms.

Lhasa momos were served with a chick pea chat and a chapatti. Another vegetarian dish from a cuisine that offered so much variety.

On the adjacent table a thick set Sikh with a ruby-red turban was enjoying his momos.

'My name is Livjot, where are you from?' He talked in a Punjabi accent.

'The North of England, my name is Miles, pleased to meet you.' I leaned over and shook his hand.

'You must know the city well to come here for the momos.'

'No, it was pure chance. Why?'

'Dawa makes the best momos outside of Tibet.'

Dawa smiled and gestured with an Indian head wobble.

We discussed the Golden Temple and my living quarters in Connaught Circus. He happened to know Vijay, the owner of the building, also a Sikh and they both worked in the film industry. It was a coincidence considering there were millions of people living in Delhi. He told me Indira Gandhi's government had recently set up an initiative called Project Tiger to protect the species and he would be assisting the ministers with a documentary on the subject.

After the momos he offered me a lift in the sidecar attached to his motorcycle. As we tore along the avenue next to the Red Fort, the late afternoon sun illuminated the dressed stone into a wondrous salmon pink hue. Although I appreciated the ride, sitting so low to the ground had its disadvantages. Fear being one of them. It was reminiscent of a fairground ride, especially when tackling roundabouts. Clambering out of the bullet shaped sidecar, Vijay greeted Livjot and they were still chatting hours later when I peered down from the balcony.

The next day Vijay summoned me to his office located through an arch in the colonnade. When I arrived Livjot was sitting in an armchair looking dapper in a light grey suit and a royal blue turban. Helle and Torben, travellers from Denmark, had also been asked to attend and we sat together on the sofa.

Vijay poured the chai, 'We have some special work for you.' Livjot gave a wide grin, took a deep breath and exhaled excitedly. 'In a Bollywood movie.'

Vijay smiled, 'It will be a wonderful experience and on location at a luxurious hotel. With free food, and, you get money.'

Our role would be as extras, mingling and chatting at a drinks party but we must be available for two days from 8 a.m. to 9 p.m. We were to be paid twenty rupees which equated to one hours work in England during the 1970s.

'Why not!' We spoke in unison and signed the forms. Livjot would be our driver and mentor.

On the first day of the shoot, I squeezed into the sidecar with Helle and Torben sat behind Livjot on the motorcycle. With a jolt, we pitched into the traffic flow. Helle squealed at each twist and turn throughout the journey. Finally we roared through a pair of majestic iron gates, shuddered over some cobblestones and came to rest outside the grand entrance of the hotel. We were jammed inside the bullet, unable to move, Livjot and Torben uncorked Helle by pulling her out by the legs. We decided I would sit at the rear on the way back as she was too tall for the compact space.

After months of grimy rooms and third class travel the opulence of the Imperial Hotel was bewildering. The serenity inside this regal building with its colonial charm from the days of the Raj was alien to the chaos and reality outside.

It was in this very building that the key decision makers had convened during the lead up to independence in the 1940s, when the subsequent decision to partition India took place and Pakistan was founded. The lounges displayed the original art and antique furniture. Corridors of panelled ebony flanked the marble flooring. Plush Persian rugs lay under cut-glass chandeliers suspended from vaulted ceilings. I felt an overwhelming sense of history and considered the tortuous decision making process which affected hundreds of millions of people.

In a fitting room Torben and I were given black trousers, white shirts, creamy dinner jackets and red bow ties. After some adjustments we were ready to join the party, but the film crew took a further four or five hours to set up. We passed our time seated in walnut-brown leather armchairs, chatting and nibbling from bowls of mini-samosas which we dipped into mint yogurt. Waiters with cherry-red turbans and beige evening wear served tea from a Victorian silver service.

Helle and Torben gave us a rendition of travellers' tales from their eight month overland journey from Copenhagen to Delhi. After the shoot, they intended to visit Nepal before gradually making their way south to Goa for the winter. They were a lovely couple, laid-back and easy-going. One of the Indian extras introduced himself as Grumk, a dumpy entrepreneur from Patna who knew every trick in the book. His small satchel was full of hotel paraphernalia, shampoo bottles, soaps and hand towels. He was looking for anything that would fit into his bag. Helle asked Grumk for advice, as to where she could buy papier mâché figures for her mother who collected Indian art and crafts. It just so happened Grumk had a cousin in old Delhi who was a manufacture of these items and he would take her to visit the factory.

Later in the day, more people arrived and together we formed a crowd, milling around in a palatial glass domed atrium with an elaborately decorated water fountain at its core. We were instructed to talk in small groups without sound but using expressions and gesticulations. The words 'action' and 'cut' were repeated again and again until around 10 p.m. when they shouted, 'That's a wrap.' A queue gathered outside the fitting rooms and the smart clothing were replaced by our dusty rags. Helle and I squashed into the bullet for the ride home in the dark. A similar schedule followed the next day. We never did see the finished movie, *Naya Din Nai Raat*, but our spell in Bollywood was a fun memory.

Two days later Torben, Helle, Grumk and I met for breakfast in Connaught Circus to visit his cousin's papier mâché business in Old Delhi. In the café, Grumk ordered a communal bowl of chole bhatwe, a moreish mix of chick peas and spices served hot with a light puri bread. The four of us crammed into one creaking tuk-tuk for the thirty minute ride to a back lane in a gloomy slum. The factory entrance was a one metre high metal grate at the base of a towering brick wall. We crawled through the hole into a labyrinth of narrow alleyways and compact courtyards where hundreds of families lived in cramped conditions. We followed Grumk to a darkened room where fifty or so people sat on the floor moulding papier mâché figures. His cousin failed to materialise.

'A German guy smuggles cannabis resin in these figures and makes a fortune with no risk at all,' said Grumk.

After the visit, we told Livjot the story.

'It's one the oldest scams in India!' He guffawed.

Livjot reassured Helle he would check the goods carefully before packaging and posting them to Denmark. The Danes and I left on the same day and Livjot drove us to the station to wish us a safe journey with his customary grin and firm handshake. Torben and Helle boarded a train to Kathmandu and we agreed, if the timing was right, to meet in Goa the following year.

It felt a little strange to be on my own once again after being with fun people all day every day. The train to Agra took three hours and arrived at sundown. I could sense an altogether calmer atmosphere than Delhi. The horse and buggy softly trotted through the congested streets to a district of the town within easy reach of the Taj Mahal. In a narrow, jam-packed moonlit passageway, I clawed my way through white eyes and grinning teeth to the darkened entrance of a guest house. Inside, hanging lanterns spread a faint glow over two Buddhist monks in saffron robes who clasped their hands and gave a slight bow 'Namaste.' I returned the gesture. 'It's a full moon so an excellent opportunity to see the Taj Mahal in all its glory. At night!' I thanked them for the information, put my bag in the room and took a cycle rickshaw to the Taj.

In 1607 when Shah Jahan, the grandson of Akbar the Great, cast his eyes on Mumtaz Mahal for the first time he spontaneously fell in love. She was fifteen years old and he was fourteen. He immediately asked for her hand in marriage but it was a further five years before they could marry. She died giving birth to their fourteenth child. He built this monument in memory of their true love, hiring 20,000 workers for twenty-two years to complete the task. It was the immensity of love that inspired this technically perfect, symmetrical edifice which transcends the ubiquity of everyday life. I sat and gazed at the purity of white marble radiating a blue diamond lustre from the full moon. It seemed to suspend the Taj Mahal in perpetuity as if floating on air. It was the embodiment of pure love.

The Taj Mahal was all mine. There was no one at all until 3 a.m. when some workers started to arrive. As the azure orb faded into the first blush of dawn, I yearned to be impulsively captivated by an unconstrained intensity of the heart. To relish, cherish and treasure. Maybe one day it would happen to me, I thought to myself.

The next stage of my travels entailed a two day journey east by third class rail travel from Agra to Calcutta (Kolkata). After six hours sitting in the passageway I managed to grab a seat once it arrived in Lucknow. Talking to Kaifi, a Shia Muslim who asked, 'At your age, how can you afford to visit India?'

'I worked hard, saved each penny and have travelled low cost by either hitchhiking or using public transport but I must get to Australia soon to find work and replenish my travel funds.'

During our conversation, he mentioned Tamil Nadu to the south as the most populous Muslim state in India. Lucknow had the highest number of Shia Muslims and where harmony existed between Shia and Sunni. A positive statement given the fact that there is often disagreements between the two major denominations of Islam. It was Kaifi's ambition to visit the Imam Reza Holy Shrine in Mashhad, Iran and mine to visit Tamil Nadu. The train chugged east and the climate gradually changed from dry to humid, arriving in Calcutta late at night during a boisterous street procession. By the time I fought my way out of the station, I realised my appearance was the worst it had ever been, filthy, smelly and scruffy.

Calcutta in the state of West Bengal is India's second largest city and regarded as the intellectual and cultural capital of the country, located in the lower Ganges delta alongside the Hooghly River. The Bangladesh War of Independence two years earlier in 1971 had resulted in a massive influx of refugees further straining the already fragile infrastructure – this was apparent with the city's urban pollution and gridlocked traffic – on another scale again to that of Delhi.

My hand-pulled rickshaw inched its way through the masses down to Vivekanda road near to the Howrah Bridge, but the YMCA refused me entry due to the fact that I resembled a tramp covered in black soot. Feeling dejected, I lumbered my way through the darkness passing rows upon rows of beggars, who in some places, were tiered three deep. How could we allow fellow humans to suffer in this way? In a quiet suburb, I found a B & B with a lit passageway and an open door. After my experience at the YMCA, I set about convincing the owner, a smartly dressed Bengali called Mr Malakar, that I was a normal traveller and not a down and out. I gave him the train ticket with some cash to prove my point and he agreed to give me a room. At last a shower, a shave and a bed. The next day, I felt brand new and alive. Mr Malakar gave me a second glance.

'Good morning, you look younger today?'

'It was rejuvenating to have a wash and a night's sleep. Something smells good?' I yawned.

'Jhaal muri, typical food from Calcutta. It's very popular. Do you wish to try?'

'Yes please, I'm starving.'

'It has rice, peanuts, chillies, mustard oil and coconut, mixed with special Bengali spices.' He handed me a bowl with a chapatti.

I could taste the tropics in this mouth-watering spicy dish unique to this part of India. After breakfast, I explored the city. On the riverbank elephants ate whole pineapples, using their trunks to rummage amongst the heaps of fruit and select the juicy ones. It was amusing to watch as they spun them round with the tip of their trunk and wiped away the mud before munching them whole and tossing away the ferns. Stroking the elephants, I was unaware these majestic creatures were covered in hair and felt furry to the touch.

Energetic street sellers were doing a roaring trade selling hot phuchkas from rows of handcarts in the park. These light round hollow puris (crisp fried unleavened bread), the size and shape of a golf ball, were filled with spicy mashed potato and dipped in tamarind water. Individually served in tiny stainless steel bowls. The hot crunch followed by a soft smooth chilli masala flavour was a delight.

Having travelled overland from England to Calcutta with Western Australia being my final destination, the next leg would take me through Burma (Myanmar). However, in the 1970s, foreigners were not allowed passage across this country so I was forced to fly to Bangkok. I would resume the journey by train through Thailand and down the Malay Peninsular to Singapore where I would take a boat for the seven day passage over the Indian Ocean to Perth.

My first visit to India had been a spectacular experience and I now understood why it was such a popular destination. I promised myself that Tamil Nadu, the southernmost state of India, would be next on my travel hit list once I generated enough funds from working in Australia.

Malay Peninsula 1973

THE FLIGHT FROM CALCUTTA TO BANGKOK TOOK FOUR HOURS. A German traveller named Olaf sat next to me on the aircraft and we struck up a rapport. At the immigration desk we were informed by a young official in a sinister black uniform, 'Bangkok is under a state of emergency and a revolution is taking place.'

Olaf and I shared a cab into Bangkok. Protesters were erecting barricades on the streets, violence was erupting all over metropolitan area and a curfew had been imposed by the military but we made it to a squalid hotel just as darkness blacked out the city. More than seventy-five people had been killed and over 800 wounded on that day alone. The uprising was supported by a cross section of society including the middle class who challenged the ruling junta to allow a transition to democracy.

Taavi, the Thai hotel owner, was a leathery octogenarian with shrewd narrow eyes. 'You want pretty girl?' We declined, but each time we met him, be it on the stairs or in the hallway, he would ask the same question. A few days later, I returned to my room to find a naked girl in the bed. Her name was Pakpao and she told me Taavi had sent her. As the curfew was in place, I had no choice but to climb in next to Pakpao and sleep with a complete stranger.

Owing to the insurgency and subsequent brutality within the city, I decided to make my way south towards Singapore earlier than expected. I left Bangkok the following week by train to Butterworth in Malaysia close to the island of Penang. However the journey time of twenty-four hours to cover 800 miles took much longer due to an incident at the Malay border. In 1973, tourism in Thailand was minimal and local people regarded foreigners with suspicion. Communication was an arduous task even for the simplest undertaking and it took me most of the day to find the correct railway station, obtain a ticket and board the train. The carriage was basic and the seats converted to bunk beds after dark with a flimsy curtain to give some element of privacy. These berths filled the whole carriage on both sides.

The train rolled out of Hua Lamphong station and idled through the shanty suburbs interspersed with ornate Buddhist temples. Three Australians arrived from a rear carriage and threw their luggage onto the empty benches either side of me. They were two sisters, Leona and Bunkie, accompanied by Jack, a huge brawny character with an unruly mop of sandy yellow hair and a bone-crushing handshake. They were going all the way to Singapore. Jack bought a box of cold beers from a passing vendor and as the night progressed, I learned he was a renowned actor with a successful film career specialising in action movies. When I met him in 1973 he was famed for his role in the drama series, *Spy Force*.

As the lights dimmed, we climbed into our respective bunks. In the middle of the night the train slowed to a stop at the Malay border. Jack was fast asleep but the guards wanted to check his passport. To wake him they roughed him up a little but he was not the sort of guy to manhandle. He automatically leaped out of the bunk and accidently fell against the guard sending him spinning down the aisle. The commotion lasted for hours during which time the situation rested on a knife edge. The border police threatened to eject us from the train and throw us into a cell. Once they realised his film star status a suitable apology was forthcoming and the train resumed its journey. Instead of sleeping, we continued to chat. Jack had had an extraordinary life. At four years old his mum passed away and he was brought up in an orphanage. Although his image was that of a macho man, he had bohemian qualities and loved the arts. His polyamorous relationship with Leona and Bunkie was unusual but it would successfully continue for another fifteen years.

At Butterworth, Jack lent out the window and threw me the last bottle of beer as the train left the station. I stood and observed three pairs of hands waving from the window and thought to myself, 'What a lovely family.' I boarded the ferry for the three kilometre sailing to Georgetown, the capital of Penang Island, and booked into a dilapidated house hotel close to the town centre. The following morning, I discovered it was also a brothel but the girls were chatty and helpful and my room was comfortable, clean and cheap. It had a high ceiling and a wide fan, perfect for the warm humid nights.

Malaysia was officially Islamic and the population comprised of three quarters Chinese with the remainder split between Malay and Indian. On the island there was an open mix of Taoism, Buddhism, Islam, Christianity and Hinduism. These religions were juxtaposed peacefully and displayed their own identity with pride. I sensed a more relaxed and friendly atmosphere to that of the mainland.

The capital, Georgetown, was a charming cosmopolitan city noted for its British colonial buildings with the Penang Museum being a dignified example. During my stay I ate from the outdoor markets where communal tables were positioned around food stalls. I collected my dish and sat amongst the other diners. On the first night, I chose a local fare called Penang rojak as it appeared so different from anything else on display due to the dark red colouring. A deep-fried doughnut sprinkled with cubes of bean curd, bean sprouts, white fish and pineapple were covered in a thick crimson syrupy peanut sauce. It was delectable. There was such a variety of tastes in Southeast Asian cuisine.

A Chinese family invited me to try their lok lok, skewers of shrimp, crab and mushrooms, blanched in boiling water then dipped in a chilli soy sauce. They advised me to take care on the streets at night due to an unsavoury element within the city, opium addicts, mostly from the West, who wandered around the town in a sorry state. Apart from committing street crime, they hustled for money and gave a bad name to travellers in general. The following year, 1974, the government would throw them off the island prior to the construction of hotels in preparation for a growth in tourism.

The sea beckoned so I made a decision to travel to the north of the island and find a quiet place to enjoy the beauty of nature. On checking out of the brothel, I opened my bedroom door onto the landing and a short-nosed fruit bat flew past my head. It was the size of a baby fox and as it fluttered back and forth the working girls screamed. The poor creature was in distress. I managed to open the blinds at the far end of the corridor and had the satisfaction of seeing it soar to freedom. I had never seen one so close, it was beautiful.

A cycle rickshaw took me to the terminal where I boarded an aging and battered bus destined for the coastal village of Batu Ferringhi. The vehicle was full of farm workers with their round cloth bundles and caged livestock. It meandered from village to village through a mosaic of paddy fields before the road ended at a clump of palm trees three miles from the coast. The only means of transport to the water's edge, other than walking, was by donkey or hand-pulled rickshaw. As the pathway looked quite rugged I chose an unusually large mule with a glossy chestnut coat; after numerous stops to graze, she eventually ambled onto the white sand. I walked up and down the bay and found a tiny room to rent in a flimsy wooden chalet for three ringgits a night. It was a few metres from the sea and home to a local fishing family. The toilet was a small wooden squat, heaving with maggots, in a tiny doorless outhouse behind the shack. They spoke Malay and we communicated with hand gestures and smiles. The head of the household was Irfan, his wife Nurul and their little boy, Irfan junior.

In the early morning the wooden sampans sailed out to sea for their daily catch and on their return everyone in the community helped haul these heavy nets up the beach. In addition to the grilled fish, our diet consisted of guavas, papayas and Nurul's speciality, pancakes smeared with peanut paste. Occasionally, Irfan would swap fish for a mammoth jackfruit. These greenish yellow rugby ball shaped fruits could be one metre wide and weigh up to ten kilos. The orange flesh tasted of a hybrid between pineapple and banana while their fawn coloured seeds resembled water chestnuts.

Irfan junior's pet monkey, Normah, lived in the wild but spent her days hanging around the hut. The macaque sat at the bottom of my string bed and waited for me to throw her a banana. She caught the fruit in one hand, peeled and ate it before throwing the skin back with incredible accuracy. If it bounced of my head she jumped about and shrieked. Prior to leaving, I asked a local artist to sketch Normah and frame it in driftwood as a parting gift. Nural was overjoyed and placed it in a prominent position above the stove. The family insisted on escorting me to the bus stop and together we rode the three miles on bicycles.

Batu Ferringhi is a natural paradise and I was fortunate to have experienced living amongst a sustainable community before it was lost forever. When I look at that area of coastline today, I am horrified. It looks more like Benidorm rather than the emerald green nirvana I remember so well and I often wonder what happened to the fishing families.

After leaving Penang, I arrived back to Butterworth on the mainland and boarded a train for the 430 mile journey through the tropical forests of Malaysia to Singapore. In the 1970s, the most effective way to communicate internationally was by post and on arrival in Singapore I made my way to a nominated Post Restante and collected a letter from James, the older brother of a friend from the USA. He was on assignment in the city and staying at the Pan Pacific Hotel on Orchard Road. I booked into a pension in Chinatown and hailed a rickshaw to his five star hotel. After Irfan's hut, it was another world. There was a door on the toilet and no maggots in the bowl. Monkeys and parrots were nowhere to be seen and the air conditioning made it feel like Canada. James introduced Fowler, a visitor from his home town, New York. We dined on the roof terrace overlooking the city before taking a cab to a jazz venue in the Raffles Hotel, a colonial gem regarded as the 'Grand Historic Hotel of the Far East.'

Chilled Tiger beer was served in the long bar steeped in a colonial ambience and as James chatted to a lady colleague, Fowler told me his life story. For over a decade his profession was as a television game show host in Los Angeles. One day by accident, he discovered his wife was having a long-term affair with his agent. Soon after, the IRS unearthed discrepancies in his tax return due to the fact that the accountant had syphoned off six million dollars from the estate. Both of these events occurred just before the TV show was axed. As a result, he sold up all of his remaining assets, bought a fifteen metre yacht and started life from scratch, sailing around the world. He came across as being stress free, happy and having retained his nutty sense of humour. In the early hours we strayed into Bugis Street, famed for its transgender theatricals, and ate skewers of goat meat with cucumber from a street vendor. In the morning, I visited Fowler on his yacht, Legarde, and we drank tea and chatted in the sunshine until it was time for me to board the MV Eastern Queen for the passage to Australia.

05 Western Australia

'The land is sacred; it belongs to the countless numbers who are dead, the few who are living, and the multitudes of those yet to be born.' ABORIGINAL SAYING

Perth 1974

THE MV EASTERN QUEEN PLOUGHED ITS WAY THROUGH THE tropical waters of the Indian Ocean, accompanied for the greater part of the journey by flying fish. Their streamlined torpedo-shaped bodies gathered enough underwater speed to break the surface and become airborne; gliding through the air with their enormous pectoral fins like the wings of a bird. During the passage of seven days, we crossed the equator midway and docked at the port of Fremantle, Western Australia, the port city which forms part of the Perth Metropolitan area.

The state of Western Australia covers an area of one and half million square miles which is equivalent to sixty-four countries the size of Holland, inhabited by a mere two million people. Although it has over 12,500 miles of coastline, it is made up of mostly arid Outback which is why the majority of the population are concentrated in the fertile south-west corner where the capital Perth is located, next to the Indian Ocean and alongside the Swan River. Although it is one of the most isolated cities in the world, it is a futuristic conurbation which is not only sophisticated and cosmopolitan but easy-going and pretty.

After my year-long overland trip from the UK, the primary purpose of my visit to Australia was to obtain work and top up my travel funds. I decided to apply for difficult and dangerous work in the Outback, mines or fishing boats which were well paid and included accommodation. While I was waiting for the right opportunity I would look for something temporary in Perth.

At Fremantle, while waiting in line to pass through immigration, I wondered why my disembarkation card had different markings on it to that of the other passengers. The explanation became apparent soon after when I was escorted by uniformed customs officers to a private room. They informed I had been randomly selected for a strip search. During the process they deliberated as to whether to remove the heels from my boots, as they could be hiding drugs. I told the officers they were my only footwear. After several hours they allowed both me and my boots entry into the country. I took a room at the YMCA hostel in the centre of Perth on the hottest day of the year in January at the height of their summer.

Ever since I left Northumberland, there had been a recurring image in my mind of running down an Australian beach and throwing myself into the Indian Ocean. The thermometer showed 47ºC when I left the hostel and caught a bus to Scarborough Beach, a coastal suburb ten miles away. As I stripped off my ragged clothes to reveal an emaciated body, the result of protracted third world travelling, I stood out as frail and pale among the copper-coloured surfers with their six-packs and trendy surf boards.

The mountainous sea of white horses rolled gigantic breakers towards the seashore which slammed onto the sand with a thunderous roar. It was far too rough for a shark net to be deployed effectively but I had waited a year for this experience. I took off at a blistering pace in the same way as a terrier chases a rabbit and dived through the ten metre high curling wave; emerging from the other side into a dramatic swell which lifted me up like a bungee jump in reverse. From the apex to the trough, the surfers below resembled crawling ants. The safest way to exit the water was to body surf a wave onto dry land. I stretched out below the foaming crest but the strength of the turbulence beneath gripped my feet and pulled me under. I held my breath as the gushing force took control and twirled and twirled my body like clothes in a tumble dryer. The huge volume of water crashed onto the shore and cartwheeled me up the beach. I lay face down in the searing heat and squeezed the burning sand through my fingers – panting to get my breath back – covered in scratches and abrasions but exhilarated.

'Pleased to meet you Australia!' I kissed the ground.

That first night was the hottest experience of my life, even though the room at the YMCA had a high ceiling with a wide fan. I must have taken ten cold showers during the hours of darkness. I would lay on the bed dripping wet, hoping to fall sleep before the fierce temperature baked me bone dry. But soon after, my body began to swelter excessively and need yet another cold shower. Although the dry heat in Western Australia was preferential to the humidity of the Far East, at this level it was difficult to manage and further compounded by the scorching north-east winds that swept across the Outback. The Perthians claim the city to be one of the windiest in the world. There is a cooling sea breeze from the southwest, referred to locally as the Fremantle Doctor, but it would be three weeks before it changed to an offshore and dropped to a moderate 30ºC.

After a few days at the YMCA, I met two Dutchmen, Kobus, an artist and Wim, a musician, who had rented a four bedroom ground floor apartment in Mount Lawley, a suburb of Perth. They offered me a bedroom and I jumped at the opportunity due to the difficulty of obtaining work without a residential address. The cost of the bond and the first month's rent left me with nothing but change in my pocket.

I bought a newspaper to view the situations vacant and sat in a telephone box making calls until the last remaining five cent piece was all that I possessed in the entire world. The Parmelia Hotel advertised for a kitchen porter and as the coin clinked into the telephone, my whole body constricted with nerves. I talked to a pleasant woman, Ms Fenwick, who invited me along for a face-to-face interview. Later the same day I started work in their kitchen. My first chore was to clean the toilets, so I took the approach that whatever I do in life, do it well. I rolled up my sleeves and got stuck in. They worked an eight hour shift system from early morning to late at night with the inclusion of free meals. As it was a five star hotel the food served to the guests was also given to the staff, so I ate choice steaks, crayfish and beautiful cakes which soon put the weight back on.

A month later, the personnel manager, Ms Fenwick, invited me to her fiftieth birthday party at her home in Subiaco on the other side of the city to Mount Lawley. On arrival at her suburban bungalow, she opened the door and greeted me with a radiant smile. She was wearing a micro bikini and holding a frothy glass of bubbly in her right hand as her left caressed my cheek. 'Come on in my darling, your timing is impeccable, the champers is perfectly chilled.' She sauntered suggestively through the house to a contemporary open plan kitchen and dining area at the rear which stretched out through the folding patio doors into an enchanting garden. As she poured the champagne, 'You're not going to believe this Miles but my birthday is tomorrow and that's when my friends and family arrive. I gave you the wrong date which is why you are the only guest, I do apologise.' She spoke coyly.

'Shall we celebrate the last day of your forties instead? Happy forty-nine years and 364 days!' We smiled and clinked glasses.

Although she was thirty years my senior, she became somewhat amorous before opening the third bottle and suggested I stay overnight. Soon after this encounter, I was promoted to front of house. In my new position as bellboy, I had to report to the head porter by the name of Mark Brown, a tubby American from Chicago, who had made a career as a concierge in premium hotels. He took his work seriously and had a team of four bellhops. His nickname was Lard which referred to his portly characteristics and propensity for meringues with cream. An arrogant man with greasy slicked back mousy hair, waxen skin and a hawkish nose flanked by pink ferret-like eyes.

We stood in pairs at the front desk in the grandiose marble foyer, wearing pale blue monkey suits with two rows of brass buttons which ran up the centre of the chest and onto the shoulders and ended at the epaulettes. The outfit was topped off by a matching oval rimless hat with a gold band. The uniform reminded me of something that a South American military dictator would wear at a parade.

Part of our remit was to meet and greet the arrivals at the imposing entrance by opening their car doors; make them feel welcome and carry their luggage into the hotel. Mark took the guests to their room so he could pocket the tip while he allocated me the task of taking the vehicles to the multi-story car park. There was an endless stream of high-end cars and before long I was behind the wheel of Aston Martins, Rolls Royce's and Ferraris. I would cruise along the highway in these plush marques with the radio blasting *Midnight at The Oasis*, Maria Muldaur, *I Shot the Sherriff*, Bob Marley and *Waterloo*, Abba, while taking them on a circuitous route to the parking lot.

Every Friday afternoon at 4 p.m. the bellhop team crammed into the guest's cloakroom for a meeting. On my first attendance, Mark embarrassingly reprimanded me in front of the others for wearing yellow socks instead of the requisite black. He tugged at my trouser leg to prove his point. Further humiliation was forthcoming at our apartment when Kobus used his artistic skills to draw a man-sized image of a chimpanzee dressed as a bellhop on the living room wall.

Later that month Swinko arrived on a flight from England with the intention of working in Australia for two years. He was a friend from Newcastle, a burly English Pole, who rented the fourth bedroom. As it was a Sunday and a free day, Kobus, Wim and I decided upon a pub crawl to introduce Swinko to Perth. The first watering hole we visited was a dark and dingy aboriginal hostelry. We were the only non-aborigines and regarded with suspicion. Bambam, the albino barman, made us feel welcome and in all of his fifteen years we had been the first pommies to visit. He took a shine to Swinko and kept brushing his hair with his hand each time he brought a jug of chilled Swan lager. These jugs of beer were receptacles intended for sharing into smaller glasses called shetlands, or ponies – a slightly bigger version.

Our next port of call was a typical working man's bar clad with clinically-white ceramic tiles from floor to ceiling which resembled a public toilet and echoed our voices like being in a cave. After a few more in the Irish pub, Durty Nelly's, we tipped into a busy hotel where the tables were fixed to the floor and it was not long before we discovered why. The place erupted into a drunken brawl as chairs and anything else that was loose flew in all directions. Needless to say, we took the earliest opportunity to quietly escape out of a side door.

During conversations with the locals, there was talk of earning big money working manually in the Outback. On the grapevine, we were told of a German called Bruno who was recruiting a four-man gang for a three month stint of land clearing in the bush. It involved the removal of small trees and shrubs to allow cultivation and crops to be planted. The job was located 700 miles north of Perth. When we met with Bruno, a mountain of man with a bushy red beard who had twenty years of experience in this type of work, he impressed upon us he only wanted hard-working men to join his team. We were to be paid by the acre split four ways and live in a caravan in the desert. It was 150 miles to the nearest shop. The fourth member of the gang was a smooth talking ex-SAS Brit called John Bower. A tall, stringy, bald man with thick blond-gingery sideburns and a glint in his eye. Bruno addressed the group as his hit squad and stressed the success of the mission rested upon each and every one of us pulling our weight. Retribution would be in order for anyone failing to keep up.

After submitting one week's notice to Frances Fenwick, my friend and personnel manager at the Parmelia Hotel, she kindly offered to put me up at her home when I returned to Perth. I banked the apartment bond and by the time I left for my new project, the balance in the account was beginning to look healthy.

The Outback 1974

THE FOLLOWING WEEK, WE CLIMBED ABOARD BRUNO'S EIGHT LITRE four wheel drive Holden for a journey through the last true wilderness on earth. His vehicle had morphed into an expedition truck with: six metal water containers, spare parts, shovels, machetes, general tools, food, medical supplies and two rifles carefully stowed onto a sturdy roof rack. An ominous metal structure called a kangaroo bar was fixed to the front and two spare tyres to the rear. We had acquired wide-brimmed hats, several pairs of working gloves, protective sun lotions and two weeks of food rations. Bruno banned alcohol as we would be working, eating and sleeping – nothing else.

After we left the cultured city and drove into the Outback, the song we listened to on the radio before losing contact was, *When Will I See You Again*, by The Three Degrees. The tarmac road changed to a brick red earth and ran straight as an arrow to the horizon. Either side of the track was an expanse of dry arid desert. Occasionally, the monotony would be interrupted by a shimmering mirage of a triple trailer road train which suddenly appeared and flashed past with a roar and an explosive cloud of red dust.

Bruno had a passion for the Australian wildlife and as we had time to spare I asked him, 'How would you best describe a marsupial?'

'A mammal whose distinctive characteristic is it carries its young in a pouch. They are endemic to the southern hemisphere and range in weight from ten grams for the Tasmanian pigmy possum up to ninety kilos for the red kangaroo.'

'What on earth is a wombat?'

'It's a burrowing plant-eating marsupial which looks like a small bear with short legs, about one metre long, similar to a badger without a tail.'

'What other marsupials are there?'

'There are so many. The Aborigines used to hunt most of them. They include grey kangaroos, wallabies, possums, koalas and numbats. We have to be especially careful not to crash into the kangaroos at night as it could be fatal. The roo bar helps protect the engine if we hit one.'

'I've never heard of a numbat?'

'It's an anteater but they're rare and most are found near Adelaide in South Australia.'

As the hours rolled by and the truck cruised the undeviating line, we took it in turns to drive or doze. At around 5am the following morning we stopped travelling on a linear course and turned right up a smaller track. Around twenty miles later arriving at a decrepit caravan next to one acacia tree in the middle of nowhere. It was surrounded by a sea of desert wilderness covered in pockets of mulga scrub. We stepped out of the truck into silence, the air was still and a red orange sunrise spread over the wide sky. We looked up towards the sound of whooshing from a flock of ringneck parrots as they swarmed in symmetry like daubs of black paint against a radiant light.

'We refer to them as 'twenty-eight' parrots because of their distinctive 'twentee-eight' call,' said Bruno.

By 6am, the beauty had vanished and the air was filled with bush flies which buzzed around our heads and into our ears, eyes and noses. We pulled our hats down and tied our scarves over our faces in an effort to keep them at bay.

Bruno explained, 'It's the female bush fly that pesters us because she wants our saliva, mucus and tears, it's how she gets her protein. She needs it to breed and that's why she's so persistent and so in our face.'

I laughed at John who looked akin to a mad man on a mission to flail himself to death as he tried to keep the bush flies away; whereas Bruno simply ignored these annoying insects when they crawled around his face. The rustic caravan was old, tired and smelled fusty. Bruno meticulously checked the crevices and hideaways for snakes and venomous bugs. The rest of us gave it a full valet to remove the grease and dead flies.

The briefing from Bruno was simple – work from sun up to sun down – eat then sleep. He allocated each person an exclusive en suite bush to use as their own toilet. Ablutions had to be completed before 6am, when the flies joined us for the day, and definitely not after dark as we could tread on a deadly nocturnal creature.

I worked alongside Bruno to see if I could cope with the pace. He didn't walk but ran to the first clump of bushes and feverishly hacked at the vegetation with a machete, cutting it into pieces. He made bonfire pyramids with the loose scrub and ran to the next group of bushes. After three days, my feet were covered in egg sized blisters and the running was reduced to a hobble. Over yet another tin of mince and potatoes, Bruno exercised his medical expertise and attended to our feet; we all placed our blistered tootsies onto stools as he dipped his bowie knife into boiling water and punctured each of the pustules with amazing dexterity, draining them of fluid. I wish I had recorded the squeals.

At two week intervals Wally the farm hand arrived in his pickup with our food supplies. On his first visit he complained about our lack of progress. The next time Wally made the delivery, we tied him to the acacia tree and used his truck to drive across the desert and light all the bonfire stacks to improve our productivity. Wally was upset with his treatment and became aggressive. Bruno picked him up in a bear hug and threatened to rub his head in the faeces under Swinko's bush. He was much more respectful after that altercation.

Each one of us at some point had issues with Bruno and the pace in which we had to work but we remained good friends and a team spirit endured the day to day hardship. Sleeping was not an issue, as soon as our heads hit the oily pillows we were gone until Bruno's gruff voice woke us at 5am. One night, I heard the sound of something strange scuttling over the caravan floor. I called out to Bruno who shone his torch onto three scorpions before kicking them out of the door with his bare feet. We had left the door ajar.

After two months, we began to suffer from not only fatigue but cabin fever being stuck in the same place with the same people, night and day. We had become more muscular, fitter, darker skinned and had grown shaggy beards, to say nothing of our calloused hands. Although cleanliness lapsed and we washed once a week, I made it a rule to clean my teeth daily. Sometimes the wind would pick up to gale force and we would have to work throughout the day in a sandstorm. It stung our skin, gritted our mouth and gave us itchy red eyes. When we walked into the wind the flies would seek protection by gathering on our backs covering us with a shimmering metallic sheen like a lizard's skin.

One evening in the fading light of day, there was a sudden knock at the door, normally an everyday occurrence at home, but 150 miles from the nearest house, it made us all jump. I opened the caravan door and standing there was an Aboriginal elder with salt and pepper hair tied into a ponytail. He wore a red bandana, a white shirt and black trousers and wanted to buy a blanket. His name was Gumaroy and he had set up camp nearby.

We sat around the dying embers of the fire with mugs of coffee while John located a spare blanket. We were enthusiastic at having a visitor, especially an Aborigine, and I wanted to ask him many questions about his culture. He told us that the Aboriginal people had been in Australia for sixty-five thousand years before the white man arrived. They had the longest continuous cultural history of any group of people on earth. Each one of their 600 tribes had a different language which extended through to over 3,000 dialects. Gumaroy related the Aboriginal dreamtime stories which describe the travels of their mystical ancestors, who were integral to Aboriginal spirituality and covered the past, present and future; he told the story of the rainbow serpent who had given birth to all of creation: the lakes, rivers, mountains, sun and fire. This spoken dialogue was a way in which to pass down knowledge to the next generation.

I asked Gumaroy where to find the witchetty grub, a large white, wood-eating larvae similar to a big caterpillar that was a staple foodstuff of the Aborigines. He pointed at the ground where we were sitting. They lived underneath the soil, inside the roots of the acacia tree. When he left our camp, he walked into the darkness without a light, I ran after him with a spare torch but he dismissed the gesture with his hand and pointed at the moon.

Not long after Wally had unloaded our supplies late one afternoon, I was beavering away feeding the bonfires when a brown snake, over one metre long with an orange underbelly, slithered between my boots. I shouted over to Bruno and pointed at the snake which prompted him to run in the opposite direction towards the caravan to retrieve a phial of anti-venom from the first aid kit in case it attacked.

'It's a Western Brown Snake. They're super-fast, highly venomous and can be aggressive when disturbed,' he said.

Sometimes, the morning sky would fill with flocks of budgerigars which would scatter when the wedge-tailed eagles hovered high in the sky. These eagles were the largest bird of prey in Australia and had been known to hunt young kangaroos. One evening, when I was throwing wood on the fire, I found a black scorpion hanging by its pincers from my gloved hand and managed to knock it into the fire with a stick as it crawled onto my bare arm. Quite often the poodle-sized sleepy lizards stood close by and stared. These reptiles looked vicious but were harmless.

John, Swinko, Bruno and I began to show signs of agitation with each other towards the end of our third month. Two more weeks to go and the farmer would arrive and price up the work. We were to be paid in cash as self-employed contractors. The Australian revenue had automatically reimbursed most of the tax deducted from both jobs because I was leaving the country. Three month's work in the bush amounted to a whole year's salary in England. The combination of incomes had replenished my travel fund and it was ready to be deployed. The big day arrived and we each collected our swag-bag of cash from the farmer amongst hoots of laughter. We looked forward to returning to the human race, itching for some edible food and a cold beer.

Perth and Adelaide 1974

DRIVING BACK TO PERTH, THE ATMOSPHERE INSIDE THE TRUCK WAS buzzing as we chatted incessantly between bursts of *Waltzing Matilda*. When the futuristic skyline of Perth appeared on the horizon, we were like children on Christmas morning. Bruno parked the filthy truck on Hay Street. When we clambered out the pedestrian flow steered clear; not surprising given the fact that we resembled hillbilly tramps and had failed to shower in three months.

Swinko and I were invited to stay at John's flat in Subiaco where we took a long hot shower and changed into some city clothing. The four of us met at the nearest bar. The table was covered in empty beer jugs when we left to visit an Italian restaurant. Everyone ordered steak, or two steaks as was the case with Swinko and Bruno. On the table opposite, a balding plump gentleman had fallen asleep on his folded arms next to a steaming pizza. Swinko scooped it up with his hand and laid it carefully on his egg-shaped head much to the amusement of the other diners. The searing heat eventually roused him and as he jolted upright the pizza flew half way across the restaurant. To add insult to injury, the poor man was noisily evicted from the premises. Seconds later he was at the window with his nose and hands pressed hard against the glass, scowling at us, and the top of his bald head glowed bright red.

During the course of the evening Bruno got into a fight with three bullies. They had threatened a Maori by the name of Rongo, so Bruno exchanged blows with the thugs while we stood by as spectators. A police car pulled alongside, 'G'day boys, we're going to drive round the block and whoever's on the street when we return will be arrested and locked up for the night.'

We ran into a nightclub with Rongo and left the hooligans nursing their wounds. The next morning I woke up with a monumental hangover and found Rongo asleep on the kitchen floor.

The effect of returning to civilisation with the boys became apparent so I decided to escape and stay with my risqué friend Frances Fenwick, the personnel manager from the Parmelia Hotel. Frances turned out to be a brilliant chef and my display of appreciation was an ongoing source of amusement to her. At the weekend, we visited the wallabies at one of Perth's nature parks where we lay alongside these endearing marsupials stroking their bellies in the sunshine. Above us in the branches of the karri trees, pairs of enchanting Galhas, rose-breasted cockatoos, groomed each other as they perched in long rows facing the warm breeze.

She shared her passion for Aboriginal music. The Noongar people of Western Australia are one of the nation's largest indigenous groups and Frances took me to a musical workshop they were giving in Wanneroo. We listened to their performance with the famous didgeridoo and a bullroarer; a piece of wood shaped like a sword and attached to a length of cord. They whirled it around in a circle to make a low-pitched rumble like a sports car revving its engine. One elderly member placed a gum-leaf between his lips and blew over the surface – causing it to vibrate and produce a high pitched sound – originally used to mimic bird calls. At the rear, boomerangs were played as high-density hardwood clapsticks to effect a well-defined percussion. What a delightful experience to listen to them as an ensemble.

Francis allocated me some space in her home to research my travel master plan. I would make my way through Malaysia to the island of Penang and take a boat to Tamil Nadu, a state in South India. I had no particular agenda other than to wander within the Indian Subcontinent until my funds were depleted which I calculated to be in the region of one year. Beyond that, I wanted to return to Australia and work a full season on the cray fishing boats and maybe a further six months in the opal mines which would enable me to buy my own house outright in England. An embryonic vision of being self-sufficient.

I reserved a berth on the MV Eastern Queen to Singapore and set about preparing myself for the journey with a full body service which included visits to a dentist, a barber and the doctor for updated vaccines. There were two weeks to go before I left Australia. That night, Frances gave me a task. The Parmelia Hotel had bought two minibuses from a dealership in Adelaide and it was cheaper to send someone to collect rather than have them shipped by trailer. A paid opportunity and Swinko would be the second driver. We realised the distances involved when collecting the train tickets from the travel agent. It was 1,700 miles from Perth to Adelaide over the famed Nullarbor Plain which equated in mileage to that of London to Athens. I now understood why Perth was the most isolated city in the world.

We took the Indian Pacific train for the three day and two night journey to Adelaide which was the longest single stretch of railway in the world. As the train left the gold mining town of Norseman, it passed through the western gateway into the Nullarbor Plain. A flat featureless, treeless and monotonous semi-arid landscape which stretched 1,000 miles to Port Augusta in South Australia. The luxurious air-conditioned cabins were en suite and the bench seats converted into bunk beds at night. In the morning the attendant brought tea at 7am, and for breakfast the restaurant carriage served steak and scrambled eggs with real orange juice. The lunches and dinners were also of a similarly fine quality.

We were pleasantly surprised by Adelaide, South Australia's coastal capital, smaller than Perth but a cool city with a long beachfront. Frances had told me it ranked highly in terms of liveability and boasted a thriving arts scene. While the minibuses were being prepared, we took a swim in the calm sea of the Great Australia Bight from Glenelg beach and afterwards visited an Aboriginal art exhibition.

The Aboriginal people have no written language of their own. Their paintings are in effect a visual story used as a means of passing on vital information to the next generation and for the preservation of their culture. Originally their artwork appeared on tree bark and rocks but once it moved to canvas they adopted a style called dot painting; a technique used to obscure the symbols underneath and hide secret information from the white man. The nucleus of Aboriginal philosophy derived from their long-term survival in a hostile environment. It is rich in spirituality, cultural behaviour and knowledge therefore belongs in museums and of course, galleries.

Once the vehicles were ready the dealership foreman, Connor, gave us a pre-trip briefing, 'Rule number one, if an emu, camel, dingo or kangaroo moves to the centre of the road, don't swerve or you roll. If you roll, you die! Don't drive at dusk, dawn or during darkness if you value your life.

Beware of road kill at all times. Each bus has a container with fifty litres of water and I suggest you drive in a convoy taking it in turns to be the lead. Good luck.'

That afternoon we made the first leg to Port Augusta, 200 miles away and slept in the vehicles. Soon after daybreak we reached the National Highway and drove all day, every day during daylight hours for three full days crossing the grim wastelands of the Nullarbor Plain. Each night we parked the buses by the roadside. When we arrived in Perth, we pulled into the main entrance of the Parmelia and handed the keys to Mark Brown, the head porter and took a shower. Francis and I returned to her home and during the week that followed I assembled my travelling kit and wrote letters to my parents, relatives and friends.

The boys organised a farewell party on the Friday night before my departure on Sunday morning. At 3am, we staggered out of the nightclub and fell into Rongo's souped-up Holden coupé. I realised he was incapable behind the wheel when he drove into a sapling in the car park. In fact, none of us were capable but I made the stupid mistake of taking the wheel. On the way home, I drove the wrong way up a one-way street and at the T-junction two policemen waved their arms high above their heads gesturing for me to stop. If I was charged with drink driving my trip would be cancelled. There would be months of hanging around for the court case in addition to the costs and the stress. All of which flashed through my mind in a flurry of images.

I jerked the steering wheel to the right and accelerated down a narrow backstreet at speed. The car shot out of the alleyway like a bullet, skidding sideways across the main avenue before gaining traction and squealing towards Subiaco. The police cars were 200 metres behind so they were too far away to see our number plate. Up to 100 mph kept them at a suitable distance. Fifteen minutes later we roared into the cul-de-sac and hit a speed bump launching us like a missile through the apartment block entrance. I braked hard as the coupé slid across the lawn and wedged itself between two trees, making both doors inoperable. We climbed out through the sun roof.

The next morning my first thought on awakening was, 'Did that actually happen?' Before pulling back the curtains and there it was, Rongo's car sandwiched between two eucalyptus trees and elevated ten centimetres from the ground. I looked in the mirror and told myself firmly to grow up. It took six of us to rock it back and forth and eventually free it from the tree trunks. Rongo was delighted we had outrun the police because of his fragile work permit status, especially if legal proceedings had progressed. He would happily attend to the damage himself.

On my last night in Australia, I took the lovely Frances out to a fish restaurant which specialised in barbequed crayfish, her favourite. Over dinner, I gave her a gift of an original Aborigine painting of a wallaby as a thank you for her support, kindness and friendship. The waiter asked if it was my mother's birthday which had us both howling with laughter.

After boarding the MV Eastern Queen in Fremantle, I looked down at the throng of people standing on the quayside waving enthusiastically to their departing families and friends. At the front of the crowd stood Frances, Bruno, Swinko, John, Wim, Kobus and Rongo gesticulating with their hands when suddenly something flew through the air and clattered next to my feet – a can of Swan lager. I opened it with a hiss as the ship gave two long deep blasts of the horn and with a tear in my eye toasted farewell to my special friends and to Australia. The vessel swivelled round and glided through the harbour entrance into the Indian Ocean *en route* to Singapore. Australia had given me a great appreciation of how tough life could be and how resolute the Aboriginal people are in the face of adversity. As Gumaroy said, 'The more we know, the less we need.'

06 Indian Summer

'We can't change the direction of the wind, but we can adjust the sails.' INDIAN PROVERB

Tamil Nadu 1975

THE OCEAN GOING MV TAMIL NADU STOOD PROUD FROM ITS mooring as it dominated the harbour and cast a shadow over the terminal. The ship was docked in the town of Butterworth on the western seaboard of Malaysia in readiness for the six day sailing over the Bay of Bengal, through the Andaman and Nicobar Islands, to Madras (Chennai) in India. Droves of impatient Indians with their worldly possessions gathered on the quayside in an unruly fashion jostling for position to board the aging vessel. When the whistle blew and the gantry lowered, the mob swarmed into the bottleneck and the boat began to list to an unhealthy angle. I decided to retreat to the café and be one of the last to embark.

Aboard, there were no safety drills and the lifeboat signs pointing towards the muster stations were obscured by rust. With a rumble from the shuddering engines, a booming fog horn and plumes of black smoke, the boat edged its way out of the port and into the open sea.

On each of the six levels, there were immense poorly lit dormitories laid out with fifty metal cages, each containing four bunk beds. During the hours of darkness the smell and noise in these communal areas got the better of me and I brought my sleeping bag onto the open deck. There was a cosy concealed area to bed down between a life boat and a capstan. I unfurled my bedroll, folded my jacket into a pillow and stared up at a cloudless night sky shrouded in navy blue and ablaze with celestial constellations. There was a warm sea breeze flowing over the bow - a gentle rolling motion as it glided through the calm waters - a guttural moaning and monotonous vibration from the engines below. I was soon asleep.

On the third night, I caught sight of a shadowy figure with spiky hair moving between the lifeboats and who nearly tripped over me.

'Sorry, I didn't see you.' He talked with an Essex accent.

'Are you English?'

'Yes, I'm from Ilford.'

'I thought I was the only westerner aboard. I'm Miles from Newcastle.'

'You gave me a fright. I didn't think there was anyone on deck. Hi, I'm Richard.' He shook my hand.

Richard was a Ten Pound Pom, an Australian term given to British people who had relocated to Australia via an assisted passage scheme during the 1970s. He was on his way to Madras to experience India before flying home to London. After five years in Melbourne working as an architect's technician, he wanted to return to his homeland. He had also decided to sleep in the open air as he felt claustrophobic and overly hot in the cages down below. He rolled out his sleeping bag next to mine and struggled to remove his black winklepicker boots. We gazed at the shooting stars and talked of fish and chips, real ale, Coronation Street, Bob Dylan, and of course, the weather. He reminisced about his passion for playing the mandolin and hoped to reignite his musical skill one day. The next morning, the winklepickers had vanished. They were his one pair of shoes and he would arrive at Madras in his socks. We visited the ships bursar and the subject matter caused much hilarity in their office, which in turn made me laugh as Richard stood there in his knee length hosiery. Members of the crew formed an orderly line each clutching their spare footwear, and after much deliberation, he purchased a pair of used flip flops.

On the fifth day, we anchored at sea a mile offshore, 200 miles to the south of Madras next to the coastal village of Nagapattinam in the state of Tamil Nadu. A wooden rowing boat pulled up alongside and a net full of small fish was hauled up. I instantaneously made a decision to leave the ship via this boat. It would save me a rail journey from Madras as I was heading south to Ceylon (Sri Lanka). I gripped the swaying hessian ladder that followed the motion of the vessel and began my descent, the end of which did not quite reach the little boat. The ladder was a metre or so too short. When the ship rolled from one side to the other I let go on cue as the two Indian crew reached up to grab my legs and we tumbled into the tiny craft. As the rope lowered my rucksack, I looked up at the gigantic ship and noticed the faint silhouette of Richard and his spiky hair waving goodbye with his arms high above his head.

The creaking timber craft pitched and rolled into the pocket-sized seaport. On the jetty, two officials with peaked caps performed a military salute in unison before escorting me to a wooden hut where I was interrogated for three hours; for no other reason than being the first non-Indian to arrive at this harbour since the war. At dusk, they ceremoniously stamped my passport and I hurried along a dirt track into the forgotten town to find it empty. There were no cars, two abandoned handcarts and a lone donkey. The silence was broken briefly by a handful of chattering people walking past followed by a meandering cow. There appeared to be no bank and it was a Saturday night.

I sat on a wall pondering what to do when a young Hindu on a bicycle stopped in front of me. He also performed a military salute. Out of courtesy, I returned the greeting.

'What are you doing in Tamil Nadu?'

I told him why I left the boat and my subsequent lack of rupees.

'The nearest bank is in Thanjavur, fifty miles away and the money changer in Nagapattinam is not open until Tuesday due to the state holiday.' He gave an Indian head wobble.

'Three days without money,' I thought out loud.

'Come and stay with my family,' he insisted.

Prabhat worked as a clerk in the railway station and I was grateful to be invited to his home, a single story round house with two rooms made from mud bricks and covered by thatched reeds. He introduced me to his wife, Kusuma, who nodded a welcome and disappeared to make the food. I sat on the earthen floor next to a plastic table cloth on which Prabhat placed a banana leaf. He ladled two scoops of white rice onto the leaf accompanied by an aluminium pot of yellow lentils with fingers of okra and placed a chapatti on the side. I sat alone and ate with my right hand while Prabhat, his wife and three small children sat bunched up in the other room.

My bed was a piece of straw matting outside the hut, under a thatched overhang where I rolled out my sleeping bag and retired early to give the family some space. The first morning, I awoke to an audience of inquisitive children with wide brown eyes who followed me everywhere while holding their hands over their mouths and giggling.

Kusuma collected water 100 metres from their home and used a heavy wooden bucket tied to a rope fed through grooves in the well. As she poured the water into an aluminium container shaped like a milk churn, frogs jumped in all directions. Once filled with twenty litres, she gripped the handles and with one swift action lifted it up and positioned it on her head. A rolled up tea towel cushioned the load. She refused offers of help by waving an arm dismissively and walked to the hut in a steady poise.

The family always seemed to be happy and their neighbours and friends greeted one another with warm smiles. Prabhat and I discussed lifestyles and he suggested they were wealthy. I questioned his logic but he was referring to spiritual wealth as the reason for their contentment.

'A satisfied life is better than a successful one. Because success is measured by others whereas satisfaction is measured by our own soul, mind and heart,' smiled Prabhat.

It was second nature for everyone in the village to help each other. He told me about their cousin who worked in a café seven days a week for two free meals a day plus a pittance of a salary. Each Friday, he cooked a large pot of dhal and distributed it amongst the homeless from a steel box on his moped. I thought to myself that whenever help is needed, it is invariably those who are needy themselves who give.

Early on Tuesday morning, Prabhat suggested I stop in Thanjavur and visit the one thousand year old Brihadishwara Temple which is India's most famous Hindu shrine. I changed my Australian dollars for rupees and went directly to the market and bought: lentils, rice, bunches of garlic, some cardamoms, nutmeg, mustard seeds and a carton of sweets for the children. I hired an enthusiastic driver with his hand-pulled rickshaw to deliver the foodstuff to Prabhat and Kusuma's home where we stacked the provisions neatly alongside the stove. They found it strange I wanted to give something as a thank you but it was the least I could do for their kindness. The same rickshaw took me to the station.

In Thanjavur I rented a room overnight and, as per Prabhat's suggestion visited the Brihadishwara Temple, a Hindu shrine dedicated to Shiva, one of the three major deities of Hinduism. It was the world's first granite temple with the tallest tower in India. When I entered the walled complex the air thickened to a fusty church-like atmosphere clouded by fireflies. In this place of worship my thoughts mulled over the variations between what I had been taught of Christianity at school in England and that of the Hindu religious teachings which Prabhat and Kusuma's children would undertake.

Christianity segregated mankind from the rest of the natural world. The nature of God was deemed as transcendent and essentially different from creation whilst learning was channelled through prophets and popes. The human world was emphatically not the sphere in which the moral destiny of the individual was played out, rather, rewarded or punished him or her for their earthly activities only after death.

Hinduism regarded each and every sentient being as having value. The Divine was inherent in all of creation and the source of awareness came from within the individual. The spiritual principal of karma would influence the future of that person as the actions of the human were the subject of cause and effect.

In an enclosed courtyard, I stretched out in a quiet corner and took some chai while listening to a musician play a four metre long woodwind instrument. It was positioned between his legs and sounded eerily of a melodic fog horn. Behind the instrumentalist towered India's largest statue of Nandi, Shiva's sacred bull with yellow garlands around his neck and sculpted from an enormous chunk of pink granite. As the light faded, the temple changed colour from a pinkish hue to orange and then to an orange-red. The atmosphere was sublime and made a lasting impression.

The train from Thanjavur to Rameswaram on Pamban Island took most of the day, stopping at each station, even though it was a mere 150 miles. At one of India's most southerly points, the train left the mainland and rattled over the sea on a single wobbly rail track called the Pamban Bridge onto Pamban Island. The distance to Ceylon from Rameswaram over the Gulf of Mannar was twenty miles but there was one problem – the monsoon season was underway – and the ferry had been mothballed for the season. Local fishermen offered to take me over if and when the wind eased. In the meantime I found a room in a wooden house with a pier that extended into the sea.

In Rameswaram I became a regular visitor at a café whose speciality was bhelpuri, a puri bread served with: peanuts, green chilli, tamarind, coriander, ginger and mango. Presented as a thali on a stainless steel platter with six little bowls arranged around a mound of puffed rice scooped from a shiny silver bucket. At the end of the main street and adjacent to the sea stood the majestic white stone tower of the Ramanathaswamy Temple where hundreds of people in dhotis and saris immersed themselves in the water up to their waist. It was a Tirtha – a Hindu place of watery pilgrimage.

As the week progressed the weather worsened and the wind increased to gale force making the boat passage over to Ceylon seem remote. While wandering around the island I discovered a peaceful stretch of beach to myself and sheltered from the driving rain under a cluster of palm trees. In the distance I could see a lone, shaven-headed Buddhist in an orange robe walking in my direction and as he came into focus, I recognised him as a Caucasian.

'Namaste,' I shouted.

'Vanakkam,' he responded and walked over. 'The greeting namaste is from Northern India and in Tamil Nadu you must use the term vanakkam.'

'You speak English.'

'Yes, I'm from Gatesheed.'

'That's astonishing!'

I had not met a single westerner since the chance encounter on the ship. Here I was on a forgotten beach in a remote location on the most southerly tip of India during the monsoon season chatting with a Buddhist Geordie. He introduced himself as Derek, who had been studying his religious craft on Pamban Island for three years. As we ambled into Rameswaram I asked what had attracted him to Buddhism in the first place. He went on to explain his passion for a way of life which taught wisdom and respect for all forms of life and the importance of being moral, mindful and understanding. It had given him a code of practice to live by and helped him understand the meaning of his own life. Since he had lived on the island, his spiritual development had evolved into a true contentment and this serenity radiated from his persona.

In his early years, Derek had worked as a fitter in the Tyneside shipyards. He was brought up as a single child in a high-rise block of flats overlooking the River Tyne. When he was seven years old, his father left home to work on the oil rigs and they never heard from him again. His mother died in her early fifties from cancer caused by heavy smoking. Buddhism gave him a purpose in life and helped him recognise the injustices, inequalities and lack of compassion which existed around the world. He wanted to use his new powers to help others and perhaps work for an international charity one day.

Derek looked after an elephant by the name of Moti, owned by a charitable trust who hired her out as a working animal. She also assisted with a variety of Buddhist ceremonies. Moti lived nearby and he took me to meet her. A towering creature who loved bananas. She lifted her trunk and curled it round my shoulder as a thank you for the treats.

'Apart from fruit what else does she eat?'

'She feeds on roots, bark and grass.'

'What sort of volume.'

'About 100 kilos a day.'

'How long does it take for her to consume all that?'

'Most of the day.'

'Is she intelligent?'

'For sure! When we're in the forest, if the fruit is too high she wraps her trunk around the tree and gives it a shake.'

'That's funny.'

'She's so sensitive and loving. Last week I was feeling low and she gently stroked my back with her trunk. Moti is a truly affectionate animal.'

'What a lovely creature.' I gave Moti a pineapple before we left.

At the bhelpuri café, Derek, a vegan, ordered paruthi paal. A sweetened milk made from cotton seeds.

'I don't think I shall ever return to England as my heart is in India.'

Sometimes travellers stayed overseas for too long and it tipped the balance to the point they became a stranger in their own country. Tantu, an Indian friend of Derek's who was brought up in England told me that in India he was English but in England he was Indian.

Derek invited me to join him at a session with his spiritual teacher and guru. He described meditation as a vital part of the process towards enlightenment, from where I would gradually warm to the tranquillity of thought which this practice brought about. We sat cross-legged on a smooth wooden floor in silence as we prepared our minds. The guru told me to focus on my breathing, not to think of the future or the past but to disengage from my thoughts. If my mind wandered, not to become anxious, but to gently escort it back into the present in which to reach a state of mindfulness. It will remove negativity of thought and prepare for meditation. I found it both intriguing and therapeutic, and to this day I allocate time to meditate.

After several weeks, the wind refused to abate and the heavy rains turned the narrow lanes into a sea of mud. As there were no boats willing to sail or row over to Ceylon, I decided to continue with my journey to Madurai. From where I would gradually make my way up to Bombay (Mumbai) via: Bangalore (Bengaluru), Mysore (Mysuru), Mangalore (Mangaluru) and Goa.

When the rickety train left the station, Derek's image stood out as a solitary blob of bright orange among a plethora of brilliant white as he stood waving from the bustling platform. The locomotive wobbled along the single track a whisker above the heaving ocean spitting sea foam through the open windows like a snow blizzard. It stopped at every station and took most of the day to reach Madurai.

Madras is the capital of Tamil Nadu but Madurai, one of the oldest cities in India, is the heart and soul of Tamil culture. The city straddles the mighty River Vaigai which originates in the Ghat mountains to the west. The nucleus of Madurai has to be the Meenakshi Amman Hindu Temple, one of the biggest complexes in India and proportionately surrounded by fourteen opulently embellished pyramidal towers referred to as gopurams.

This magnificent Hindu temple is dedicated to the female deity, Meenakshi, who represents fertility and love and is known as the fish-eyed goddess because of her exquisitely shaped eyes. The Dravidian architecture depicts thousands of vibrantly painted stone statues of gods, animals and demons which cover the walls of these lofty gopurams.

My yellow rickshaw led the way from the station through the pandemonium of the city to the temple and adjoining market. It overtook the dawdling carts pulled by twin oxen and steered clear of the lone cows which sauntered through the crowded streets and alleyways. They would lift their tails and deposit their dung outside of newsagents and hardware stores.

Outside the entrance to the temple, I heard the musical peal of hand bells accompanied by light percussion. I waded through the multitudes towards this beautiful sound, surprised to find it was, in fact, a mechanical box from which protruded: four drumsticks, three hanging bells, one small drum and a cymbal. At the front, the drumsticks oscillated at different speeds to create the beat and on the top, smaller pads rocked back and forward to ring the bells. The gadget was perfectly synchronised and produced a professional sound. It must have been invented by a mad musical professor.

In the market, I drank a jiljil jigarthanda, a vanilla milk drink with a rose flavoured syrup and also tried a palm sugar version called panangkarkandu paal, both of which were rich, sweet and exclusive to Tamil cuisine. From the milk stall, I observed a skilled barber in a roofless salon use a gleaming wet razor with great dexterity to shave the beard of an old man. With a smooth chin, he crossed the road and deposited his own faeces in the gutter in full view of a disinterested public.

After several days in this restless city, it was time to leave, not only Madurai, but Tamil Nadu for the 300 miles train journey directly north to Bangalore.

Karnataka 1975

BANGALORE — WHICH MEANS BOILED BEANS IN A LOCAL DIALECT — IS the capital of the state of Karnataka and positioned on the Deccan plateau 900 metres above sea level. It is one of the highest major cities in India where the climate is more moderate. Throughout South Asia it is regarded as a progressive metropolis and home to India's aeronautics industry. Bangalore was purely a transit point from which to connect by rail to Mysore in the same state, situated at the foot of the Chamundi Hills, peppered with lakes and famed for its age old Devaraja Market and Palace of Mysore.

At the station in Mysore, a betel nut seller persuaded me to pop a folded green leaf into my mouth. I did want to try one at some point but there is never a right moment for this experience. It tasted similar to cough medicine and by the time I spat it out, my lips, teeth and tongue were stained a dark red. It had the same effect as having too much coffee and I felt overstimulated and on edge.

In the centre of the city I rented a room above an ironmongers overlooking Mohalla Square and its ornate water fountain. It was situated a few miles from the vibrant Devaraja Market which became psychedelic in the run up to Diwali — the Hindu Festival of Light — which celebrates the victory of light over darkness. Cone-shaped heaps of flour, ground rice or sand in lurid colours of: fluorescent pink, dazzling yellow, gaudy green, brilliant blue and flaming red. These powders were used to make Rangoli, traditional Indian decorations and patterns spread over the floor.

Darkness fell and the essence of curry leaves emanated from the simmering sambar being cooked in all the cafés and on every handcart. This hearty vegetable chowder was served with dosas, a type of pancake made from rice flour and ground pulses. The other local speciality was Mysore pak, a delicious buttery sweet made with cardamom flavoured ghee.

On Sunday night, I viewed the Palace of Mysore illuminated by 100,000 lights. Its architecture had blended styles from

Hindu, Islam, Rajput and Gothic but I was especially fond of the crimson marble domes. Under the pale moon, these ruby coloured arched roofs were gilded by the soft golden threads from strings of lightbulbs which formed delicate trellis patterns over their surface similar to those found on Fabergé eggs.

Mysore was an impressive conurbation. It was cleaner and more organised than most cities I had visited in India. The train ride from Mysore to the coastal city of Mangalore on the Arabian Sea took four hours and covered 100 miles. There was a welcome offshore breeze as I walked via the beach to the Post Restante to collect my mail.

There was a postcard from Torben and Helle, the Danish couple I had met in Delhi the previous year when we appeared as extras in a Bollywood movie. They were travelling overland from Nepal and would meet me on the east coast. My plan was to rent a house in Goa for four or five months prior to taking a boat 400 miles up the beautiful Koncan coastline to Bombay and flying back to England.

I hailed a tuk-tuk to go to the railway station in Mangalore as an American tourist barged me out of the way and took it for himself. I caught the one behind instead, driven by a Sikh who was enraged by this incident. He held the driver responsible and a confrontation between the two tuk-tuks morphed into a race. They slowed down on the ascent due to the overweight tourist, but for the same reason travelled faster downhill. We were neck and neck as the angry Sikh edged closer and closer to the other vehicle and forced the Hindu driver to shoot down a narrow crowded alley at full pace. Never agitate a Sikh was the message and we both laughed all the way to the terminal.

Goa 1975

MANGALORE TO GOA IS 250 MILES VIA THE COASTAL ROUTE however, it took close to twenty-four hours to complete the journey due to a mix of train delays, mechanical problems and missed ferry connections. It was well after dark when the trishaw slowed to a stop outside of Sani's ramshackle bar on Coco Beach where a closed sign hung from the shutters. I sat on the sand and gazed out at the twinkling night lights of small fishing boats scattered over the silky-smooth black Arabian Sea under a soft moonlight. It was tranquil and warm. The beach was empty so I decided to find a hidden spot and bed down. I laid out my sleeping bag away from the coconut trees, but close enough to the sea to hear the hypnotic ebb and flow of the wavelets and I was soon asleep.

A sharp jolt of pain in my ribs abruptly roused me from my slumber. Wide-eyed and confused, I stared up at three policemen in chrome aviator sunglasses, khaki uniforms and black berets peering down at me.

'What the hell!' I screamed as I struggled to free myself from the sleeping bag. 'You kicked me,' I shouted in anger.

'Sorry sir, but you are alive unlike the fellow next to you,' said the stocky one.

'What?' I glanced in the direction of a lifeless body protruding from a bedroll a few metres away and felt numb.

'Is he dead?' I stared at my own reflection in their aviators.

'Yes, he's dead, sir.'

'Has he had a heart attack?'

'Come with us, sir,' said the young one as he seized my arm and escorted me from the beach to a black jeep nearby.

Inside the vehicle there were four Europeans who told me the man had been murdered and his throat was slit but he had been dead for some time. Someone had dumped the body during the night and the police had no idea of his identity. He did not appear to be an Indian. They drove us to the police station in Panjim, India's smallest capital with Goa being their smallest state liberated from the Portuguese in 1961. When it was my turn to be questioned, they showed me a photo of a bloodied face. I told them of my arrival the previous night, gave them the bus and train tickets and signed a declaration that I did not know the dead person. Soon after, they released me along with the other westerners.

Local Indian people put my mind at rest saying Goa was a peaceful place, and this was something which may have happened as far away as Bombay. They told me that no one in the area locked their doors at night. However, I stayed away from that section of coastline and took up residence in the south of Goa.

On Colva Beach, I rented a room from Oli and Ingrid, a Dutch couple from Utrecht. Their three bedroom bungalow was twenty metres from the water's edge and when they left, I took over as master tenant with the approval of the owners, Chakor and Wafa, a husband and wife team from Panjim. They lived in a splendid Portuguese style bungalow, painted yellow with wrought iron window grilles, ornate balconies and oyster shell windows. The diffusion of light through the oyster shell was enchanting and atmospheric. Other colonial style houses in the area were coloured green, blue, and pink.

On the first day in my new home, I came face to face with a deformed rat which poked its withered head out from a bag of rice in the kitchen. At that point, I spent several days scrubbing the floors and walls. After which, I sublet the two spare rooms to visiting tourists and lived rent free. The house had a basic kitchen of one sink and a wood-fired stove. It was connected to the electricity but the water had to be collected from a communal well fifty metres away. The shower was a bucket attached to a length of rope which hung from a tree and tipped the water over your body. The lavatory was a wooden stand-alone. It resembled an English telephone box in shape, raised from the ground by three steps and positioned twenty metres to the rear of the house. Inside the toilet a round hole was cut in the floor, over which one would adopt a squat position. As soon as the door closed, a thunder of hooves indicated the pigs were charging towards it – their snouts appeared bunched together through the hole – grunting enthusiastically. I had to advise visitors not to sit too low as the hairs from the pig's snouts would tickle their backside. No faeces ever reached the ground.

One evening a young American from Atlanta, named Brenda, booked in for three days. Her father had given her a flight ticket to Bombay as a birthday gift and told her to go and see the world; however, she hated India and was visiting under sufferance. The following morning, I was taking tea in the garden when the toilet door suddenly burst open and a screaming Brenda bolted out over the grass and through the palm trees with oinking pigs in hot pursuit. She immediately checked into a local hotel. During the months that followed I must have had every nationality stay at the house, from Palestinians to Brazilians, some of whom were great characters; Farooq from Gaza with his repertoire of hilariously funny jokes and Carmen from Salvador whose traveller's tales from South America had us all transfixed.

One of these personalities was Polly, a pretty Welsh girl with sparkling china-blue eyes, pale complexion and a mane of lustrous red hair. She had hitchhiked overland to India through Syria with her boyfriend but they fell out in Kerala and he had flown home to Cardiff. She alluded to the fact they had grown apart anyway. They were childhood sweethearts and after she moved to London to attend university he continued to work on the family farm. She loved India and he hated it. Polly gave the house a female touch – flower displays were strategically placed here and there – the drab furniture was brightened up with her artistic designs. She became friends with numerous Indian women at the well who would pop in with gifts of food and give us the local gossip over tea. It became a home from home.

When Torben and Helle arrived, the Danish friends I had met the previous year in Delhi, we celebrated at the tumbledown beach bar until the early hours. As I was leading the way back through the jungle, a flash of light suddenly appeared out of the darkness followed by a thud to the chest which knocked me backwards into the foliage. Two Indian teenagers were holding an oil lamp and clubbing something on the pathway. It was a king cobra snake crossing the track where we were just about to step. They had been following it and drop kicked me out the way which may have saved my life. During the night, Polly climbed into my bed for a cuddle; she dreamt of being eaten by a giant eel and was frightened.

Helle bonded with Polly and they became good friends. Helle was a tall Dane who had a peaceful approach to life and together they learned from each other's skills and knowledge. The girls would paint, draw or read while Torben and I would help the fishermen drag their heavy nets, laden with small fish, out of the water. On a weekend, we visited an old fashioned theatre in Margao, our nearest small town, to listen to a local folk band play Goan and East Indian music. Everyone ended up on the dancefloor including members of the band. It was great fun.

Each week we ate vegetarian food at our local bhelpuri house. At the restaurant, we heard an unpleasant groaning sound coming through the open window. It was made by a disabled person moving along the road on his hands and feet, upside down like a spider, but with his face looking up. We felt desperately sorry for this individual who was obviously in discomfort and without any mechanical aids or human help. Two Goan ladies on the next table told us he had been born with the condition but his family did look after him.

'How anyone can complain about our health service is beyond me,' said Polly.

That night, Polly climbed into my bed once again but this time she dreamt she was a solitary head with no body and was frightened.

Vahin was a Goan street seller whose reputation for the finest samosas made him a local celebrity and he often parked his handcart in front of the house. One morning Polly invited him to join us for tea. On the table, he slowly untied the string from a white muslin bundle to reveal a genuine Nepalese temple ball complete with an identifiable gold seal. He insisted it was the best cannabis resin in the world which was soft, pliable and smelled pungently fresh. None of us wanted to smoke, so he took it away and two days later brought it back having made the squidgy lump into a selection of sweet samosas.

Polly asked me to hold her bath towel while she showered under the tree. After dark, I crawled into her bed and told her I had dreamt that I was a bee, being chased by a giant bee-eater and was frightened.

As time passed by, the world seemed a different place. Some days we emerged late, read, sat on the beach, read some more, talked and went back to bed. One month blended into another. We would munch a samosa and sit for hours on the sand watching the sun go down, talk and talk, then reconvene at the water's edge to view the sun rise. I read all the classics, the history of the world and copious volumes of poetry using Chakor's registration card at the Margao library.

A glittery Christmas card arrived from England with the illustration of a red telephone box topped with fluffy snow and a robin standing on the handle of a garden spade. It made something click inside my head. Torben and Helle would be going home soon and Polly had a new position in the City of London. My funds from working in the Australian Outback were running low so the time to move on had arrived and I prepared to wind up my trip of almost three years. Polly was the first to leave, taking a train to Kochi in Kerala for her return flight to Cardiff. She left the house spotlessly clean and arranged to meet me in England. Torben and Helle departed a week later by train to Delhi for their flight home to Copenhagen.

I handed over the keys to Chakor and Wafa who were delighted that the house was tastefully decorated and cleaner than when I took possession. They gave me a lift to the port of Panjim to catch the sailing to Bombay, a service provided by Mughal Lines whose boat was a compact ten metres in length with a lightweight canvas top. The journey of 375 miles took four days due to the choppy seas and strong head winds. I ate the last of our sweet samosas aboard, reminisced about my experiences in India and slept on the open deck. When the vessel reached its destination we moored alongside the Gateway to India, which in effect was the front door to Bombay; the most populous city in India and the capital of Maharashtra state. Leaving the boat felt like stepping from an empty cathedral into a football stadium. The meditative lifestyle of the Goan coastline disintegrated by means of an ear-shattering city.

Bombay and West Germany 1975

INDIA PRESENTED A KALEIDOSCOPE OF DIFFERENT FACETS TO THE traveller: the Punjab, Bengal, Tamil Nadu, Kerala, Karnataka, Goa and Rajasthan, to name but a few, with Bombay being yet another dimension from this cultural prism. In this tumultuous city I took a basic room with paper-thin walls in a youth hostel and prepared myself for yet another culture shock; my return to the UK. The cheapest flight to Europe was via Bahrain and Beirut to Cologne in West Germany.

Roaming around the street markets, I carried out some market research and asked the sellers which products were popular with German tourists. Multi-coloured leather shopping bags were the item at the top of the list. I could afford 200, which, together with the baggage excess left just enough money to kit myself out with a new wardrobe of warm clothes and buy my flight ticket. All booked up, I had my last feed of egg masala and chapattis with copious quantities of chai and hauled the boxes of shopping bags up to the airport.

The flight took twenty-three hours which included two stopovers in the Middle East before landing in Cologne on an icy cold Friday night in December. In the airport terminal, I sold two bags to an Englishwoman which gave me enough money to rent a room in a typical German townhouse hotel overlooking a square. The goose down quilt felt cosy to snuggle under and stopped me shivering. As my head sank into the wide pillows, I drifted off into the longest sleep ever, through two nights and all of Saturday. I was awoken early on a Sunday morning by the sound of tolling church bells. I drew the curtains to a sunny blue sky and pushed open the double-glazed windows with a sharp intake of breath on a crisp winter's day. Glistening white frost clung to the trees and hedges. I swiftly crawled back under the duvet and lay there listening to the pealing bells – ding-dong, ding-dong – followed by their lingering harmonic chime. I contemplated my time in Asia but found it comforting, warm and homely to be back in Europe, my domicile.

After soaking in the first hot bath since leaving England, my thoughts turned to food. At the breakfast buffet, I asked the friendly owner, Felda, if I could have some eggs. She chortled and pointed to a row of tiny woollen bobble hats placed over the hard boiled eggs to keep them warm.

I dragged the boxes across the square next to the Christmas market and spread the contents onto the pavement. They were selling fast but the line of customers scattered when the police arrived and demanded to see my permit, by which time, my pockets were stuffed with money. I made an excuse that the trader with the correct paperwork had failed to turn up and I quickly packed away the goods.

One of the stallholders caught my attention before leaving the area and bought most of the remaining stock. I still had twenty bags to sell but now that my funds had been replenished, I spent the remainder of the day touring the city. At the post restante there was a postcard from Polly to say she was waiting for me in London.

My meat-eating habits returned and I chewed my way through a mighty schweinshaxn, (part of a pig's hind leg), sitting at a long wooden communal table in a Bavarian brewery and served by a fräulein in traditional costume. She dished up the ham hock of monstrous proportions with crispy skin adding dumplings, sauerkraut, boiled potatoes and a bubbling dark gravy. I staggered out through the purple flock curtains and frosted double doors into the winter night air with my stomach bulging. I stood there oblivious to the chill and thought to myself how strange it was to end my trip in a German ale house; considering my first adventure after leaving England three years earlier had been at the hofbräuhaus in Munich with Andrew and Martin.

Walking through the silent streets to the townhouse, I strayed into a parkway hugging the Rhine. An icy wind howled up the watery gloom and froze my skin. Beams of warm orange light shone through the small rounded windows of the river traffic and their reflection shimmered like fireflies on the pitch-black flowing water. I sat on a bench and wondered how my reaction to life in Northumberland would manifest itself after the length of time away – all the changes within me - and the effects of adapting to so many cultures.

I travelled by train to Ostend across the dark wintery wonderland and boarded the cross-Channel ferry to Dover. Aboard the ship, the remaining bags were sold except for one. The sailing arrived on time to catch the first train to London St. Pancras. On the frenetic platform, Polly waved a red scarf above her head amongst swarms of commuters. I pushed my way through the hordes, lifted her up and gave her a long kiss and a big hug before ceremoniously presenting her Christmas gift from India – the last remaining leather bag.

MILES & MILES ~ A LIFETIME OF TRAVEL IN ASIA AND LATIN AMERICA

Australia overland to Europe

07 Turkish Delight

'If the Earth was a single state, Istanbul would be its capital.'
NAPOLEON BONAPARTE

Istanbul 1980

THE 1950s CADILLAC LURCHED FROM SIDE TO SIDE ON ITS SPONGY suspension as it squealed round the corner into the serene square. The corner of my eye noticed the red ragtop over the pink bodywork hurling towards our expedition truck outside the quaint hotel in the centre of Istanbul. The car pulled alongside and two burly Turks jumped out running. 'What the hell!' I screamed as one grabbed my arms, the other gripped my neck and together they manhandled me through the open door onto the rear seat. I suddenly found myself jammed between two suited thugs with matching purple shirts as the ageing Cadillac raced away over the cobbles.

Struggling to move, claustrophobia swamped my mind and rapidly morphed into a blind panic. Like a startled rabbit I stared up into their dark cavernous nostrils and pleaded, 'You've got the wrong person. I'm just a British tourist. Please, please let me go…' The purple shirts remained stony-faced. In the confined space the more I wriggled the tighter it became and the stench of my own fear mingled with the dank fruity aromatics of their coal-black oily hair. I tried to catch the attention of the driver, 'Let me move my arms, I'm trapped,' I shouted as his beady rat eyes appeared in the rear view mirror but their stoicism prevailed.

Shock turned to rage. Feeling the pointed end of a metal comb in my back pocket I became less fearful and more confident. Considering it was a cabriolet in the city centre during daylight, I adopted a limp posture and waited patiently for an opportunity to lash out and make a run for it through the busy streets.

It was surreal, why would anyone abduct me in a pink Cadillac. My thoughts raced. It cannot be a kidnapping as I am worthless. It must be mistaken identity. On the other hand, they could be the authorities. That thought provoked the worst of my fears.

This was the second trip to Istanbul but the first time working for Trekeast Expeditions as their driver and guide taking a party of fifteen people on a three month tour of the Near East and Europe. Normally the brief states that we must use the campsite on the edge of town but I had asked the group if they would prefer a change from camping to something more comfortable after six weeks on the road. They agreed wholeheartedly so we checked into the two star accommodation in a quiet location downtown Istanbul and close to the Blue Mosque.

A few months earlier, Turkey had endured its third coup d'état. It was led by four military commanders who overthrew the civilian government, abolished the parliament, suspended the constitution and banned all political parties and trade unions. A feeling of hope had arisen among the international banking community that this military coup may have opened the way to greater political stability; a prerequisite for the Turkish economy to be revitalised. However, the coup had come at a price as hundreds of thousands of people were arrested and subsequently detained and tortured. I prayed not to be a mistaken victim from one of these mass round-ups.

The Cadillac slowed to a stop up an alley, not that far from our hotel. The purple shirts bundled me out of the vehicle while keeping a tight hold of my arms and marched me through a café entrance into a darkened room at the rear. In an armchair, their controller sat in the half-light sipping tea from a tulip-shaped glass in his left hand while clutching the hose from a hookah pipe with the other. I could not make out the facial features but the frizzy mane of afro tresses was unmistakable. He pushed himself up from the chair to reveal a Herculean stature whose body appeared to be covered in a mass of black curly hair – some of which protruded from his shirt like a ripped duvet – and gravitated upwards over the Adam's apple to seamlessly join with his impenetrable beard, wide sideburns and fuzzy thatch.

The minders released their grip but continued to stand alongside. He introduced himself as Muzaffar, the manager in charge of the tourist division within the Turkish Mafia. This may sound crazy but it was a relief not to be thrown into some obscure cell by the authorities on a trumped-up charge. It was preferential to be with the mafia. Muzaffar barked a command to his henchmen and they left quietly. He sat back down and gestured for me to take a seat.

'May I offer you tea Miles?'

'Yes please Muzaffar. That would be great.'

How did he know my name?

Silence followed with the exception of a mild gurgling from the hubble-bubble pipe. An old man poured the dark red tea into a transparent pear-shaped glass on an ornate plate and placed it on the table. I sipped the hot liquid and felt my energy returning.

Muzaffar directed his gaze towards me and smiled, 'You must be new to this?'

'It's my first solo trip as a driver with Trekeast. May I ask you why I'm here?'

'Of course, and the reason is simple. You did not obey our rules.'

'Sorry Muzaffar, it wasn't intentional, where did I go wrong?'

'You failed to use the designated Trekeast site and travelled with your group into the city without my consent.'

'I will undo the situation right away get the team together and take them to the right place. I apologise for the incorrect way in which I have handled my first trip to Turkey.'

'Well, now that you're here, I welcome you to Istanbul and will allow your expedition to stay at the hotel.'

'Thank you.'

'A pleasure.' He shook my hand firmly with his enormous palm.

That was too easy, I thought.

'There is however, one condition,' he mused. 'I want one of your beautiful blonde girls and furthermore, I will take my blonde girl and you to dinner this evening to see our wonderful city at night.'

'I can't give you a girl Muzaffar, they're not mine to give, but I can ask the group if one of the ladies would like to join us.'

'I want a blonde girl,' he insisted.

'I promise to ask Morag when I return to the hotel. I will let you know her response when we meet later,' I implored.

Muzaffar changed the subject and asked how many visits I would make to Istanbul during the summer season. He pondered my response when I told him two perhaps three more trips. As he rummaged in a back office, the aging waiter topped up our teas. On his return, Muzaffar clutched a leather-bound notebook. He carefully manoeuvred his bulk through the tables and reversed into the cosy chair.

'I have a business proposal for you.' His voice took on a pragmatic tone as he flicked through the pages.

'What do you have in mind?' I asked with trepidation. Maybe an opportunity to mitigate his obsession with one of my fair-haired passengers.

'There's a possibility to bring items from England. Products we cannot purchase in Turkey. We'll discuss the detail over tonight's dinner when I show you the city.' He smiled broadly displaying his gold and yellow stained teeth.

'Don't be concerned.' He spoke reassuringly. 'It's legal and you will be paid a commission.'

Muzaffar snapped his fingers and the two brutes reappeared. He instructed them to return me to the hotel with immediate effect. We would meet at 7 p.m.

The return journey was a great deal more dignified and I took pride of place in the front seat, slithering around on the red leather. The group were having tea in the courtyard and I related an amended version of events to avoid worrying them, but I was honest with regard to Muzaffar's status within the city. To my surprise Morag readily agreed to the evening out, and to complete the foursome I asked Emilia, a Swedish girl from Stockholm, to be my date. A passionate mountaineer with short ginger hair and an ear-piercing laugh. Not the type of girl Muzaffar would be attracted to, I guessed, and as such, less complicated a scenario for me to manage during our jaunt into Istanbul's nightlife.

At 7 p.m. prompt, Muzaffar strode into the hotel beaming a golden smile like a corn on the cob. His soot black wavy tresses tumbled down over his sky blue velvet jacket. Our eyes were immediately drawn, not only to his personal presence and stature, but to the bright yellow and red chequered trousers which seemed to be at war with his jacket. For a moment, he reminded me of an oversized Turkish version of Rupert the Bear. He could have easily been mistaken for a long lost friend while giving us all a hug with a kiss for Morag and Emilia. However, the look of terror in the hotel owner's eyes indicated something different as he nervously poured the teas. Although I worried about Morag's security, he was charming, talkative and made us laugh. We began to relax in his company.

As the evening progressed he told us many fascinating stories of Turkey and in particular, Istanbul, his stamping ground. I could see that Morag felt comfortable in his presence. She was tall and athletic with straight, ash-blonde hair to her shoulders, a hawkish nose and steely blue eyes. Morag could be feisty when it suited her, whose profession as a Glaswegian pub manageress meant she could handle drunken Scots, so I assumed she would qualify as someone who would manage 'The big man.'

Muzaffar and I had a good rapport as we travelled around the city in a succession of taxis which popped out of nowhere the moment he snapped his fingers. We walked to the front of queues without any objection, were given the best tables with panoramic views of the city and no money changed hands. He instructed the musicians at one of the venues to sing a Turkish folk song which had represented his country at the Eurovision song contest earlier that year. Emilia whispered in my ear that the Turkish entry had come eighteenth out of twenty contestants. We feigned enthusiasm during this awful melody and clapped our hands with gusto at the end of the performance.

At his favourite restaurant, our table was located next to the window on the seventeenth floor overlooking the Bosphorus, where famously, the East meets the West. A watery link between the Black Sea and the Mediterranean on which we could see the glimmering night lights from swarms of shipping traffic.

When the girls went to the bathroom, Muzaffar took the opportunity to talk me through his proposal for our business venture, importing goods into Turkey on the roof of my truck. I had travelled through the Greek Turkish border several times and it was always an unsettling experience because of the problematic relationship between the two countries. On one occasion, due to a slight administrative error, officials in gold braided uniforms had dragged two French tourists from their Citroën 2CV and banged their heads on the bonnet before refusing them entry. I recalled instances when luggage was randomly searched and the contents strewn over the road. Any form of reaction would invoke a brutal response. I never wanted to be involved with any form of smuggling but under the circumstances I had to hear him out and respond with reasoned argument. In essence, his list of items seemed to be legitimate. These obscure commodities included photocopying ink, marine engine parts and strangely enough, instant coffee. All of which could be imported up to a certain value upon presentation of an original invoice.

The expedition vehicle was a stretched, reinforced Ford transit van which accommodated a total of sixteen people including myself. The roof rack was a sturdy and substantial piece of equipment, accessed from the rear by a fixed metal ladder. It held everyone's luggage and their sleeping bags plus eight two man tents, one communal tent, a large metal tool box, spare parts and cooking equipment. They were neatly stacked and strapped together under a heavy canvas tarpaulin. There was capacity to add another tier to the load for Muzaffar and he wanted me to accept his proposition without delay.

'I will agree on one condition.'

'And that is?'

'You allow Morag to choose whether she returns to our hotel or goes home to your place.'

He thought about it, took several sips of raki and reacted with a rambunctious laugh which shook the table. He threw his enormous hairy arm around my back and pulled me close to his matted barrel chest, 'It's a deal Miles. You have my word.'

'Your word is your bond and that's enough for me Muzaffar.'

The aroma of his Middle Eastern Jadayel hair oil reminded me of events earlier in the day.

'Let's toast our partnership,' he thundered.

We lifted our glasses of Raki, 'Serefe!' I cried.

'Cheers!' He bellowed and our glasses clinked.

We slugged the clear aniseed firewater in one and slapped our palms together with a high five.

The meze arrived, a Turkish appetizer of brightly coloured hot and cold dishes. Spread out on the table were: rice-stuffed vine leaves, artichokes with a chilli tomato paste, lamb-filled aubergines, fried squid, sheep's cheese and a herby yoghurt with black olives. A mouth-watering mix of different tastes.

As we ate, Muzaffar continued to entertain the girls, who laughed and giggled, especially when his huge frame leapt up and down as he emphasised certain aspects of his funny stories. To stay in control, I refrained from drinking any more Raki just in case I needed to handle what may have unfolded during the evening. To my relief, Muzaffar ordered a tray of Perge beers.

In the centre of the table, a large platter of sizzling lamb kebabs on a bed of grilled peppers was accompanied by a stack of wafer-thin pitta breads. Somehow, we cleared the entire dish after which and to our delight, they brought the speciality of the house, a freshly baked Baklava. We quietly munched our way through the syrupy, nutty and doughy flavours of this phenomenal sweet. Muzaffar suggested that this was probably the best Baklava in Turkey and we believed him.

After 2am, Muzaffar took us to his regular hookah café close to the Blue Mosque which, even at this late hour, was full of men smoking the hubble-bubble pipes. The Turkish water pipe is a tradition spanning five hundred years and the flavours of tobacco are extensive: apple, peach, strawberry, banana, mint and many more. Referred to as a nãrghile, I now understood its social relevance in cultural terms to the Turkish people. The hookah bar was equivalent to our coffee shop or pub and as such, a place to meet friends and relax. Although it was a male domain, the men accepted and respected the women in our group. Muzaffar motioned us to sit around the hookah and explained the rules of using a water pipe in a communal café.

'Be quiet. If we speak louder than the sound of the bubbles, it's too much. Leave the pipe to one side for the next person to pick up, as and when they are ready.'

Each of us were given a detachable mouth piece. Glowing oak charcoal heated the black coffee flavoured tobacco and as we gently sucked on the hose the smoke cooled in the pipe as it travelled through the water. Emilia caused some amusement when she coughed and blew the burning contents all over the floor.

When we arrived at the hotel, Muzaffar flung his arms around Morag. To my surprise she responded in kind but soon after left the cab and Muzaffar kept to his word. Although Morag was an adult who could make her own decisions, I had a duty of care as the team leader.

The following day, the group paid a visit to the Blue Mosque while I met with Muzaffar to be briefed on the deal. During our rendezvous, he gave me a list of products to bring from the UK on my next trip together with some upfront cash. The exchange rate with sterling and the Turkish lira was substantial, something in the region of 1,000 lira to the pound. He handed over two carrier bags bulging with notes to take to the bank and change into British pounds. I was accompanied by the same two henchmen who walked either side of me but this time they were my bodyguards. I left the bank with £800 in £20 notes, a small wad by comparison. It was a considerable sum at the time, equivalent to three month's salary in Britain.

As the years progressed, I completed three further trips to Turkey and on each occasion delivered a consignment of goods to Muzaffar. It was lucrative and always included a night out on the town. Muzaffar and I continued to keep in touch after I left Trekeast and every Christmas for ten years he sent a box of Turkish delight scented with rosewater, to my mother's home in Northumberland. She in turn, would post him a Christmas cake and a classic British Christmas card of snowflakes tumbling onto a red London double-decker bus stuck in a snowdrift on Oxford Street.

In 1992, the Turkish delight never arrived. I wrote to his home several times and in the summer of 1993, I received a sad postcard from his sister to say that Muzaffar had been wounded in a gunfight and had died of his injuries. She went on to say he was an innocent bystander in the wrong place at the wrong time.

08 Through the Iron Curtain

'It's better to see something once than hear about it a hundred times.' RUSSIAN PROVERB

Poland 1981

THE OVERNIGHT FERRY FROM ENGLAND DOCKED IN THE BEAUTIFUL city of Gdańsk, Poland's principal sea port on the Baltic coast situated next to the Russian enclave of Kaliningrad. The city has had a complex political history having changed hands several times between Poland and Germany, as well as a period of self-rule and free city status. Since 1945 it has been part of modern day Poland.

The Motława River, which connects via a delta to the Vistula River linking Warsaw to the sea, flows through the city alongside the colourful facades of narrow buildings with stepped or triangular peaks. The oldest preserved houses date back to the middle ages but the majority were reconstructed after World War Two, influenced by Dutch architects in the same style as Amsterdam and Copenhagen. Ulica Długa, Long Street and Długi Targ, Long Market, pronounced Ooleetsa Dwooga and Dwoogee Targ, form a wide pedestrianised thoroughfare flanked at both ends by elaborate city gates and are part of the old town.

After a few days in Gdańsk, Swinko and I caught a train to Poznań, Poland's fifth largest city and 200 miles from the seaport. We had worked together in the Australian Outback during 1973 and were long term friends. Swinko was an English Pole whose anglicised nickname from Polish meant piglet, which had been given to him by his British schoolmates due to his hefty appetite. Although I normally travelled solo, on this occasion I adventured with an experienced traveller in Swinko and together we had left Newcastle upon Tyne by train to Hull where we boarded the ferry. His parents were Polish immigrants who escaped the Nazi occupation during World War Two and had taken up pig farming in the North East of England. His first language was English and second Polish with a good understanding of Russian.

From a western perspective, the Soviet Union existed as a secretive and dark group of countries which had posed a constant threat to world peace throughout our lifetime. Aged eight, I remember the Cuban missile crisis of 1963, the trepidation at home during sombre news bulletins and grim warnings. The recurring questions that were never fully explained; why did the Soviet Union forbid its citizens to visit other countries? Was communism a more favourable dogma? Why did the two lifestyles conflict? However, we were not looking for in depth answers. Our passage through the Iron Curtain presented an opportunity to witness life under Soviet rule and as an alternative overland route to reach the Far East, in particular, the Philippines – a beautiful location to scuba dive.

We visited in the late spring of 1981, which was a year of change in the Republic of Poland with waves of strikes by workers across the country ultimately resulting in the founding of Solidarity; an independent trade union under the leadership of Lech Wałęsa, an electrician. Seven months later, the Poles would wake up on a wintry Sunday morning in December to find their country under Martial Law, imposed by a Military Council. The Soviets had felt threatened by the first independent trade union behind the Iron Curtain and therefore pressurised the Polish government to de-legalise Solidarity and defend socialism. Thousands of activists would be arrested and imprisoned without a legal process. Borders were sealed, airports closed, road access to main cities restricted, telephone lines disconnected, TV and radio suspended and a curfew imposed. Sea ports, trains stations, health services, power stations, coal mines, and public administration were placed under military management and the schools and universities closed. The junta eventually lifted Martial Law in July 1983 but the popularity of the trade union movement continued to grow in strength ultimately forming part of an opposition which challenged Soviet rule.

Swinko's cousin Linik, a weathered farmhand, picked us up at Poznań station in a 1970s Polski pick up which rattled through meandering country lanes for several hours before arriving at the family farm. Uncle Tomasz and Aunt Franciszka, pronounced Tomash and Francheeshka, greeted us fervently as Linik poured shots of homemade vodka according to the Polish tradition of hospitality.

'They slaughtered a pig in preparation for our visit,' Swinko translated.

The welcome celebration began in earnest. Aunt Franciszka laid out a feast of pork meat, pork fat and cherry juice as more relatives and friends streamed into the farmstead to make up the party which continued until the early hours. Many of the older folk, including a ninety-two year old, left the farmhouse riding ancient heavy bicycles without lights into the sub-zero moonless night.

Early the next morning, Aunt Franciszka make a new batch of cherry juice on a wood fired stove by boiling water filled with morello cherries. She referred to the mix as a kompot and served it with breakfast: slices of pork, cubes of clear animal fat, eggs, potato pancakes and hot baked bread.

'Why do I have three eggs on my plate and the others have two,' I asked Aunt Franciszka through Swinko.

'Because you are too skinny and need building up.'

Most days at lunchtime, she would prepare bigos in a wide pot, one of Poland's national dishes – a stew made with cabbage and sausage meat. Their unique family version was a recipe from her great grandmother. The difference to the regular dish was the use of their own pig meat and specifically, the shoulder, plus their own herbs to make the spicy sausages. A further process of reheating the mix during the following day improved the flavour.

At each mealtime, she would say, 'For you Miles,' and pass me the largest plate of food. All visitors to a Polish home were shown this exceptional kindness, in fact, there is a Polish saying, 'Guest in house, God in house.'

A week later, we push-started the old truck and with many tears and hugs, Linik drove us with full stomachs into Poznań. Located on the Warta River, Poznań was regarded by many as the birthplace of the Polish nation and one of the oldest cities in Poland, dating back to the tenth century. After the Franco-Prussian war of 1871, the city and province had been annexed by Germany and made part of the German empire. Consequently the city was officially named as an imperial residence which led to the construction of the royal castle and opera house.

However it was best known for its Renaissance style old town. We sat in the cobblestoned marketplace surrounded by colourful merchant houses: vermillion, blue, green, purple and butterscotch. Each day at noon, inside the clock tower of a splendid town hall in the middle of the Old Market Square, two mechanical goats emerged and butted heads twelve times. The billy goat legend stemmed from the sixteenth century when the governor was invited to a celebratory feast. The chef burnt the venison which he replaced with a pair of goats. They escaped to the top of the building where they began butting heads much to the amusement of the crowd and the governor decreed that they be added to the clock.

We looked forward to sampling the famous St. Martin's Day Croissants but they were nowhere to be found. This may have been due to the time of year or the lack of ingredients, especially almonds and poppy seeds. Unlike French croissants, they were crescent-shaped sweet rolls traditionally served on November 11th for an ancient public celebration of patron saints.

A great place to eat hearty food throughout Poland were the milk bars. Low-cost canteens where bigos, stews and broth are simmered in huge aluminium pots. These milk bars had their own hot and steamy atmosphere where large ladies with large ladles served up substantial dishes in deep ceramic bowls. The dish of the day was a cabbage and sauerkraut mix called gulasz myśliwski, translated as hunters stew, or rabbit bigos. As we gulped our stew in people watching mode, it struck me how powerfully built and sturdy the Poles were on the whole. No wonder Swinko's aunt thought I was undernourished. In my experience of Polish people from both England and those I met during this trip, I found them to possess a remarkable work ethic, as well as being constitutionally strong, proud, spirited and stubborn.

Leaving Poznań, we boarded a train for the 150 miles journey to Warsaw, a city surrounded by mile after mile of bleak residential apartment blocks. On arrival at the main train station, the Warszawa Centralna, we exchanged money on the street. The cash transaction was swift, out of sight from watchful eyes and at 230 złoty to the pound sterling was much greater than the official bank rate of sixty. I had hidden a small amount of undeclared notes in my sock and took them through immigration at Gdańsk for this reason.

We took a Trabant taxi to an inner city guest house in a residential area within walking distance of the old town. On the way, we discovered a period bar in the Bristol Hotel, built in 1901, still with its original ruby-red velvet flock curtains over each door. Vodka was the only drink available and served in a tall thin glass with a dash of tonic. The mixer was a great deal more expensive than the hard liquor and subject to availability. To our surprise, a succession of Libyans flowed through the curtains into the bar area. We were aware that Colonel Muammar Gaddafi, the Libyan leader, was a close ally of the Soviet Union during the 1980s which no doubt explained the presence of these young people who studied at Warsaw University.

Through a mix of alcohol, pretty girls and the crowds, Swinko and I became separated during the evening. My knowledge of Polish was miniscule as I wandered aimlessly through the city having lost all sense of direction. There were queues forming on Piwna Street outside a butcher, probably not open until the morning. I came across many of these grim lines, tightly packed and silent. A vivid reminder that Poland like most other countries under Soviet rule, in my opinion, was an enslaved nation. A compassionate Pole who spoke some English helped me find the terraced guest house before daybreak.

During World War Two the Nazis bombed the old town and the Royal Castle to smithereens. They would be faithfully rebuilt, brick by brick, and financed by public donations. As a result, UNESCO granted World Heritage status to the old town in 1980 and in 1981, the Royal Castle restoration was underway and scheduled to be completed by 1988.

The złoties were a valid currency exclusive to Poland so we threw our remaining bundle of notes and bag of coins into a startled busker's hat before leaving Warsaw station. As the train glided away from its platform, we settled into our claustrophobic two berth cabin and arrived at the Russian border at midnight.

Russia 1981

THE SOVIET UNION IN THE 1980S WAS STILL A HERMETICALLY sealed unit which had yet to open up to the rest of the world. Leonid Brezhnev had been in charge since 1964 and his tenure as General Secretary was second only to that of Joseph Stalin in duration. Brezhnev would decide against Soviet military intervention in Poland during the unrest later this year but it was to be a further ten years before the demise of communist rule in 1991.

The Olympic Games had been held in Moscow the previous

summer, 1980, but they were boycotted by eighty nations due to the Russian invasion of Afghanistan in 1979. Britain and France attended but voiced objections. The games turned out to be a showcase for Soviet athletes on their home soil who won an astonishing 195 medals, eighty of which glittered gold.

At the frontier, the first Russian officials aboard were three wide men in bulky uniforms who had difficulty squeezing into the couchette. They were the military to search our bags and look under the mattresses, followed by two immigration officers who checked the visas and stamped the passports. Finally, a customs officer confiscated my magazine, indicating with his finger that it contained a banned photo of a banana.

The train was jacked up and a different gauge of wheels replaced the Polish ones to enable it to travel on the Russian rail system. As it pulled away from the checkpoint, there was a subtle change of percussion from a clickety-click to a clickety-clack as it rumbled on through the remainder of the night.

The journey from Warsaw to Moscow took twenty-eight hours including hold ups and the lengthy wait at the Russian border. We arrived in Moscow late afternoon by which time the station was crowded with busy commuters. As we stepped onto the platform, a young man with a slight Yorkshire accent met us in person. He introduced himself as Maarav from Intourist, the official state-run tourist agency which all foreign visitors had to use when travelling in the Soviet Union. Joseph Stalin founded this organisation in 1929 as a division of the KGB. Maarav took us by metro into the city and on foot to our hotel.

Our first impression of Moscow, the capital of the Union of Soviet Socialist Republics or its acronym the USSR, was the grandiose designs and gloriously ornate vaulted ceilings of the scrupulously clean metro stations. We emerged from the underground in downtown Moscow to cross expansive avenues, wide boulevards and vast sanitised squares. On the streets thirsty Soviet citizens bought glasses of kvass poured from cisterns delivered around the city each morning. Kvass was a sweet fizzy drink, light brown in colour and made from rye or black bread with a tiny amount of alcohol. Or they dropped a one kopek coin into soda pop machines located all over Moscow, which dispensed a type of fizzy water called gazirovka. It was drank from a communal glass which they turned upside down on a grate for a splashy rinse after use.

The Hotel Metropol was an imposing structure. We sensed the days of old which this building, its furnishings and décor had lived through since the beginning of the twentieth century. A silent witness to the many historical and political events which shaped Russian history. Close to the Kremlin or Red Square and a few minutes' walk to the Bolshoi Theatre. In 1986, it would undergo a major refit so we were lucky to have experienced and captured the moment prior to the next stage in its evolution. At check-in, two plain clothes KGB officials probed our bags before porters carried them to our room on the third floor. On each level, a stern looking matron dressed in funeral black sat behind a strategically positioned desk next to a 1950s black bakelite telephone and a square register to log the guests in and out of their rooms.

Russian visas allowed for a maximum stay of two weeks so each stage of the trip had to be pre-planned. The Trans-Siberian railway that we were about to embark upon took eight days to travel from Moscow to Vladivostok, the port city where the ship sailed from the mainland to Japan. We would visit Khabarovsk *en route*, the capital of Siberia, which left us three days to spend in Moscow.

Our first stop was the Kremlin, which in the distant past had been a self-contained medieval town covering twenty-seven hectares. In Sobornaya Square, the middle point, there were three cathedrals and two churches; the domes of these fabled buildings shone with gold and were once the stage on which the Tsars were crowned. In Ivanovkaya Square, we met twin

Russian sisters sipping kvass outside the magnificent pillar of Ivan the Great's bell tower. Lana and Inna accompanied us to Red Square and through Swinko's translation, they gave us an insight into its long and fascinating history.

In the Gum Department Store which at the end of the nineteenth century had been the largest shopping mall in Europe, we witnessed the legendary queues of people patiently waiting their turn.

'The top floor is home to Section 100, a secret clothing emporium only open to the highest echelons of the Communist Party,' whispered Lana.

Lana and Inna were identical twins who wore the same grey trouser suit and twisted topknot bun hairstyle. Both had kind eyes, a pert nose and bore an indistinguishable wistful expression. During our conversation, we mentioned that we had hoped to try the celebrated Russian borscht. In unison they invited us to their home in the suburbs to meet their mother, Lyosha, who would cook her special version of the dish. A taxi drove us to their grim apartment on the third level of a concrete block overlooking a busy road. The furnishings were pre-war but their apartment was spotless. The kitchen comprised of a three ring electric hob sunk into a table in the living room and a sink in the hall. Lyosha served an eye-catching crimson soup which tasted homely after which Inna gave me a list of her Mum's ingredients: beetroot, cabbage, potatoes, meat stock and if possible, carrots. Once back at our hotel, the black bakelite phone rang out like a 1950s movie. It was Maarav from Intourist who asked if we enjoyed our visit to the outskirts, no doubt to confirm that we were under constant surveillance.

Having sold a pair of Levi jeans to a hotel worker for a bundle of rouble notes, we decided on our last night in Moscow to thank Lana, Inna and their mum for their kindness and treat them to dinner at the Metropol. The waiter gave us each an enormous menu board with an impressive list of main courses but only one dish was available – salted sea sturgeon with pickled cucumber – served with neat vodka. As we chewed the grainy fish, the girls expressed a wish to bid us farewell from Moskva Kurskaya Station. The following day, our two-tone cream and red Trans-Siberian express rolled into the terminal and within fifteen minutes we were ready to board. Lana, Inna and Lyosha stood on the platform waving both hands high above their heads as the train chugged out of the station. Swinko and I were happy to have met and enjoyed time with genuine Muscovites.

There is no other train journey anywhere in the world to this day that compares to the Trans-Siberian. The distance spanned is immense, almost 6,250 miles, further than a direct flight between London and Los Angeles and covers seven time zones. This was not a tourist special resembling the modern day Orient Express but a working service used by ordinary Russian people. We shared traveller's tales over glasses of vodka with Tatar traders, Russian soldiers and a Chechnya dentist. Built across some of the most challenging terrain in the world, the Trans-Siberian Railway is one of the greatest engineering feats of the nineteenth century. It took all day to pass Lake Baikal alone, 400 miles long and the deepest in the world up to 744 metres, located above the border with Mongolia and within the mountains of Siberia. In fact, the total journey time from Moscow to Vladivostok, including twenty-eight hours of unexplained hold ups, amounted to 203 hours of continual rail travel.

There were several types of carriages. Some were dormitories fitted from end to end with bunk beds whereas others had rows of cabins which slept four people. The train included standard seating coaches and a restaurant car. Together, they formed a steel ribbon – the Trans-Siberian Express. At the end of each carriage was a fixed samovar dispensing hot water and almost every meal from the restaurant was dominated by boiled eggs. We were fortunate to have elevated bunk beds in a cabin which Swinko and I shared with two brothers from Khabarovsk who drank surgical spirit when the vodka ran out. During the hard liquor drought, the stress manifested by the occasional scuffle or argument erupting in the aisles. I read *The Magus* by John Fowles, twice, during the eight days and spent a great deal of time reflecting on life induced by the endless Russian tundra linked with the monotonous metallic rhythm of the train.

Due to our late arrival, we did not have enough visa time to visit Khabarovsk. Vladivostok was temporarily out of bounds for unknown security reasons so the train terminated instead at the port of Nakhodka, located on the Trudny Peninsula adding a further seven hours to the journey time. Before leaving Russia we were allowed to change roubles into a foreign currency to the maximum value of £7 per person so again, as in Poland, we gave away fistfuls of notes but this time to an old woman on a bicycle.

We boarded an older but stylish ferry decked out with mahogany wood and polished brass fittings. The Japanese crew took three days to sail 625 miles over the Sea of Japan between the islands of Hokkaido and Honshu to Yokohama, a port city thirty miles from Tokyo. It was a comfortable journey in a warm two berth cabin with a shower. The onboard café was basic and had a compact galley but the food was tremendous. Each day, steaming bowls of dashi broth made from dried kelp and thinly sliced dried fish were served with noodles or rice. Adjacent to the kitchen there was a small self-service buffet of sea food and salad.

During our travels in Poland and Russia under the restrictions of communism it was sad to witness individuals confined to one location. Soviet citizens reminded me of caged birds yearning to soar in the sky or energetic dogs on a short leash longing to run free. Arrival in Yokohama produced a flood of emotion – the extreme contrast of the dreary Soviet cityscapes to that of the glittering neon illuminations was overpowering – it produced an eclectic feeling of liberation.

Swinko and I checked into the YMCA and early the next morning we sat in the sunshine on the 7th floor with an aerial view over the whitewashed city. Glass pots of emerald green tea were brewed to an exact 80°C with a typical Japanese breakfast of steamed rice, soft boiled eggs and a variety of fermented and pickled vegetables. We were in heaven.

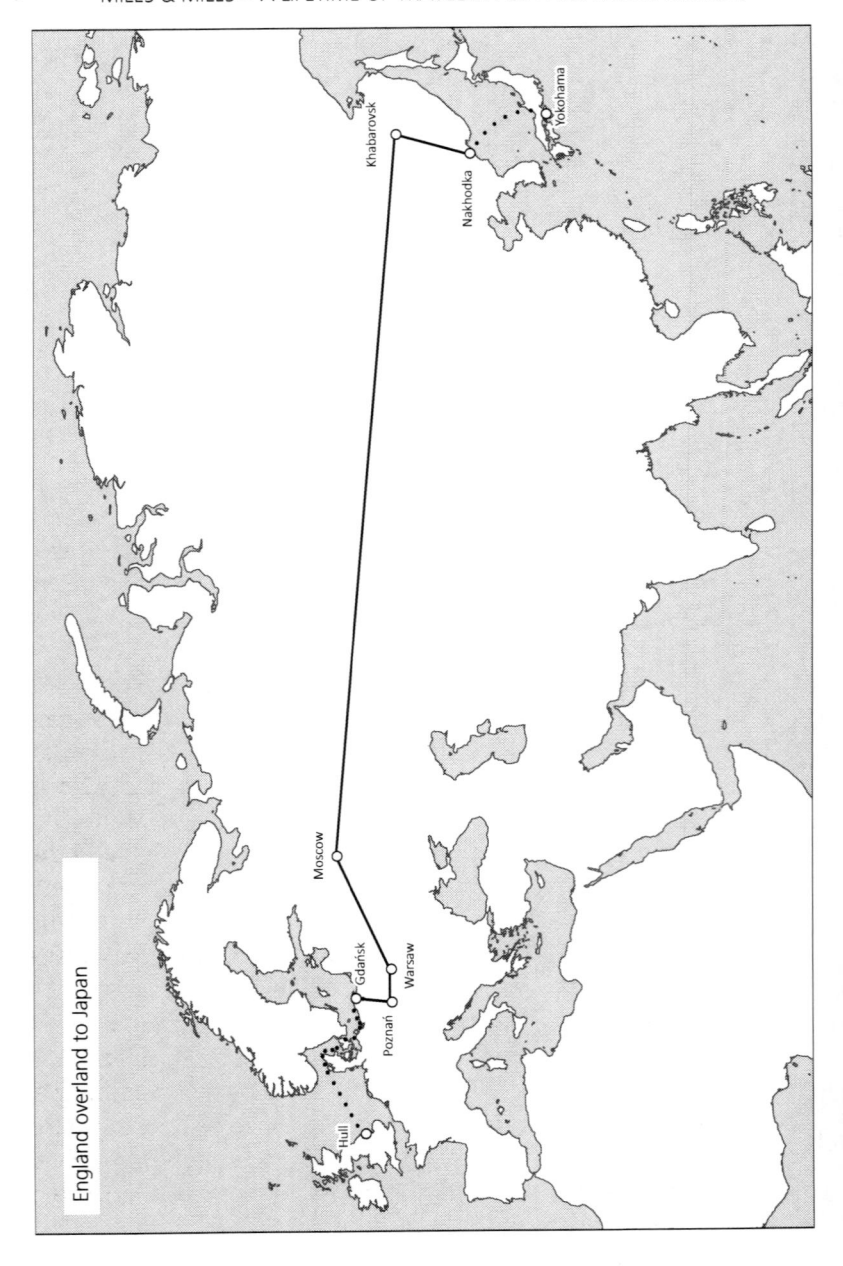

MILES & MILES ~ A LIFETIME OF TRAVEL IN ASIA AND LATIN AMERICA

England overland to Japan

09 Quezon City

'Like all great travellers, I have seen more than I remember and remember more than I have seen.' BENJAMIN DISRAELI

The Philippines 1981

WHEN THE AIRCRAFT DOOR SWUNG OPEN AT MANILA International Airport we were engulfed by a warm blanket of humidity from the diesel-charged breeze. As we made our way through immigration to the jeepney station a fragrance of shrimp paste impregnated the stifling night air.

London has the red double-decker bus, New York, the yellow cab and Manila, the jeepney – a stretched American military jeep which seats about twelve. It is the most popular means of public transport in the country and a ubiquitous symbol of Philippine art and culture.

Swinko and I had travelled overland from Europe through the Soviet Union and Japan with the intention of spending several months scuba diving in the tropical waters of the Far East. The Philippines was a low cost option and recognised as a diver's paradise in a country made up of more than 7,000 islands.

Our packed jeepney was adorned with a profusion of aluminium-made miniature horses protruding from the bonnet. It honked its way around Manila Bay to Quezon City known as QC, the erstwhile capital from 1948 to 1976 and the most densely populated area of the Metro Manila urban sprawl. The bench seats faced each other and a Filipino sitting opposite advised us to beware of kidnapping.

'It's a popular source of income and foreigners are of particular interest to the abductors. Nobody and nothing is safe, especially after dark. Last week, a commercial oil tanker vanished from Manila Bay.' He gave a wry smile.

In the centre of QC, we scrambled out the rear of the jeepney and found ourselves in close proximity to a violent altercation on the street. The screams were disturbing and the ominous shroud of threatening tension triggered a feeling of anxiety and apprehension. We scurried down a back lane into our seedy third-rate hotel. On entering the room, the door slammed shut behind us with a dull thud caused by an excessive array of locks and bolts making it disproportionately heavy. I systematically secured the door while Swinko opened the shutters to ventilate the hot stuffy room, three floors above a side street overlooking a commercial district.

When we were ready to face the city, we strapped on our money belts and stashed the passports under the carpet behind the wardrobe. I had a habit of padlocking my rucksack and putting the key under the mattress.

'What do we have here?'

There was a bulging jiffy bag shoved into a crevice between the mattress and the base. I pulled the sizable padded envelope from its hiding place and emptied the contents as hundreds of folded paper sachets spilled out onto the bedspread.

'What the hell are they?' Swinko blurted.

'I have no idea, they have words written in German scribbled on them.'

I carefully unfolded a sachet to reveal five or six grams of a brownish powder.

'By all accounts, this must be heroin,' I whispered.

'Holy cow! We need to get rid of it and fast,' Swinko muttered in a strained tone.

We looked at each other and our facial expressions acknowledged that we had a major problem which struck us like a bolt of lightning. Question after question flashed through our minds. Did a German traveller back out from a smuggling run at the last minute? Was it a set-up by corrupt police? Were the mafia coming to collect it? The horror and realisation took hold and we could sense our imminent demise and death.

Consider the setting. A sweltering night in Quezon City, 1981. The Philippines were ruled by President Ferdinand Marcos and his corrupt authoritarian regime under the premise of martial law. Imelda Marcos was the Governor of Metro Manila and the American military were still resident in Subic Bay. Crime and corruption had reached epidemic proportions, virtually no tourism existed and hand guns were commonplace. Street gangs operated with impunity and gunfights were the norm. One of the most vicious and famous organised crime syndicates, Bahala Na, had their headquarters on Roxus Boulevard overlooking Manila Bay. It was next to the impregnable fortress of the American Embassy indicating their status within the Filipino political framework.

In this lawless and densely populated city of Metro Manila, there we were, two Brits, holding several kilos of someone's heroin in our sweaty hands and not knowing a single person in the country. I carefully folded and sealed the open sachet and put them all back into the jiffy bag while Swinko paced up and down in an anguished state.

'Let's stay calm and consider our options,' I said quietly as he continued with his tormented gait. I was relieved the door had so many locks.

'We cannot risk taking the drugs out of the hotel to put them in a rubbish bin especially if it's a trap. For the same reason, it's too dangerous to bring it to the attention of the sleazy hotel owner as they may be part of the scam,' I said.

'We're on the top floor, can't we stick it in the guttering and check out?' suggested Swinko.

'It's an idea but the drugs would still be here and to leave now considering we arrived two hours ago would seem strange and draw attention our way.'

We both stood staring out of the window.

'Maybe we can fling it over the street onto that flat roof opposite?' Swinko pointed at the target.

'Good idea. What other choice do we have?'

'None! This package is a death sentence.'

'Your arms are the longest. Can you throw it that far?'

Swinko wrestled the package into the shape of a boomerang then lifted it up and down to feel the weight.

'I think so.'

'OK, let's go for it but remember we've only one chance.'

I shifted the chairs and table to clear the way and maximise his chance of a good throw. With his back to the wall in a trial run, he sprinted towards the window like a gazelle but kept a tight grip of the jiffy bag. The second time, he set off at a meteoric pace with a determined look in his eyes and hurled the drugs with all his might towards the roof opposite. Momentarily, because of its shape, I thought it might spin round and fly back into our room. We stood silently and watched it soar through the air in what appeared to be slow motion.

We must remember that the Philippines is a beautiful and fascinating nation state. Although a South East Asian country, it was a Spanish colony for three hundred years which accounts for eighty per cent of the population being Catholic. The third largest Catholic country in the world after Brazil and Mexico and one of only two in Asia, the other being East Timor. The Philippines has a distinctive South American temperament to its personality and the Filipinos are warm hearted people who laugh readily and openly express their emotions.

The package swivelled from side to side as it flew over the street and eventually landed on the edge of a parapet that surrounded the flat roof. Like a tightrope balancing act it continued to tremble either way until it finally tipped over onto the far side and slipped out of sight.

'Close the window and shutters,' I spoke in a more relaxed tone as I moved the furniture back to their original spot.

Our sense of relief was short-lived by a sudden and aggressive banging on the door. Swinko ran towards it, 'Don't open it!' I barked.

'Why not?' he replied in a panicky voice.

'Because there may be more hidden drugs and it's the police. Keep them busy, tell them to wait five minutes and I will search the place.'

I combed every inch, crevice, nook and cranny, in and under the dilapidated furniture as the knocking continued.

'OK, unlock it now, I'm sure it's clean. Please don't let it be gangsters with guns wanting their heroin,' I prayed.

The door opened wide and standing there was a toothless pimp beaming a broad smile with a girl on either side. He announced himself as Rodrigo, our new friend with two beautiful women at best rates for the whole night. Danica, a pretty girl, who looked directly at me, and Bianca, a stout woman who took an immediate shine to Swinko. We were so relieved that we quickly nodded our heads in agreement.

Prostitutes were not our style but given the circumstances, our best defence was to act normal. We agreed a deal and both girls entered the room. As I counted the pesos into Rodrigo's open hand I noticed a single tattoo of a ball on his left wrist, maybe a symbol of something sinister.

When Rodrigo left the hotel, we wandered down to the local bar, chatting and laughing with Danica and Bianca who were fun personalities and from whom we learned much about the country. They explained that the wrist tattoo indicated one's status within a gang and the ball on Rodrigo's arm was quite low down the scale with a question mark being the highest. The girls were somewhat bemused when we wished them a good night, nevertheless, they gave us their private number should we need help.

At first light we checked out and left a false trail at reception by claiming to be American Jesuits *en route* to Cebu Island. For extra security, we caught a jeepney to the docks and another to the main bus station. With no definitive destination in mind other than to leave by the first available bus and find a good diving location, we chose one going to Olongapo City. It was close to Subic Bay which was a departure point for hundreds of small islands.

'Let's immerse ourselves in nature and leave the colourful chaos to another day.' Swinko nodded and smiled as we boarded a geriatric vehicle with glassless windows.

The journey took ten sweaty hours over bumpy roads while resting our feet on cages of clucking hens. There were endless stops to unload and pack again. Exhausted, we arrived in Olongapo City by nightfall and found a guest house close to the terminal. The following morning we travelled up the west coast until dusk and by default discovered a small secluded island with no name.

The retreat was in the province of Zambales, thirty miles north of Iba. There were several log cabins and a tiny café bar on the water's edge adjacent to the islanders' main business, a saltwater crocodile farm. We slept until late morning and emerged into a tranquillity and beauty which took our breath away. Our hut overlooked the turquoise sea rippled by a soothing westerly. Ramon and Jessica were the friendly owners who made us feel welcome and in an instant, we decided to stay on this beautiful island for a few months.

There was a floating extension to the seating area with a type of raft which Ramon made from tree trunks, secured to the pier by a long rope. The idea was to pull it over to the jetty, climb down a short wooden ladder, release the rope and float out into the bay. The homemade raft became our living room, laid out with comfortable hessian chairs, hammocks and a table under the shade of a thatched roof. On the first morning, we ate breakfast of the sweetest mangos and Jessica's moist coconut buns.

As we relaxed the incident in Manilla began to fade from our memories. During the months that followed, Swinko and I discovered a multitude of uninhabited islands in the area. We explored the extraordinarily rich underwater flora and fauna while scuba diving through the multi-coloured coral gardens. The transparent water felt comfortable at 25ºC in stark contrast to a 6ºC and cloudy North Sea back home in England.

The Philippines has one of the most diverse ecosystems on the planet where one can find the biggest fish in the world, the whale shark, and the smallest, a pygmy seahorse. We observed a variety of marine creatures which inhabited this area of the South China Sea including turtles, tuna, and red snapper. Shoals of jackfish were not alarmed as we swam amongst them, indeed, sometimes their curiosity brought them right up to the mask like a dog sniffing your face. We marvelled at the silvery abstract shapes that the glistening shoals of sardines would make as they twisted and turned in perfect symmetry. I often returned to a gnarled outcrop of tomato-red coral to study the antics of a hairy frog fish, which reminded me of a splayed toilet brush, furiously digging up the sea bed.

We had a pleasant surprise during Jessica's birthday celebration when a Scotsman strolled into the bar. Walter was a travelling salesman who sold marine paraphernalia to the local fishing community. He had been on the road continuously for forty-six years without ever once returning to his homeland in the Highlands of Scotland. During this time he had lost his parents and both sisters. A stout man in his early sixties with long flowing, smoky white hair and matching beard topped off with a faded panama hat. Walter was the only British person we met on this trip, but his eccentric personality more than made up for it as he regaled us with his humorous traveller's tales.

It was rare to have strangers visit the island. Most were local people known by Ramon and Jessica with an exception one Sunday afternoon of a group of rowdy young men who docked at the pontoon in a rigid inflatable boat. They placed their handguns on the table in the same way we do with our smart phones. Ramon became agitated by their loud voices and aggressive posturing until they departed well after midnight and the smile on his face returned. The incident reminded us of the lawless state that existed on the mainland.

After several months of blissful living, we were diving at our favourite spot and as I drifted to the surface, I felt something hard hit my leg and the emerald water suddenly turned red. Hands gripped my arms and Ramon hauled me out of the water onto the boat, blood spurted into the air from a main artery with alarming force. Swinko made a makeshift tourniquet from a t-shirt and pointed my toes towards the sky. A fishing vessel had not seen us in the water and the propeller from its outboard motor had taken a chunk out of my foot. Our Barangay (a traditional craft with outriggers which acted as stabilizers) chugged back to the island at full speed. When we docked, I was especially lucky as the mayor had parked his jeep next to the jetty and it was the only vehicle on the island at the time. He drove for an hour over rugged tracks to a medical station in a jungle clearing.

A cheery Filipino doctor leant over as I lay on the concrete slab, 'You have cut through a main artery and have lost a great deal of blood. Do you want a transfusion?'

'How much blood have I lost?'

'Three beer bottle,' he said.

I tried to visualise the volume without success. To avoid further confusion, I rephrased the question.

'Will I die without one?'

'No.'

The medic dressed the wound and I spent the final few weeks fishing from the raft and reading while Swinko continued to dive. On the weekend before our departure, Jessica cooked a red snapper banquet. Local fishermen, the mayor and some of his friends from the mainland joined us for the celebration and the party lasted until dawn. It was a wrench to pack our rucksacks and say goodbye to Ramon and Jessica. Our friends who had treated us as family. We would never forget this pretty and undeveloped Philippine island.

An elongated jeepney took us for the protracted bumpy ride to Olopongo and we transferred to a regular bus onto Manila. Benjie, an amiable Filipino sat next to us on the journey. He worked at the Stone House Hotel on East Rodrigo Avenue in Quezon City and lived with his family in a poor barrio on the edge of town. Benjie booked us into the Stone House at Filipino rates and we accepted his kind invitation to visit his home the following day.

Benjie arrived late morning and took us on three jeepney rides to the barrio. From our final stop, we walked through ever narrowing alleyways between single-storey breezeblock homes with corrugated iron roofs and others made from plywood and plastic sheeting. We squeezed past wandering pigs, stepped over sleeping dogs and through gangs of feral children. By this time, the rancid smell of sewage and decaying garbage was beginning to have an effect on my stomach. The entrance to Benjie's home was a one metre high padlocked grate through which we crawled to access a ruinous complex of shanties. Inside their home, there were cages where we would normally have food cupboards. The toilet was a hole in the ground which drained into a stagnant canal at the rear but their living quarters were immaculate.

Benjie proudly introduced us to his wife, Camille, Uncle Jemuel and four cousins. Their two children Yumi and Claude, a boy and a girl, had just returned from school in bright white shirts and wore their shiny black shoes with dignity. We sat in a semi-circle on the polished wooden floor and ate a simple rice dish, accompanied by a glass of hot sugary tea and a sweet called ginatan made from jackfruit, with its distinctive aromatic flavour. We brought toys for the children and a teapot for Camille. As a thank you, Yumi and Claude sang a song which made my eyes well up with tears. Despite their circumstances, pride in themselves made a big difference to their outlook on life. Each adult had regular work or ran a lifestyle business and together they created a happy family unit even though they were surrounded by hardship and danger from all quarters.

Camille showed us her photos of the visit to Manila by Pope John Paul II as he travelled through the city waving to the crowds from a jeepney which reflected the Spanish and Mexican traits of vivid colours. These vehicles forever celebrated something Filipino.

The first jeepney we caught back to the city was an impressive work of art, expertly spray painted with two-dimensional owl imagery. The second had a neat row of garishly coloured car horns on the bonnet which resonated at different pitches. The driver called it his 'boom box,' which was connected to a deafening sound system blasting out *Ghost Town* by The Specials and *One Day in Your Life* by Michael Jackson as we motored through the crowded streets.

We had a few days left in QC before our departure. My flight home to the UK had a stopover in Thailand and Swinko was travelling to Tennant Creek in the Australian bush for his new job working in a tin mine. We called Danica and Bianca to arrange a farewell celebration.

The party night arrived and the four of us visited the Cultural Centre of the Philippines on Roxus Boulevard. The CCP was a key music venue for many famous Asian artists. It was a magnificent show followed by a late dinner downtown where I tried the pork adobe for the first time. A regular dish in the Philippines cooked in soy sauce with vinegar and garlic. It was rich and succulent and reminded me of Chinese sweet and sour with the addition of caramelised meat. After dinner, we strolled around the late night food markets taking in the different aromas and jovial atmosphere. The girls wanted us to try balut, a fertilised duck egg, boiled and eaten after the embryo is half developed. We gave this street delicacy a miss to avoid any possible stomach complications on our respective flights.

At the end of the evening, we stumbled into a seedy club. We were sitting at a table in front of the exotic dancers when a group of gangsters arrived and the mood darkened. Danica held my head in her hands and whispered in my ear not to look in their direction. Later, when I went to the bathroom and stood at the urinal, I felt a pair of strong hands massage my neck and shoulders. I spun round to decline any further pummelling and gave the masseur a peso. He smiled and returned to his chair in the corner. As I was running my hands under the tap, I saw the door open in the reflection of the mirror and three thugs walk into the grubby toilet. The masseur walked out. Two of them stood either side of the entrance while the obnoxious looking one with a pot belly stood and stared at me with a silly grin.

'What you doin' here Yankee?' he snarled.

I dried my hands on the paper towel, I had no fear. I knew Swinko would arrive soon if I was away longer than expected. I offered to shake his hand.

'I'm English, not American, and visiting your beautiful country.'

When he gripped my hand, my eyes instinctively homed in on the question mark tattooed on his left wrist. I then did something totally out of character, in a moment of madness, and slapped his fat belly making a joke about his lack of exercise. The two henchmen drew their breath in sharply with a hiss, thin-lipped and poised – a long eerie silence ensued – like waiting for the smouldering fuse of a firework to explode. Maybe this time I had made a fatal error, been over confident and accidently pressed the self-destruct button.

Fatty finally reacted with what I can only describe as a raucous, maniacal laughing fit. He wrapped his arms around me in a bear hug and I could feel his hot breath in my ear when he asked if I loved the Philippines. I froze, half expecting a long sharp knife to be driven into my abdomen but he continued to guffaw as we left the bathroom. He even sent over a tray of complimentary beers. Soon after we quietly slipped out of the club making sure to avoid eye contact.

The next morning at the airport with Danica, Bianca and Swinko, I was taking the earlier flight to Bangkok so it was my turn to say goodbye first, not only to Swinko and the girls but also to the Philippines. As the aircraft left the runway, I scanned the blue pearlescent arc of Manila Bay and the smoky megalopolis of Quezon City. The envelope given to me by Danica at the last moment lay on my lap. As I unfolded the sheet of yellow paper a symmetrical apricot-coloured pearl rolled into my palm. Scrawled in red ink, 'A small piece of the Philippines to stay with you forever xx.'

On most journeys, I often go through a myriad of emotions before, during and after the adventure: anticipation, excitement, joy, fear, belonging, frustration, appreciation and sadness all play their part. When my relationship with each country comes to an end, a small token or souvenir can galvanise and represent that affinity. Sometimes it is harder to come home than to go away. Danica's gift of an apricot pearl was symbolic of my experience of the Philippines.

Thailand 1981

A GENTLE HUM PERVADED THE RESTAURANT AS DINERS CHATTED and gesticulated with their chopsticks during the twilight zone, between a red orange sundown and nightfall. It was a quality Thai restaurant which overlooked a floating market in a smart classy area of downtown Bangkok. I sipped my Tom Yum soup, a favourite of mine in Thailand which tasted of an exotic perfume with a distinctive sour, spicy, hot flavour giving it that special Far Eastern identity.

Wannaporn, Halina and Ukrit were Thai friends of old. Wannaporn was the wise one, a kind and caring person, devoted to the Buddhist community and well known for making fragrant rice dishes for their many festivals and celebrations. She was a diminutive, cuddly, unpretentious individual who allocated her time for those who were less fortunate. She had spent fifteen years of her life living in the North of England married to a British accountant. When he died unexpectedly she returned home to Thailand. Halina and Ukrit were cousins of Wannaporn who played the viola and the cello respectively in a successful string quartet. They performed various styles of classical, folk and even K-Pop and their venues ranged from farmers markets to the Tokyo Metropolitan Opera House.

The peaceful ambience was shattered by a fracas nearby. We looked in the direction of the raised voices and a group of five or six young Thai men were standing up, sitting down and banging the tables with their fists. As the argument escalated, a teenager appeared from a back room baring his teeth, holding a tall thin glass in his raised hand, running towards their group and smashing it into the head of one of the youths embedding it in his neck and shredding his own hand in the process. Blood splashed in profusion onto the crisp white tablecloths. The group chased each other around the restaurant, punching and kicking in Thai boxing style, hurling glasses and knocking furniture over.

We slid from our bench seats to under the table as fragments of glass peppered the surface like hailstones. Screams and panic erupted from the diners as they rushed for cover. The brawl moved closer to the front door with some activity outside on the street but we continued to stay where we were for safety. When I peeked out from under the tablecloth, a Latino girl stood nearby, motionless and in a state of shock. I grabbed hold of her arm and pulled her next to us while Wannaporn removed a small piece of glass from her shoulder. The poor girl was trembling but calmed down once in our midst. Her name was Alba from Rioja in Northern Spain. After what seemed an eternity, the disturbance subsided and we emerged from underneath the table as a lone policeman in shorts ambled into the restaurant flicking through his notebook. An adolescent lay on the floor gushing blood from his neck and within a few minutes, he gurgled and died.

Alba was taken away by her Thai hosts and soon after, all the diners were shepherded to a room upstairs. Our drinks and food were laid out as a buffet but everything was still covered in shards of glass. The atmosphere remained highly charged and unsettled. The young men who accompanied Alba stared at me with hostile eyes. Wannaporn suggested it was tarnished machismo having failed to save Alba and to avoid their gaze. An hour or so later we were allowed to leave.

Thailand was a stopover on my way home to England after several months in the Philippines where I had contracted a tropical infection from a diving wound. The doctor at the clinic confirmed it would require treatment on a daily basis for seven days. Wannaporn invited me to stay at her bungalow in a pleasant suburb of Bangkok.

After a visit to the medic, Wannaporn and I boarded a disintegrating tuk-tuk for the ear-splitting journey down to Central Pier on the Chao Phraya River. This river is an integral part not just of Bangkok but all of Thailand and flows through the city into the Gulf of Thailand. There were an assortment of express ferries to different landing stages throughout the waterways as destination points for specific districts of the city.

Our ferry belched dark fumes as it forged its way through the floating debris and surface plant life bobbing around on the grey polluted water. The speed of arrival and departure was unnerving and the entire crew, with the exception of the helmsman, involved one man with a rope and whistle. As we journeyed up the river, muscular tugboats hauled enormous barges and claimed the widest passage. A multitude of smaller craft criss-crossed their bow narrowly avoiding collisions, especially the flat bottomed boats that skimmed diagonally from one river bank to the other.

We floated past some of Bangkok's most wonderful buildings like the stylish Japanese style pagodas which were dotted along the bankside and displayed their tiered towers with multiple eaves coloured maroon and canary yellow. The view of the Grand Palace from the water was majestic with its enormous footprint of two square miles. The light suddenly disappeared when we sailed into a long shadow cast by the daunting eighty metre ornate Khmer-style tower of the Wat Arun temple.

However, Wannaporn's favourite was the Wat Kalayanamit, famed for its Golden Buddha which had its own jetty on the west bank and where we docked via a ferry that traversed the river from Ratchinee pier. Not a spectacular edifice as the Wat Arun but a stunning example of a royal temple nevertheless. It had been built in the 1820s on land donated by an aristocrat family whose remains were enshrined in a pagoda-style chedi within the grounds. As we entered the main hall, the tallest in Thailand and built in traditional Thai style, Wannaporn whispered, 'You are the only farang in here.'

'What's a farang?' I murmured.

'A term we use for foreign people.'

The colossal Golden Buddha was stupendous at fifteen metres high and twelve metres wide sitting in the Subduing Mara posture where the right hand is bent over the right knee and the left hand rests on the lap.

'What does the pose represent?'

'It signifies the attainment of enlightenment.'

'What's it made of?'

'Limestone, painted in gold leaf...follow me.'

We knelt in front of the Golden Buddha and bowed three times as Wannaporn paid homage by reciting an adoration.

During the week that followed I helped Wannaporn with her catering duties as she prepared for a festival. We collected rice, fish sauce, palm sugar, tamarind, shrimp paste, chillies and coconut milk from a variety of warehouses and markets.

When the doctor gave me the all-clear, my plan was to visit Koh Sichang, a small island in the Gulf of Thailand. I would live in a cottage next to the sea among the fishing community and absorb the culture. Within a few days, Wannaporn drove me to the mainland ferry terminal and on the way we visited her niece, Bun Ma, in Pattaya, which I found to be an unsavoury beach resort brimming with sex tourism, noisy bars and gaudy advertising. The boat sailed for two hours before docking at a picturesque harbour where an old gentleman greeted me on the wharf. I sat as a pillion on his rasping motorcycle and we rode along the waterfront to my new stilted abode set back twenty metres from the sea and walking distance from the coastal village. Shaped like a hen house and built from a rich brown teak it had two small rooms and a tiny balcony with one easy chair overlooking the ocean. I soon fell into a daily routine.

Each day, I strolled into the village and sat by the harbour, chopsticks in hand, slurping noodles with locally caught fish or crabs while watching the sunset. After dark, I sat on the balcony and viewed the diamond dust of night lights from the small fishing vessels bobbing around on the glossy charcoal water.

At the market, I bought two hand carved meditating Buddha's, one as a gift for Wannaporn and the other for my desk at home. Four weeks soon led to six, which finally ended up being eight as I psyched myself into readiness for the challenges which lay ahead. I dragged myself away from this beautiful and peaceful island back into Bangkok for my flight home to England.

On my last night in Thailand, I invited Wannaporn, Halina and Ukrit to a celebratory night at one of their favourite restaurants, without incident, and the following morning Wannaporn drove me to the airport. Before I boarded the aircraft, she held my hands tight and looked through my eyes, 'You will be successful in your chosen venture but please remember one thing. If a person speaks or acts with a pure mind, happiness follows them like a never-departing shadow.' She was a special person and a close friend.

QUEZON CITY

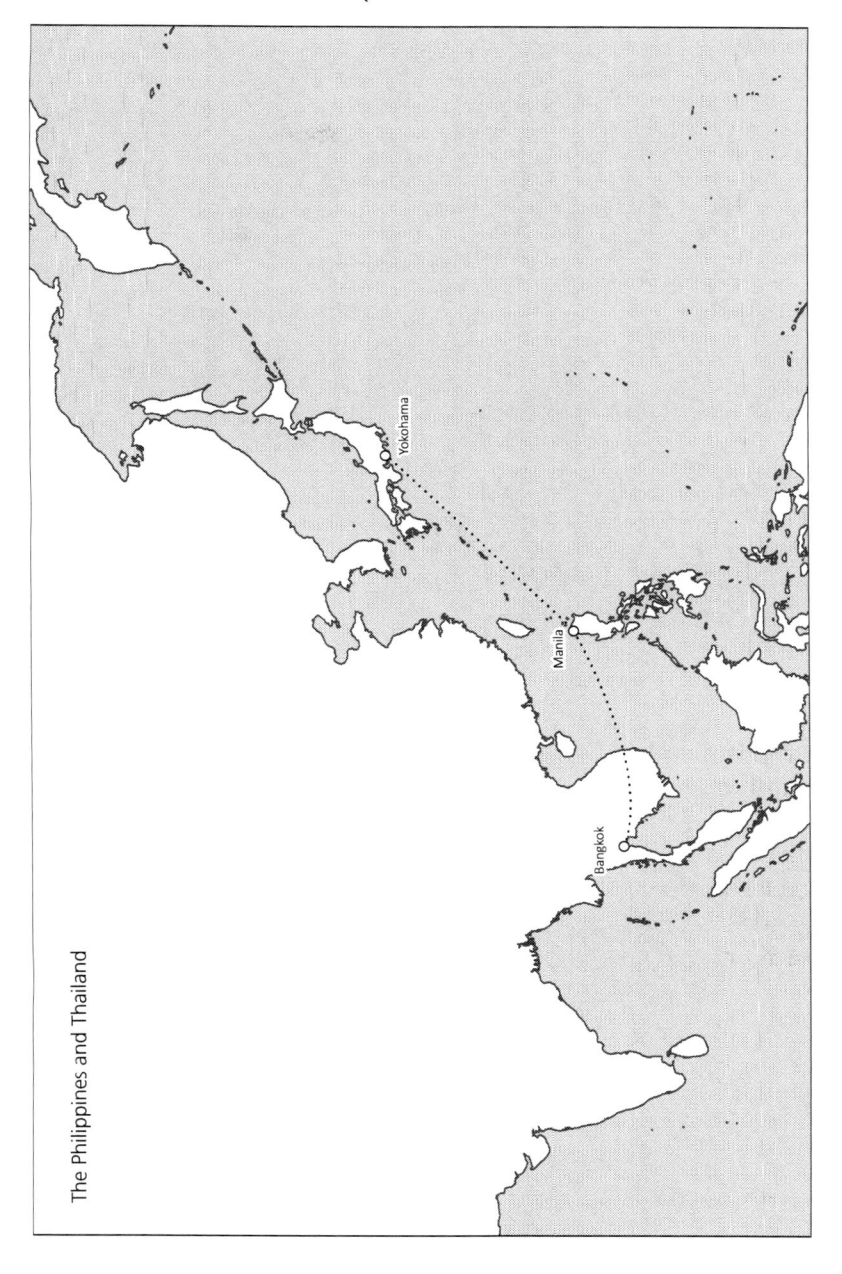

The Philippines and Thailand

MILES & MILES

On Assignment

10 El D.F. – Federal District of México

'Travel is the frivolous part of a serious life and the serious part of a frivolous one.' ANONYMOUS

Mexico City 1998

THE ROAD AHEAD WAS BLOCKED BY FURNITURE, BUILDING debris and a burnt-out pickup. Armando hung out of the car window to communicate with the rioters huddled together in groups next to small fires. Their faces obscured by bandanas and masks. He bellowed to be heard above the loudhailers, car horns and general mayhem, 'Te apoyamos. Pasamos por favor.'

'What's he saying Bob?'

Bob was an American who knew Mexico well but appeared more nervous than we would have preferred.

'He's asking to be allowed through the barricade but they refuse. Holy shit...they are threatening to t-t-t-turn the vehicle over.'

Armando reversed at speed and spun the car into the opposite direction. He drove slowly towards a seamless row of dark anti-riot-shields and black shiny helmets with batons to hand – flanked by truck-mounted water cannons – supported at the rear with clusters of armed militia. We rolled to a stop in front of the military cordon. Within 200 metres we had moved from pandemonium to a ghostly silence.

Armando left the car to talk to the soldiers but five minutes later he was back behind the wheel.

'They won't allow us to cross the line or even guarantee our safety,' he sighed.

We were trapped in a silent void of tense hostility between the two opposing sides. It was unnerving to see the armed forces involved in domestic security. The riot was due to teachers' pay and conditions but it felt a great deal more brutal than an educational dispute.

'What are we fucking hanging around for, let's get out of here now man!' shrieked Bob.

'OK, OK, Bob, calm down, what do you suggest?' Armando replied.

'We go straight back to the compound and lock ourselves in your office.' Bob mopped his brow.

'Agreed, but let's give it one more try on the other side.'

Bob was not at all happy with the idea but Armando swivelled the car away from the military blockade and cautiously motored towards the one remaining exit. We pulled alongside the protesters manning the obstruction and he leapt out to talk to them. While Armando negotiated with the ringleaders, men wearing balaclavas and scarves began to surround our vehicle in a threatening manner.

Latin America in 1998 contained forty-three of the fifty most deadly cities in the world, excluding warzones, and registered one third of all murders despite having only eight percent of the population. Mexico was in the final throws of seventy years of continual rule by the Institutional Revolutionary Party (PRI). Ernesto Zedillo was the President and during his six year term in office, he had paved the way for the country to break away from its past. Two years later, the Mexican people would appoint Vincente Fox as their first elected President.

Our day started early when Simon and I dashed through Miami airport to board the morning flight to Mexico City. Simon was my business partner and together we owned a British toy company. He had picked up a stomach virus in the USA but decided the illness was short term and he would be able to complete the trip. Simon was the quintessential Englishman whose doppelganger was Simon Templar, as played by Roger Moore in the 1960s TV series, *The Saint*. He was identical in height, had a surprisingly similar intonation and hairstyle who carried himself with the same panache as the fictional character.

It was our inaugural visit to Latin America and on arrival at Benito Juarez International airport, the formality of their customs authority was governed by two metal pipes hanging from the ceiling. They were plugged at the base with red and green buttons which we pressed for something or otherwise nothing to declare prior to being allowed entry into the country.

More rowdy demonstrators congregated next to the car and blocked our light. It became noisier inside and uncomfortably claustrophobic. The vehicle began to sway with the movement of the jostling horde and we could hear the rhythmic cracking of gunfire in the distance. Simon wore a terrified expression, Bob had his head in his hands and an acrid smell of fear permeated the air. My stomach welled up with panic as if something horrendous was just about to happen. It gave me the overpowering urge to force open the door and run for my life. Armando's welcome face suddenly appeared at the window as he struggled with the mob to squeeze into the car.

'There's no chance of the roadblock opening up but they don't regard us as the enemy,' he panted.

'Well, keep the fucking doors and windows locked man before they change their fucking minds and let's get the fuck out of here!', screamed Bob.

Simon and I were having a specialist toy made, called the power tube sound machine, which at the time was an innovative cool concept. It comprised of a stretched metal spring in the centre of a metre long cardboard tube with a plastic handle at one end and an amplifier at the other. A range of sci-fi cosmic sounds oscillated as the children shook, rattled or rolled it. Professionally it was used to create tonal effects in the film industry. Armando and his team were the manufacturers and creative owners of the toy in question and Bob was their US distributor, based in Iowa.

Armando gently manoeuvred the car backwards without running anyone over and continued into the void where his offices were located in a colonial building within the historic centre close to the Presidential Palace. He used the rear bumper to force open the arched wrought iron gates. Bob and I jumped out to heave them back into place. We scampered over the cobbled courtyard into the handsome edifice and locked the doors. Now that we were safely inside, Bob rushed over to the drinks cabinet and retrieved the Don Julio tequila. He drained two glasses before pouring everyone a shot. Simon took his medication and was given a bedroom to lie down while Armando sat at the piano. Mariano, his first lieutenant and the two administrators, Alicia and Maria gathered around him as he began to play.

'What do we do now?' I asked Bob as he handed me a glass.

'We'll have to sit it out for a day or two, I expect. I've been to Mexico City many times but this is a first for me. It all happened so quickly.' Bob gave a relieved smile.

'Why do they call the city, El D.F., and the people who live here, Chilangos?'

'The Mexicans have always referred to their capital as, The Federal District of México, or El D.F. for short, and the term Chilango is slang for someone from Mexico City.'

Bob's outward appearance was akin to a stereotypical mad professor with long, unkempt, frizzy grey hair which framed his dark brown crazy-looking eyes. He wore an ill-fitting tatty suit over his tall, thin and slightly stooped stature. In all other respects Bob was perfectly normal and an honest, hard-working businessman.

The offices were in fact Armando's home. His furnishings were made from natural materials: soft leather sofas, hessian chairs, rosewood tables including rattan stools and wood flooring. Fresh flower displays were in abundance and added to the ambience. The terracotta painted walls were adorned with fascinating black-and-white imagery of 1930s Mexico which his father had shot with an early Leica 35mm. He had spent fifteen years of his life walking the length and breadth of the country amassing a collection of 30,000 photographs.

Armando was playing *Summertime* by George Gershwin and his staff sang along as an ensemble. We relaxed with our Don Julio while listening to the melody but the music stopped abruptly when he took his hands away from the keys and stood up to make an announcement.

'It's time for lunch and there's an exceptional birria restaurant at the end of the avenue.' Armando's suggestion came as a complete surprise given the circumstances.

We left Simon asleep in his room and walked through the noisy gathering outside the gates, into the silent vacuum, before setting foot in a restaurant, which was not only open but in full swing and only ten metres from the ominous military blockade. An eight piece mariachi band greeted us at the entrance and within seconds we were absorbed into the party spirit, in complete contrast to the events outside. Trays of chilled black Modelo beers arrived and the fiesta was underway.

By Mexican standards, Armando was an enormous man. He was tall and plump with an unruly bouffant of oily black hair and an overgrown droopy moustache. His facial expressions alternated between a little-boy-lost to brooding contemplation. It was he who had invented the power tube sound machine and had lived in a creative bubble most of his life.

Armando was mentor to Mariano who had a sharp wit and an astute business brain. A little man with a shock of dark curly hair sitting uncomfortably on his head and whose hawkish eyes flicked all over the restaurant in a permanent state of alert.

Mariano ordered for all of us, the speciality of the house, lamb birria. The preparation took two hours before a reddish-brown baked stew, exuding an irresistible aroma of spicy meat, was served in finely decorated terracotta dishes. Followed by sides of red rice, avocados, corn tortillas and chipotle. Chipotle is a relatively mild, smoke-dried red jalapeno chilli with an earthy spiciness and a unique, distinctive smoky flavour which is indispensable to all Mexican households and restaurants.

The mariachi played with gusto in their traditional Charro attire. Charro is a term which refers to horsemen or Mexican cowboys from the state of Jalisco where Guadalajara, Mexico's second city, is located. Their outfits were a creamy combination of a short slim-fit jackets with waistcoats – tight pants adorned by silver thread and studs – topped and tailed with the famed Mexican sombreros and cowboy boots. Their musical instruments included: a vihuela, a slender acoustic guitar with double strings, a requinto guitar which is a smaller and higher-pitched version, one violin, three trumpets and a ukulele.

Every Mexican knows the words to hundreds of mariachi songs and they sing along to their favourites. One of my best-loved is *El Niño Perdito*, the lost child. They perform this melody in an unusual way. Initially, the trumpeter walks away from the other musicians and begins to play from afar. A whispery haunting sound in the distance. The sound amplifies as he gradually returns to the band and generates a powerful and stately crescendo for the grand finale which symbolises the return of the lost child.

The passionate vibrancy of the restaurant culture in Mexico City was a habitual lunchtime event where Chilangos transcend the hurly-burly of daily life. Mariano settled the bill and as we stood up to leave our table was taken by new arrivals. After four hours of merriment I had hoped to find the streets returned to a modicum of normality. We emerged red-faced, flushed and in good humour but the sound of mariachi music faded and the rows of dark shiny helmets continued to stand to attention. The blood-orange sunlight from the late afternoon shimmered on their body shields and made for a striking image. I took out my camera but the look on Bob's face quickly forced it back into my pocket.

We walked among the rioters once again and through the rounded iron gates into Armando's home where we found Simon attempting to placate his rumbling stomach by eating a soft boiled egg while chatting to the girls. After several coffees and much deliberation, Armando and Mariano went back onto the street to talk to the protesters and returned before nightfall. They had finally negotiated a safe exit with the key decision makers at the first barricade. Bob, Simon and myself were instructed to collect our belongings. We drove out of the gates but this time, as we approached the roadblock, a gap opened up big enough to let us through.

'Great,' I shouted and we finally set off in the direction of our hotel but when we neared Paseo de la Reforma in downtown El D.F., we encountered more obstacles in the road, both military and civilian. I made a decision to leave the car and walk the remaining eighty metres to the hotel providing the military gave me permission. Simon would stay with Maria, Armando's mother, until his condition stabilised.

Mariano translated as the helpful commander in charge of a group of soldiers described his love of British made films and especially *Mr Bean*. He instructed me to run down the right hand side of his squad, close to the wall, and to keep sprinting until I reached the hotel entrance on the same side of the street. The dash through the military left me wheezing in the foyer. Within a few days the riot began to peter out, Maria helped Simon recover from his illness with her homemade chicken consommé and Mariano brought him back to the hotel. However, he remained in a state of weakness and unable to work.

Each morning, Mariano picked me up in his lime-green Volkswagen beetle and we plunged into the gridlocked traffic of Mexico City. From the overpass, I scanned the vast expanse of stationary vehicles, most of which, to my surprise were also lime-green beetles including the taxis.

During the week, we visited a variety of commercial districts to inspect and qualify the suppliers of the toy components. It was apparent that security was a factor of daily life in all spheres. At one factory, a four metre vertical metal turnstile formed part of the entrance. We pushed it clockwise to access their office but it locked midstream trapping us inside. In the panic that ensued, a tinny voiceover from a hidden speaker asked us for our ID. After introducing ourselves, they released the mechanism and as it synchronised with the front door we tumbled into the building. Between meetings, Mariano frequently stopped at a tiny newsagent whose counter was a square metal grid sunk into a stone wall at head height. He would ask me to buy him one cigarette as they sold them in singles. The weekend arrived and Simon continued to improve but remained hotel-bound, the riot was history and the armed forces were back inside their barracks. Bob had gone home to Iowa so Mariano and Armando would show me the city.

The Aztecs founded El D.F. in 1325. The location had been decided upon when they observed a golden eagle land on a prickly pear plant and devour a snake. They named it Tenochtitlan. An image of the eagle appears on the Mexican flag, their coat of arms and sometimes the peso. Close to the city's zocalo, the main square, is the archaeological site of Templo Mayor, the most important religious setting of the great Aztec Empire and the centre of their capital.

Touring the colonial districts, the dominant colours of the buildings were red or burnt sienna made from tenzotle, a volcanic rock used as a facing stone first by the Aztecs and then the Spanish. My favourite inner city location and an oasis within this vast metropolis was Coyoacán. A peaceful bohemian neighbourhood where tree-lined cobblestone avenues led up to the market square with its iconic Coyote Fountain commanding centre stage. It was surrounded by market stalls of handicrafts, leather and jewellery.

Coyoacán is the birth place of Frida Kahlo, regarded as one of Mexico's greatest artists. Born in 1907, she contracted polio at the age of six and in her teenage years was severely injured in a bus crash. During periods of convalescence she began to paint and one third of her imagery were self-portraits.

'I paint self-portraits because I am so often alone, because I am the person I know best.'

Her art was influenced by the vibrant colours of the indigenous cultures in Mexico and incorporated European elements of Surrealism, Symbolism and Realism. Her work questioned Mexican societal roles of class, gender and race. After her death in 1954, her popularity continued to develop internationally.

Frida spent time living in New York and San Francisco but it was in Paris where she struck up friendships with celebrated artists such as Marcel Duchamp and Pablo Picasso. However, an unwavering passion for her Mexican identity always brought her back to her roots in Coyoacán. She lived and worked in the family home most of her life, La Casa Azul, the Blue House, now a museum, which has a beautiful courtyard garden where her xoloitzcuintli dogs ran free. They were a hairless Mexican breed which dated back from the Aztec period. She also had two Spider monkeys named Fulang Chang and Caimito de Guayabal.

Frida's tumultuous relationship with the legendary muralist Diego Rivera compounded her notoriety. By the 1970s, she had become a universal role model for a variety of groups in their struggle to achieve a more open society, governed to a certain degree by feminism and also the Chicano movement, a civil rights body for Mexican Americans. In 1977, one of her paintings sold for £12,500 and by 1995, a self-portrait achieved £2.1 million. *Two Nudes in the Forest* would fetch over £5.3 million in 2016 – the highest auction price for any work of art by a Latin American artist.

Sitting next to the Coyote Fountain in Coyoacán, I asked Mariano, 'What's that aroma coming out of the eating house?

Is it a beef stew or a goulash? Its making me salivate.'

'Pancita, a national dish which translates as little belly. It refers to a cow's stomach but only in El D.F. do they call it pancita! Throughout Mexico, it's known as menudo and served in menudo restaurants which are found in most towns and cities across the country.'

'One of my favourites,' Armando said as he walked towards the café. 'They add garlic and dried red mirasol chillies to the menudo and boil it overnight in thirty litre pots. It's a breakfast food served from 5am to noon and has the reputation as a hangover cure. Let's try some.'

They served it piping hot in deep terracotta soup bowls with oregano and finely chopped onion. I enjoyed the taste of chilli in the liquid but the offal was too sloppy. However, there was one added extra by request and that was the cow's hoof cut into tiny chewy fragments and sprinkled over the dish.

It became evident that the food in Mexico was far from what you would expect as portrayed around the world. The Americanised Tex-Mex image is misleading. What actually existed in all areas was a fusion of native and European elements which produced a sophisticated cuisine. The cornerstone of Mexican society was the family unit and crucial to this ménage was the preparation and consumption of food. Lunch at 3 p.m. was the main meal of the day and a family occasion which was an integral part of the Latino culture.

During the late afternoon, we roamed the pretty avenues of Coyoacán enjoying street tacos and black beer from the numerous cantinas. By nightfall, we found ourselves in Zona Rosa until late, a party area of the city. Driving back in the early hours, small children – who should have been tucked up in bed – entertained stationery vehicles at the traffic lights by performing acrobatics dressed in miniature clown outfits while others cleaned the windscreens.

I returned to Coyoacán early on Sunday motivated to discover more of Mexico and to acquire a collection of books on their culture and history. Mexico was a captivating blend of Mesoamerican and Spanish cultures with a slight dash of Asian. The population of 100 million included twenty-five million indigenous people, the largest ethnic group of any Latin American country. A nation admired throughout the America's, with one exception, the USA, where there existed a lack of understanding between the two cultures.

Armando had commented, 'The vast majority of American people don't own a passport and as such fail to experience other lifestyles. As a result, their opinion of the Mexican way of life is tainted by prejudice.'

Diego, the owner of El Jarocho coffee shop clarified the finite difference between the north and south of Mexico by drawing a comparison with European nationalities.

'In a German restaurant, the guttural sound of their conversation makes a thunderous noise in contrast to a French eatery where the romantic intonation creates a faint hum. In other words, the people from Sonora, Chihuahua and Coahuila on the USA border speak with a deeper resonance and as such are louder. Whereas the populous of Jalisco and further south have a softer, gentler pitch which characterise their somewhat passive and artistic demeanour. An exception to this rule are the Chilangos who have a recognisably harsh cadence.'

From these interesting conversations with local people about the country in general, I put together a wish list of places to visit on subsequent trips. To my surprise, they were mainly areas to the south of Mexico. From Guadalajara and Puerto Vallarta in Jalisco through the indigenous state of Michoacán to the Silver Cities of Guanajuato and San Miguel de Allende. Further south again beyond El D.F. to Puebla, Oaxaca and the semi-autonomous region of Chiapas bordering Guatemala in Central America.

I drew open the heavy brown curtains to a grey Monday morning on the Paseo de La Reforma and the eternal spider's web of lime-green VW beetles brightened up the cityscape.

The power tube sound machines were ready to ship and all that was left for me to do was agree a deal with the freight company and my work was complete. Our next meeting with Armando, Bob and Mariano would be the following February at the New York Toy Fair.

At the airport, Armando gave me a parting gift of something special from his father's collection. An original black-and-white photograph of a cactus, laden with prickly pear fruit, growing out from a mountain ledge. Armando and Mariano for the first time referred to us as their compadres which in Latin America signified a brotherly bond between friends. When the aircraft took to the night skies over the vast sparkling grid of El D.F., Simon fell asleep clutching his Don Julio while I updated my notebook.

Mexico had affected me in a good way. I found myself attracted to the easy going Latino lifestyle set amongst the organised chaos. The intoxicating vibrancy of the people and the way in which live music formed part of everyday living. It made me feel alive. The spontaneity, warmth and sound of laughter fed my soul. Something deep inside me had been released and in the not too distant future, Mexico would become an intricate part of my life for the next two decades.

EL D.F. – FEDERAL DISTRICT OF MÉXICO

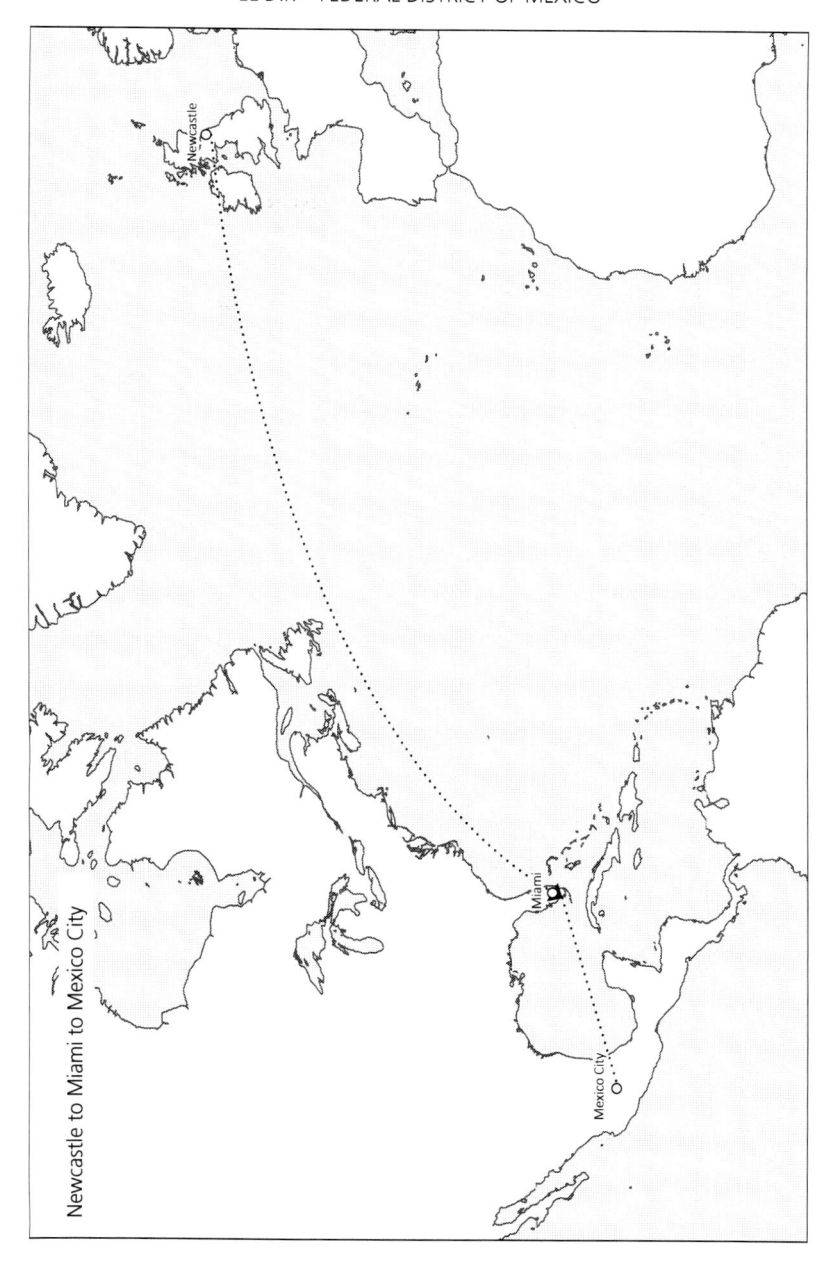

Newcastle to Miami to Mexico City

11 Pearls of the Orient

'To awaken quite alone in a strange town is one of the pleasantest sensations in the world, you are surrounded by adventure.'
FREYA STARK

Jakarta, Indonesia 2000

THE CITY OF JAKARTA AND THE SURROUNDING METROPOLITAN area, located on the northwest coast of Java, is home to more than thirty million people. Java is the third biggest island within the Indonesian archipelago, similar in size to England but with twice the population.

I regularly visited the Far East as a toy buyer and the travel persona within me enjoyed dealing with the many Asian cultures. However, these illuminating encounters would often manifest into the unexpected. From the discovery of a stunning architecture or a traditional cuisine to a romantic liaison but in some cases, a bad experience. I have selected three episodes from a trio of Asian countries to illustrate these engagements: Indonesia, Thailand and Taiwan. Flying club class and staying at top end hotels in contrast to my previous trips renting grubby backstreet rooms was not necessarily for the better. Before my meeting with a crayon manufacturer, I took a few days break to escape the five star bling of the Grand Hyatt and find the real Jakarta.

From the financial district, a taxi dropped me near to the historic area where I hailed a bajaja, a vehicle more suited to the narrow streets of the old town, Kota Tua, or Chinatown, referred to locally as Glodok. These bajaja's are a noisy and unstable motorised three-wheeled rickshaw not allowed on many of the city's main roads so they use the small lanes and back alleys instead. What the jeepney is to Manilla, the yellow and black ambassador taxi is to New Delhi, the tangerine-coloured bajaj is to Jakarta.

Aboard the bajaja, I could see the fast moving tarmac through a wide rusty hole between my feet as it zoomed alongside polluted canals where families lived above rotting garbage in the still fetid waters. Men in patterned sarongs bathed their horses near groups of women pummelling the family laundry while children splashed around in the leaden liquid.

At a warung in the old town, Timoty, a Javanese vet who wanted to practise his English helped me understand the menu. Throughout Indonesia, an integral part of daily life is the warung. A tiny, family-owned general store or restaurant which can be either permanent or mobile. Timoty recommended bakmi goring as a classic noodle dish, served hot with a thick sweet soy sauce, or, if one preferred a spicier version, mee goring, adding chilli and mushrooms. We ordered both types to share and it was an experience in itself to eat at this compact restaurant. One metre square on two rubber wheels with a pair of white plastic stools under a flip-up table big enough for two bowls of food. Behind a timber partition there was a single gas ring for frying the noodles. At a bigger warung, similar in shape to a garden shed, we devoured gleaming white steamed dumplings about the size of a grapefruit. They were light and fluffy, filled with a sweet peanut puree at their core, tasted delightfully moreish and cost twenty sen each, a few pence. These warungs were all-over the city, clogging the main thoroughfares and backstreets. Each with their gaggle of customers whose cumulative volume added to the hyperactive buzz of an already fast and furious street life.

My bright orange bajaja gurgled and coughed to a standstill up a side street on the edge of Chinatown and refused to restart.

It was in a district where the Minangkabau community lived, an ethnic group from the island of Sumatra. An unexpected stopover that gave me the opportunity to view their original architecture at an open house museum. From the pathway this impressive wooden building reached up to the sky with a dramatic curved roof structure which mimicked the horns of a water buffalo. An elderly Minangkabau woman referred to it as a 'spired roof house.' It served as a residence and a centre for meetings or ceremonial activities. Externally the patterned trelliswork flowed down from the multi-tiered gables and carried motifs of flowers, leaves and fruit that defined a harmonious relationship with nature. Internally, the decorations were infused with imagery depicting lifestyle values, customs and rituals. It was an enchanting experience of a fascinating culture which prompted me to make a note and research the Minangkabau.

In Chinatown the mood turned sombre as I walked passed rows of blackened burnt-out buildings which dominated the landscape. They were a haunting reminder of the murderous riots which had occurred two years earlier in 1998 when over 1,000 people had died. Unemployment, food shortages and economic hardship caused the mass violence and the ethnic Chinese had been a target. However, the main avenue was heaving with both Indonesian and Chinese pedestrians engulfed by smoky exhaust fumes and serenaded with a symphony of tooting horns.

As the bajaja tore through the side roads on my way back to the old town, families of three, four or even five rode alongside bunched together on one scooter without helmets. Sometimes they carried unsuitably shaped cargo such as a vertical goalpost or a live sheep draped over the drivers lap. These top heavy two-wheelers overtook us in droves as they weaved their way through the congestion like a swarm of bees. On the open road, my bajaja kept braking and swerving sharply to dodge the snail-like handcarts which dawdled across the fast flowing traffic. At a stop sign, an overladen truck on smooth bald tyres sprouting fabric cast a menacing shadow over the bajaja as it leant precariously in our direction. This was Jakarta, a chaotic melting pot of a megalopolis.

After several days, I received a message from the owner of the crayon factory, Rajasa, who informed me our rendezvous would take place the following morning. I had never met him in person but we had talked on the telephone many times and I found him to be articulate and charming. He arrived in reception at 8am, an athletic stringy man with a swept back silvery coiffure and docile copper-coloured eyes.

During the day we discussed my unscheduled visit to the Minangkabau district and it transpired that Rajasa's family were part of the same ethnic group. Their homeland was in the Minangkabau Highlands of West Sumatra and he was delighted with my interest in the culture. Over coffee he described the inner workings of his people.

'We are both matrilineal and patriarchal. The line of inheritance of land and property is handed down from mother to daughter, while the father and son are responsible for the Islamic religious affairs and politics. A principled ethos we abide by is our longstanding commitment to education. Many successful people in Asia have come from the Minangkabau. Mohammed Hatta is a good example. He was a co-founder of Indonesia and served as Prime Minister. There are numerous other successful Minangkabau, not only politicians but novelists, philosophers, athletes and composers.'

'Education certainly is the basis of a healthy society,' I said. 'Never been to Sumatra but would love to visit one day.'

'Sumatra is the biggest island in Indonesia and the sixth largest in the world. It also spans the equator. In fact, the equator itself actually runs through the centre of our village!' He gave a broad smile. 'Of course, we cannot see it but we can walk from the southern hemisphere to the north in one minute.'

'Is the Sumatran food similar to Javanese cooking?'

'Not at all! Our cuisine is unique. Tomorrow, we will go to a special place for you to try some interesting dishes from the Minangkabau.'

After our working day, Rajasa picked me up from the hotel and we drove to his favourite restaurant, built as a spired roof house, which had the enviable reputation in Jakarta for authentic Minangkabau. The manager greeted us with solemn dignity wearing a full-length, sleeveless, scarlet-and-gold sequinned jacket over a silk sarong. An Indonesian combination known as a teluk beskap and topped off with a songkok, a hat similar to a fez but without the tassel. We were ushered to a prominent table draped with a crimson tablecloth and perched on an octagonal plinth. Rajasa suggested beer but I declined in respect to his faith. Instead, he ordered fermented buffalo milk which tasted slightly richer than Indian lassi.

The laws permitting the consumption of alcohol in Indonesia varied from Bali where it was widely available, to Aceh in the north of Sumatra where one could expect six lashes of a rattan cane for drinking any type of alcohol. In Jakarta it was acceptable and available but with some mild restrictions.

To guarantee a gastronomic experience from his homeland, I asked him to choose for us both, however, Rajasa had reserved the celebratory meat dish rendang earlier in the day. It must be ordered in advance as the preparation time was somewhat protracted. Rendang is a haunch of water buffalo meat preserved initially with spices before slow cooking in coconut milk and then recooked at different stages to ensure absorption of all the flavours. He told me that a recent report of culinary experts in the USA, based upon three years research, rendang had been voted the number one tastiest fare from a shortlist of fifty cuisines worldwide.

On a side table, a cook ground shrimps, red chillies, garlic and ginger in a volcanic mortar with a stone pestle adding a dash of lime juice to create sambai, a spicy sauce – served with lemang, bamboo tubes filled with a glutinous rice.

When the rendang arrived, I was disappointed with its presentation as the meat in particular looked dry, but despite appearances, I was overwhelmed by an explosion of refined tastes which kept on unfolding. Initially I detected a perfume of ginger and tamarind followed by baked red chillies and creamy coconut, melting into a succulent, caramelised buffalo meat. I had not tasted anything that remotely resembled this dish and my expression must have said everything. The look of contentment on Rajasa's face betrayed his sense of pride.

To refresh our palettes, a bowl of exotic rambutan fruit was placed on the table. They resembled an oversized flame-red grape wrapped in a prickly, leathery skin and tasted buttery.

Our conversation turned to politics and Rajasa aired his support for the freedom of East Timor. In 1975 the Indonesian military had occupied East Timor, an independent country that was predominantly Christian and which formed part of the Indonesian archipelago. After the invasion a decades-long conflict ensued, coming to a head in 1991 with the slaughter of defenceless civilians. This was the catalyst that soured relations with many other countries and subsequently accelerated the demise of President Suharto who relinquished power in 1998. A referendum followed in 1999 in which seventy-eight per cent of the population of East Timor voted in favour of self-rule. It had been a bloody struggle which had taken the lives of 100,000 East Timorese but it would be another three years before they celebrated their day of independence.

In the morning, Rajasa accompanied me to the airport and suggested that during my next trip to the Far East, we would plan a visit to the island of Sumatra and meet his extended family who will prepare their unique version of rendang.

Bangkok, Thailand 2000

CHOMPOO, A THAI BALLOON MERCHANT COLLECTED ME FROM THE airport in an archaic Datsun Sunny without air conditioning in 38ºC of heat and ninety per cent humidity. His factory was located in a rural district near Trat, 200 miles south-west of Bangkok alongside the Cardamom Mountains and close to the border with Cambodia.

'Welcome to Thailand. No mad cow here!' Chompoo giggled.

His remark referred to mad cow disease which, at the time, was causing alarm in Europe due to its rapid growth. I had met Chompoo briefly at the New York Toy Fair two years earlier. He was a balding, rotund, middle aged businessman with eyes akin to slivers of amber ice who moved with a pompous gait. I felt uneasy in his presence and could sense a nasty side lurking beneath the surface of his somewhat pleasant demeanour.

'I like roly-poly woman for bed and for you nice young one?'

'No thanks, not for me.'

'You prefer ladyboy?'

'Strictly business Chompoo but if we have time, I wouldn't mind trying the seafood when we get to the south coast.'

The sweltering car journey of six hours terminated outside a windowless industrial plant similar to an aircraft hangar, built into the red earth and set in a jungle clearing. The balloon machine was a gigantic metal monstrosity dimensionally equivalent to four terraced houses and positioned in the centre of this commercial edifice. Making *a toy balloon* entailed a continuous stream of oval moulds, twenty abreast, and hundreds deep, moving slowly through liquid latex. The drying process followed the conveyor belt as it flowed onto the top of the machine where forty women sat either side, massaging the soft rubber stems to manually create the lips.

'You sit for women massage your stem,' sniggered Chompoo.

On the periphery larger groups of women knelt or sat cross-legged on the earth floor packing the finished product into plastic bags and cardboard boxes. The staff would avert their gaze whenever he was about and were nervous in his presence. Chompoo consistently produced each consignment to the standard required and the timing was never an issue as the raw materials from the rubber plantations were nearby. After our business discussions, he booked us into a boutique hotel on the coast.

The English speaking Thai hotelier recommended a floating restaurant, converted from a houseboat, moored in a nearby marina noted for their locally caught fish. His happy expression morphed into a frown as Chompoo arrived and rudely interrupted, 'Somsak Pu Ob is best in Trat,' which happened to be the same place.

It was a hot, humid and windless night on deck when they brought an oval platter of hoy lai prik pao, delicious chilli clams topped with sweet basil. A main course of pla tod kamin, a turmeric-coated fried catfish, had a flavour of mud but it was served with a tasty papaya and crab meat salad. Chompoo then ordered a klao neow toorian for two, sweet sticky rice with chunks of durian fruit swimming in a cloying coconut syrup. The repulsive smell of the creamy-yellow durian was astonishingly strong and reminded me of a pungent French cheese. Chompoo relished the fruit which he reckoned was an acquired taste and appeared to delight in my discomfort.

We returned to the hotel bar at midnight where he invited two working girls, Lala and Kanya, to join us for drinks. As his menacing gaze cruised their figures he slapped me on the knee, 'Lala my gift for you. She not taste same like durian!' He chortled.

Soon after, Chompoo took Kanya to his room and I was left alone with Lala, who spoke a little English and some Spanish. I gestured towards my genitals suggesting there was a problem in that area to avoid the inevitable but I indicated it would be our secret and Chompoo would pay her regardless. She nodded and smiled, so I bought her a drink and we chatted. Lala was open about her working life and told me that tourism was new to the area. I could not resist asking which nationalities were the most lucrative and she responded with, 'The squeakers,' she continued, 'Japanese man squeak three minute with good tip.'

At 3am, there was a light tap on my door and it was Kanya in a distressed state looking for her friend Lala; by the disturbed look in her eyes and the scuff marks on her neck, she must have been the subject of an unpleasant experience. I walked her to the foyer and ordered a taxi.

In the morning, I found Chompoo in reception waving his hands in the air and berating the hotel owner whose body language displayed a mix of exasperation and anger. I had no idea as to the reason for the heated debate but Chompoo instantly regained his composure once in the car so I assumed it was a ruse to lower the bill. Driving back to Bangkok, his aggression at the wheel brought about two road rage incidents, both of which were close encounters at high-speed, and he caused the death of a dog. Fortunately the animal did not suffer as it happened at sixty miles per hour but the dull thud made me feel sick. Worse again, Chompoo could have avoided the collision but instead punched the air and screamed with pleasure as if his football team had scored the winning goal. At Bangkok airport the front grill of his Datsun Sunny was a dented mess of blood and fur. I was relieved to escape Chompoo and the humidity into the air-conditioned lounge.

Taipei 2000

THE FLIGHT FROM LONDON TO TAIWAN LANDED ON THE STROKE OF midnight at Taoyuan airport in Taipei, the capital. I handed the restless cab driver the address of my downtown hotel written in Chinese characters. He slammed the car into gear and shot out of the terminal while wrestling with the steering wheel as if the accelerator was jammed to the floor. He wore white gloves and the seats were covered in the same material which I mused, could double up as a burial shroud if he persisted in mounting the pavements and overtaking on either side. The term undertaking, became a double entendre. Pointing to my heart and using my hands in a calming, waving motion did not have the desired effect. By the time we screeched to a halt outside the hotel, I was traumatised, needed a drink and the reputation of Taiwanese taxis was upheld. The reason for my visit to Taipei was to authorise a new supplier of diaries and as they were a long established family company, I expected the work element to take no longer than several days.

Mr and Mrs Ng, the business owners, arrived early the next morning accompanied by Tiffany, their translator. I was sitting in the breakfast room on the thirty-fourth floor overlooking the ultra-modern city and drinking a quality green tea which tasted of the first flush of spring. Tiffany effected the introductions with a slight bow and my first reaction was positive. A prosperous middle aged Taiwanese couple who were clean cut, professional and proud of their products. The third generation of the same family to run the factory. The couple were the exact same height with matching square faces and could have easily been mistaken as brother and sister.

'Mr and Mrs Ng have scheduled a tour of the manufacturing plant and arranged to take you to dinner tomorrow evening.' Tiffany spoke excellent English.

'That's very kind and I look forward.'

'We wish to ask you before we reserve a table in the restaurant if there are any allergies or types of food you dislike?'

'I've no problem eating most things but I'm not keen on fish.' My response was an untruth to avoid some of the stranger recipes used to prepare or putrefy seafood in Taiwan.

Mr Ng drove out of town for twenty miles to their commercial unit on a high-tech industrial estate in Keelung City. The factory visit and negotiations were spread over two days during which time the assessment of their operation satisfied all the requirements. Once the process was concluded, they suggested Tiffany be my tourist guide.

Tiffany relaxed when we left the office and in the car she leaned over, 'Are there any places of interest you wish to explore Miles?'

'If possible, somewhere that represents Taiwanese history would be interesting.'

She took me to the Mengjia Longshan Temple which resembled a Chinese pagoda in design and was the oldest Buddhist shrine in Taipei. The moment we walked through the wooden gates into the enclosed courtyard of this wondrous sanctuary I fell in love with its spirit. We sat in silence as our senses absorbed the unequivocal ambience of tolerance and peace. The perfumed incense lingered and synthesised with the mellow chanting of the monks in the main chamber. The temple was an emblematic example of classical Taiwanese architecture created in the vernacular style, where the footprint of the building followed the Chinese philosophy of balance and symmetry.

As we stepped outside having had our souls regenerated, I smiled at Tiffany, 'Thank you for that experience, it was more than wonderful.'

'It was a pleasure for me too.'

Walking to the car she bought two savoury cakes on a stick from a street vendor.

'What on earth are these?'

'It's pig's blood mixed with sticky rice and covered in peanut flour,' she laughed.

Tiffany needed to change for the evening, so we took a detour through the modern metropolis of Taipei, to her tasteful apartment in a smart and trendy downtown district of Tamsui overlooking the River Tamsui and the Taiwan Straits towards mainland China. As she prepared a pot of emerald green tea, I browsed one of her many English books on Taiwanese history and observed the river traffic from her living room window. When she reappeared, the dark drab business suit had been replaced by a little red dress. She stood in the doorway and unleashed a mane of smooth blue-black hair which flowed over her shoulders and down her shapely body. I felt an urgent need to brush my teeth after the pig's blood lollipop.

On our way back into the city Tiffany expressed her desire to become active in Asian politics, supported by her doctorate in Chinese history. Mr and Mrs Ng were friends of her family and the translation service she provided was not just a kind gesture, but helped maintain her language skills. She was a single child and her parents owned a multinational shoe retailing chain; they had homes in several countries including a property on Hong Kong Island.

Tiffany and I met with Mr and Mrs Ng at their favourite fish restaurant. I must have looked confused as they reassured me they had something special in mind and it was not fish. The evening got underway with an appetiser of oyster vermicelli which was rich and flavoursome. At this point, Mr Ng and Tiffany became embroiled in an emotional debate about some historical fact relating to the Chinese civil war. When Chiang Kai-Shek had withdrawn from mainland China to Taiwan and its subsequent relationship with both China and the USA. I was beginning to understand that her passion for politics stemmed from a belief in what was right for the people of Taiwan. I admired her tenacious ability to construct dialogue in a persuasive and positive manner especially when a sheepish Mr Ng was forced to concede his viewpoint.

The subject matter changed to food when Mr and Mrs Ng's surprise dish arrived in the form of a black and grey sea slug, the size of a rabbit, which was ceremoniously laid out in front of me by the chef. The smell and slippery texture immediately turned my stomach and I could see that Tiffany was laughing her head off under an austere pretence. They referred to it as a sea cucumber, a creature that crawled along the ocean floor on its soft cylindrical body like a gigantic marine caterpillar. I managed to work my way through the slimy slug, with a smile, a grimace and help from Tiffany's dexterity which distracted the Ng's as I rapidly swallowed lumps whilst gulping beer. When the pineapple cake was served, it helped flush out some of the oily taste.

It was close to midnight when I paid my respects to the Ng's. As our business was finalised, I looked forward to a few days' break before the next stage of my oriental trip to Hong Kong. Tiffany drove their car to the hotel and came in for five minutes to collect samples I had brought for Mr Ng. It was in the elevator that we giggled about the slug. When it rattled up to the first floor, she toppled into me with a bouquet of jasmine. As her glistening sweet-almond eyes dilated, a salvo of exploding passion-grenades shuddered through my body. Our hungry kiss only interrupted when the lift doors opened on the tenth floor and a family of chattering Chinese shuffled into the small space.

On the way down, Tiffany held my hand and beamed, 'I'm going to take some holiday and be your Taipei guide.'

'That will be lovely.'

'See you around 10am tomorrow.' She raised one eyebrow over a cheeky smile and skipped to the car in her little red dress.

The following morning I was reading the Taipei Times in the sunny dining room overlooking a glittering metropolis when Tiffany arrived with a sultry smile and looking gorgeous. Her velvety raven hair swept back to reveal long pearl drop earrings dangling next to her honey-coloured neck. She kissed me softly then brushed the contours of my lips with her finger, kissed me again and sat down.

'Did you sleep well?' She enquired.

'Yes thanks. Never moved once during the night and you?'

'I was too hot, very hot!...I left the air conditioning on all night.'

We shared a flask of light-green tea. The newspaper headlines spread over the table stated that Chen Shui-bian, the leader of the Democratic Progressive Party, had won the presidential election.

'Finally, the KMT have been kicked out of office after fifty years in power.' Tiffany smirked.

The Kuomintang Socialist Party had ruled all of China until they lost the civil war with the Communist Party in 1949 and moved to Taiwan. In his inaugural speech, Chen Shui-bian stated that he will not declare nor call for a referendum on independence or abolish their official blueprint for an eventual reunion with the mainland providing China does not attack.

Tiffany tossed the newspaper on the floor.

'Let's go to my uncle's spa,' she gave a suggestive smile.

'I'll go up to the room and collect my shorts. Is it far?'

'It's a private club about thirty minutes from here in a district called Beitou next to some volcanic springs. I will drive us there.'

We walked around the block to her scooter, a bright yellow Vespa. 'Hop onto my favourite chariot, sir.' She laughed and revved the engine.

Tiffany handled the machine with the skills of a despatch rider, zipping in and out of the traffic as I clung to her slight frame. We spent the day relaxing in steamy waters followed by a massage. The afternoon blended into the evening when we took a ride in a cable car which ascended from the riverside up to the Maokong Highlands. We had a bird's-eye view of the fading sunset hurling a spectrum of yellows and reds onto the mirrored windows strewn across the futuristic conurbation.

After dark we visited the famous Shilin night market, a lively weekend venue that showcased the range of foods available in Taiwan. In a pink booth with a water bath we used a miniature fishing rod threaded to a tiny hook to catch our own live prawns. Tiffany managed three and I, two, which they grilled on a skewer. Bright red ducks flattened out like a kipper, hung by their heads with the polished appearance of being spray painted. The tasteless duck meat had an odd rubbery texture. Baby abalone, razor clam and limpet broth carried an aroma of the sea and was delicious. A group of teenagers stood nearby scooping clear fish roe from a plastic tub as a regular street snack.

On Huaxi Street known as Snake Alley, hanging racks of snakes in varying colours, widths and lengths were displayed in preparation for cooking at a profusion of restaurants and market stalls. They served snake meat soup or eyeball and gall stew to name a few, sometimes accompanied by a glass of kaoliang, a snake wine. The more poisonous the reptile the higher the price. To extract the venom from the serpent, the live creature was gripped from behind and its head pulled back to reveal the fangs which were inserted through a paper lid into a glass jar. The deadly liquid was used to cook speciality dishes which supposedly enhanced male potency.

At midnight, we elbowed our way through the sweaty crowds to the final venue of the evening, an intimate cocktail lounge at the end of a narrow cul-de-sac. Inside, a Taiwanese folk quartet played a selection of different sized pear-shaped fretted lutes and a wooden washboard with miniature cymbals hanging from its corners. The lutes produced a higher-pitched sound to that of a banjo and were supported and balanced by the grating percussion of the washboard. Time evaporated in the fun atmosphere as we enjoyed ourselves dancing to the live music from this unusual ensemble. It was after 3am when we eventually stumbled out into the warm, humid night air.

All day Sunday we lounged around Tiffany's apartment watching movies as she cooked a British lunch of shepherd's pie not dissimilar to my Mother's recipe. On Monday afternoon at the airport we agreed to keep in touch. The flight to Hong Kong took two hours. Soon after, I arrived at the Sheraton Hotel close to the Star Ferry terminal at the bottom of Nathan Road. On checking in I was redirected to their first class reception on the third floor accessed by an exterior glass lift. To my astonishment the room had been upgraded to a penthouse suite overlooking Hong Kong Island. Whilst unpacking I thought to myself, have they confused me with a celebrity or a politician as a message was pushed under the door.

'Hello my darling, I hope our suite is to your satisfaction. My flight will arrive in the morning, your Hong Kong guide, Tiffany xx.'

PEARLS OF THE ORIENT

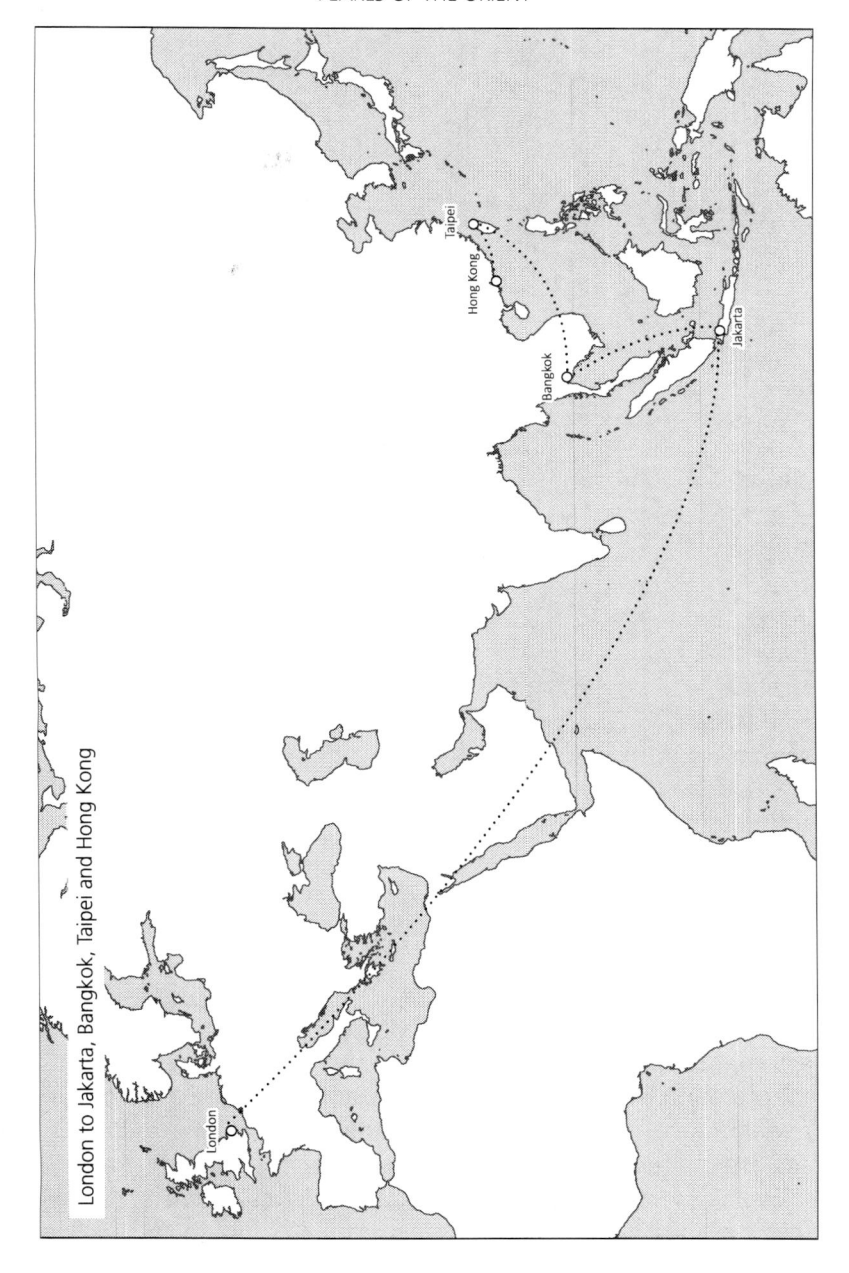

London to Jakarta, Bangkok, Taipei and Hong Kong

12 Shanghai

'Be Content with what you have; rejoice in the way things are. When you realize there is nothing lacking, the whole world belongs to you.' Lao Tzu

Shanghai 2002

'There's a call from Shanghai...a lady by the name of Ying.'
'Thank you Sarah, put her through.'
'Hello Ying.'
'He die,' she gasped.
'Who died?'
'Alfie take yoghurt drink and he die.'
'But he was fine on Sunday when he left Northumberland to travel home to China. I'm in shock.'
'I call sister but not believe and threw down phone. Please tell Alfie family?'
'Of course. How are you coping?'
'Cousin here OK.'
'What did Alfie die from? Was it a heart attack or something in the yoghurt?'
'I not know. They take him hospital. You come funeral.'
'Yes but it's all so sudden. I will be in touch once I speak to his relatives.'

I pushed back on the office chair and wiped the tears from my eyes, he had been in such fine form at the pub over the weekend. On my desk were three jars of Marmite, his favourite spread which he had forgotten to pack. It was not available in Shanghai.

Alfie was in his early sixties, born in Durham a British citizen, who lived most of his life in North Yorkshire. His career in electronics involved frequent visits to China where he met Ying two years earlier. They moved into a comfortable high-rise apartment in Pudong, a fashionable area of Shanghai overlooking the Huangpu River. Throughout Alfie's life, his ambition was to live in China and at an older age, he achieved his dream with a partner thirty years his junior.

Alfie's father had died in his fifties from circulation problems, so perhaps a genetic disorder ran in the family. I called his sister Betty who, although she had not seen him in two decades, agreed, after consulting with the rest of the family, to send Ying £3,000 to cover the cost of the cremation in Shanghai. It was a lower cost option than repatriating the body and I suspected it was what Alfie would have chosen because of his lifelong passion for all things Chinese.

Alfie was a smallish, thickset man with a paunch, protruding front teeth and a jet black comb-over which appeared to be a separate entity to that of his grey gingery sideburns. He wore gold horn-rimmed spectacles and his gait mimicked a penguin in style but what I will always remember him for, was his ability to outwit. Alfie was an enigma who thrived on mystery and subterfuge. His motive in life was to fool all the people all the time. I first met him at the Nuremberg Toy Fair in 1997 and in spite of the fact he was UK based, we hired him to source Chinese components. At the end of 2000, he relocated to Shanghai to live with Ying.

Ying was a younger version of Alfie and their relationship was built upon a riddle only they could solve. They had joined forces to create a superior deceptive force, a rogue Batman and Robin. One of their regular deceptive jaunts began with a fake secretary making a reservation at a five star hotel. She would let slip that they were Hollywood producers or owners of European hospitality publications who were travelling incognito. At the hotel, they emerged from a chauffeur-driven limousine, Alfie dressed in a mauve smoking jacket and cravat, a floppy homburg and clutching a gold-topped cane. Ying draped in a flowing silk dress with elbow length white gloves and matching chiffon scarf. They strolled arm in arm into reception as if they were on location as lead actors in a period drama. The concierge would struggle with their heavy 1930s leather suitcases while the management would offer complimentary champagne, meals on the house, extra nights for free and more. The joy of deception had been their joint passion and hobby.

I booked a flight to attend Alfie's funeral and deliver his eulogy and whilst in China, I would appoint a replacement to fill the role vacated by Alfie's demise.

The KLM flight from Amsterdam landed at Pudong International, Shanghai, on a hazy humid morning. As I emerged from the terminal it felt good to be back in the Far East. To breathe that unmistakable musky air which evoked nostalgic memories. Inside the cab on my way into the city, there was a protective device in the form of a transparent plastic shield, shaped to fit around the driver's seat, which made the remaining space within the family hatchback somewhat claustrophobic. The modus operandi of the driver was to accelerate at maximum speed towards gaps in the traffic and break violently to avoid ramming other vehicles then repeat the same motion over and over again. I witnessed accidents and near misses on most taxi journeys in China including this one. After the thirteen hour flight, followed by the drag race to the Donghu Hotel I was ready for a massage.

The Donghu was a peaceful oasis in a stylish district of downtown Shanghai known as the French Quarter and within walking distance of South Shanxi Road metro from where most prominent city centre locations could be reached by subway. The character of this great value hotel, merely four storeys high, was accentuated by the polished teak floors, Persian rugs and matching wood panelling. It had been a former French embassy dating from the colonial era and, as such, oozed elegance. Shanghai was a city of some magnitude, so a peaceful retreat was a must, and the Donghu met this criteria.

In the lobby the following day I met Olivia from the Shanghai Business Council. She was a graceful Shanghainese with intelligent eyes who would communicate with our Chinese suppliers until we appointed someone permanent.

'Ni hao, pleased to meet you Olivia.' I shook her tiny hand.

'Welcome to Shanghai Miles. Do you speak Mandarin?' She enquired with a shy smile, pushing back her glossy midnight black hair.

'Not at all, my limited repertoire extends to, how are you, and cheers.'

She glanced at her watch. 'Have you had lunch?'

'No, not yet, I've just got out of bed after my long flight yesterday.'

'OK, follow me, I will give you a guided tour of the French District on the way.'

We wandered along the small avenues through the cool shadows from the protective archways of the plane trees. She pointed out the various foods available from the street sellers, the techniques needed when crossing busy roads and the difference between genuine massage parlours and brothels. At a contemporary office tower on the corner of Nanchang Road, the external glass lift soared to the twentieth floor with breathless ease. We alighted into a chic vegetarian restaurant and sat outside in the sunshine on the roof terrace overlooking a majestic cityscape of Shanghai.

'Reminds me of a sky-high deli in New York,' I said.

'Yes,' she laughed, 'and there are so many restaurants to choose from with around 120,000 in the city.' 'How many?!' I cried.

Over a bowl of green tea noodles, Olivia suggested I meet with Shu Zhu, a prominent figure in the toy industry who would attend their annual general meeting the following week. After brunch, I walked her to South Shanxi Road metro before I took a cab to meet Ying at the Peace Hotel.

The Peace Hotel was located on the Bund, a famous waterfront promenade next to the west bank of the Huangpu River. From the water's edge, I viewed with intrigue the iconic skyline that personified Shanghai, with its unique Oriental Pearl TV tower shaped by its decorative spheres. The Hotel was a glorious throwback to the British colonial era, boasting a delightful art deco ambience, where just about everyone of any importance had stayed. It continued to host a world renowned jazz band, some of whom were its original musicians and well into their nineties, together with former members of the Shanghai Symphony Orchestra. Noel Coward had written *Private Lives* at the Peace Hotel and countless eras of debauchery from all aspects of high society were etched into its spirit.

Ying was relaxing in the Jasmine Lounge, sitting in an armchair and listening to a girl in a blue and cream cheongsam plucking the strings of a zither; a flat musical instrument that resonates an oriental elegance. Ying greeted me with a social kiss, was beautifully dressed and remembered my passion for green tea. She ordered an organic Japanese Sencha, a favourite of mine, served at 80ºC in glass pots.

'Welcome Shanghai Miles, thank you talking Alfie family. It sad time.' She snivelled.

'How are you managing after the tragedy?'

'Not good. Alfie pension go second wife. He say he wealthy. Two years life nothing.' She frowned.

'Did you get the payment from Alfie's sister?'

'Yes, family money pay funeral.'

She wrote down the address of the crematorium in Chinese characters and told me to provide the eulogy. Call after call on her three mobiles interrupted our conversational flow and I noticed that her hands were covered in gold jewellery. I asked Ying to bring to the funeral any personal effects from Alfie's estate which should go to his family.

'I'll walk you to the metro.'

'I have more meeting here. Remember, take care your best

friend wife.' She talked in a seductive tone sending a chill down my spine.

'Meet you for the funeral on Friday,' I said as one of her mobiles began to vibrate.

Walking out of the Jasmine Lounge, I thought to myself that this supposed third marriage to Ying had been yet another side of their deceptive prism and accounted for the pension transfer to Alfie's second wife.

Outside the hotel, it was an overcast and sweltering afternoon on the Bund as I walked alongside the mighty Huangpu River, 400 metres wide at this point. The junks, sampans and river ferries were careful to sail either side of the mammoth barge trains, heaped with coal and pulled by powerful tugboats. They ploughed their way through the murky water and commandeered the deepest channel. The Huangpu is but one of 700 tributaries of the Yangtze, the longest river in Asia, which travels 4,000 miles from its source on the Tibetan plateau to its mouth at Shanghai. Chinese people consider the Yangtze as a dividing line between the noodle-eating north and the rice-eating south. The river basin alone is the world's busiest inland waterway and home to 400 million people.

Alfie had loved China and anything Chinese to the point of infatuation and his favourite city of all time had been Shanghai. After my walk on the Bund, I took a metro to Jenny's Bar, Alfie's favourite watering hole and popular with expats. I had arranged to meet Brian, known as Mr Brian in the Far East, a friend of Alfie's and a resident of Shanghai for the past twelve years. He mentioned that Ying had suggested they go for cocktails one night. She was already looking for her next victim. An unusually tall Shanghainese girl entered the bar and threw her arms round Mr Brian who looked over her shoulder with a cheeky grin to say he would meet me at my hotel on the day of the funeral.

On Nanjing Road, the busiest shopping street in the world, I flowed with the crowds and sensed a togetherness in the throng which radiated an undefined confidence. There existed a feeling of serenity in numbers – an intimacy amid the hordes – where nobody was ever alone. It dawned on me why the citizens of Shanghai were regarded with a certain panache found nowhere else on mainland China. I made my way through the vast expanse of People's Square to the Peace Park, a relaxing manicured garden with pink blossom, lakes and plum trees where neat rows of Shanghainese practised their tai chi – a meditation in motion.

At the Donghu, Olivia had left a handwritten message at reception, 'Are you free tomorrow night to take in some live music at the Cotton Club and perhaps dinner beforehand?' I sent her a response to meet at 7 p.m. in the hotel.

The next evening, Olivia glides into the bar wearing an elegant cocktail dress of yellow satin.

'Now I know why they refer to the Shanghainese as the Parisians of the Orient.'

'Thank you,' she laughed and grabbed my hand, 'Let's go, I have a crab waiting,' pulling me towards the exit.

In the taxi, I chuckled at the word 'crab' as opposed to 'cab' but she repeated and giggled, 'I have a crab waiting...a hairy crab.'

I smiled, 'Am I missing something?'

'It's the hairy crab season! We're going to a restaurant to eat Shanghai mao xie which are freshwater crabs and they are delectable.' She licked her lips and rolled her eyes.

The driver stopped next to the entrance of a neon passageway which led into the popular seafood restaurant. A cast of green crabs in glass displays lined the route, their hairy pincers delicately tied with string into small bundles. These creatures were still alive and their eyes followed us as we walked past to our table. They served the cooked crabs whole with the tools needed to extract the sweet and delicate meat – a pair of scissors, two spoons and some chopsticks. On the side, there was a bowl of crab bisque with sliced ginger. As I followed Olivia's technique to dismember the crab, she told me about her life.

'I took a degree in Social Sciences at Fudan University and my first job was with the Shanghai Business Council. It's been eight years now but for three of them I relocated to our offices in San Francisco.'

'That accounts for your language skills.'

'I learnt British English at school and my ambition is to visit London one day.'

'Mine is visit a Chinese town built during the Song Dynasty. I have read about this era which covered a period of three hundred years until 1279. Is there anywhere close by?'

'I will give that some thought,' she smiled knowingly, 'Do you know that we're the oldest continuous nation state on earth? There are prehistoric characters on oracle bones, unique to China, which connect us to the distant past more so than any other culture.'

'That's why I would like to experience the real China.'

She slugged her wine, 'Come on, let's go to the Cotton Club?'

In the 1920s and 1930s, Shanghai had been famous worldwide for its jazz, glitz and glamour and that distinction was ingrained into the fabric of the Cotton Club. From the outside it looked desperate, a hidden commercial edifice without any lights or inviting entrance. Once inside, it was a time machine which transported us back to the roaring 20s. With its original wooden floors and panelled walls, festooned by black and white imagery of famous jazz musicians. Most of whom had performed live at the club, a strong sense of musical history infused the atmosphere.

We sat in the corner as the band played, *What a Wonderful World*, by Louis Armstrong and she told me all about a tropical island in the far south-west of China called Hainan – a hidden gem regarded as their Hawaii. I had never heard of it and made a mental note to do some research.

The next morning, Mr Brian arrived in good time for Alfie's funeral and a cab took us to the crematorium, a grim single story building on the outskirts of the city. Ying was smartly dressed in funeral black and her face concealed by a veil. The other mourners were men in dark suits swapping business cards. We filed into the building to find Alfie laid out on a trolley in a busy corridor wearing his golfing outfit, but no shoes, and a brown tag hanging from his big toe. The paperwork was processed on the trolley next to his head with the customary red seal approval and it was at this point I noticed Alfie appeared to be smiling.

Ying was dabbing her dry eyes with a pink handkerchief when I asked her, 'Where's the coffin?'

'Not need cremation,' she snuffled.

A small man with a white face mask wheeled Alfie into a room and positioned the body next to twin doors. Ying pressured me to rush through the eulogy before he was released into the furnace and all of us were back outside in record time. We turned our heads towards a brown puff of smoke belching out from a steel flue. Several businessmen were laughing and making jokes about a jar of Marmite in Alfie's pocket which accounted for the coppery plume.

Ying lifted her veil and grimaced, 'You say bring item from Alfie, no like, it spooky.' She handed me a white paper bag and swiftly turned round to talk to the black suits. Mr Brian reckoned it was the cheapest funeral possible and would have cost no more than 5,000 Yuan although she was paid 40,000 Yuan by his family. She had concluded her final deal with Alfie.

Mr Brian and I held our own service prior to visiting Jenny's Bar to meet Alfie's expat circle of friends and celebrate his crazy life, outrageous sense of humour and ability to step outside the box. At midnight, the wake moved downtown to a late night venue and at 3 a.m., I took a cab to the Donghu. Unknown to me, the driver was going in the opposite direction and it was not a real taxi. It stopped outside a typically garish entrance to a nightclub. In my inebriated state, I accepted the cabbie's story that he misunderstood my destination and in one hour he would take me back to the hotel free of charge. I was ushered into an empty lounge with TV screens showing porn movies and realised it was a brothel. A waitress handed me a beer as twelve scantily clad girls filed past accompanied by their madam. Two of them remained and a bill for 5,000 Yuan was placed on the table. I objected to the monstrous tab, threw a wad of notes onto the saucer and left. In the corridor, I was met by two silent men with flat leathery faces who stood either side and held my arms. I couldn't move. Suddenly a steely eyed young man emerged from a hidden door.

'You must pay!' He spoke forcefully.

'I'm not paying 5,000 Yuan for one beer.'

'Do you have the money?'

'No, I don't.'

He talked on his mobile and took orders from an invisible controller.

'We are instructed to remove your ears,' he talked nonchalantly.

'But my specs will drop off,' I joked.

The noiseless leatherheads tightened their grip and he lashed out with a striking karate blow to the stomach. A sharp pain reverberated through my body and the colour drained from my face. I squealed, 'OK, OK, Stop! I will pay, my health is more important than money. I have a credit card.'

I was now under the control of Chinese organised crime.

'Listen!' He brutally squeezed my chin and talked into my face. 'I don't have time to deal with a fucking awkward limey. I have a club to run. I'll remove your ears now!' He screamed with venom.

'Do you want a dead Englishman on your hands sir? I have had three heart attacks. Will that not disturb your evening?' I suggested calmly.

Although it was not true, my ashen face wincing with pain must have validated the statement. He was back on the mobile.

'OK we go to the ATM but it must be paid in full.'

They dragged me to a waiting cab with the same driver but this time I sat in the rear between the two leatherheads. The young Chinese climbed in the front and for the first time we began to converse on rational terms.

'The Triad, the police and the government are one and the same, there is no place to hide,' he said.

At the cash machine, the maximum I could withdraw was half the amount due to the daily limit.

'I have another card at the hotel.' As we now had a rapport, he appeared to suggest to the hidden voice we were nearly there, so we drove to the Donghu.

The situation was tense as he followed me to my room and waited outside the door which was left ajar. I was tempted to slam it shut with my foot and call reception but I thought, is that wise? At the final ATM, the balance spewed out and they sped away leaving me with my ears intact.

The next morning Olivia arrived early looking bright and cheery.

'What's happened to you?'

'Alfie's wake, which ended up being a late night I'm afraid.'

'Come on, I have the solution,' she laughed, 'A massage is what you need.'

We arrived at the parlour and were greeted by three women in white lab coats who showed us to a plush, crimson-coloured reception area. The mood felt relaxed and professional. They asked if we preferred light, medium or hard. Olivia chose light, I opted for hard and they took us to adjoining rooms. My masseur resembled a Sumo wrestler who performed an agonising foot massage which lasted one hour but it released a feeling of liberation, free from anxiety. She took a further ninety minutes to pummel my whole body with superhuman strength causing me to yelp with pain. We left in a state of levitation and the total cost for both sessions amounted to the equivalent of £10. In return, Olivia insisted on buying me a gift of a battery-operated, plastic and gold-coloured paw-waving cat.

'The fortune cat symbolises prosperity and you must keep it on your desk.'

Olivia and I met the following day at the Peace Hotel to discuss their AGM dinner and the meeting with Shu Zhu.

'It's being held at the Waldorf Astoria, do you have a tuxedo?'

'I usually hire one.'

'I'll arrange a fitting for tomorrow. In the meantime here's a copy of the seating plan. You are placed between Shu and myself.'

'Thank you for all your help Olivia, you're a star.'

'I considered your request to visit the real China and have chosen a traditional village nearby. Tongli!' She whooped, 'It's a beautiful place from the Song Dynasty which we call, the Venice of the East. I will organise the trip, leave it to me.'

'Are you sure?'

'Of course. I will arrange it for the weekend after the AGM,' she smiled, 'It will be a pleasure.'

At the Donghu, the ordeal at the hands of the Triad continued to haunt me and I asked to be transferred to a different room. I called Mr Brian and related the story. He laughed and told me of a similar incident with two friends in a club in Ho Chi Minh City, Vietnam. They had been overheard by the staff while discussing their finances and the party spirit suddenly turned hostile. The music stopped, the girls melted away, harsh bright lights replaced the sultry tones and dark suited thugs materialised as the metal shutters slammed shut. A bill was presented for £600. Fortunately, between them they had enough cash and within a few seconds the club was once again alive and rocking. I decided to put the incident down to experience.

I stretched out in my comfortable bed next to the open shutters and listened to the sound of the city at night. As I leaned over to turn out the bedside light, the white paper bag Ying had given me at the funeral lay there unopened. To my surprise, instead of Alfie's false teeth, it contained a beautiful hand-carved miniature Chinese shar pei dog made from a type of polished hardwood and appeared to be an antique. The figurine was a perfect sculpture of this dignified breed with its distinctive deep wrinkles and confident expression. It must have been important to Alfie, perhaps reminding him of his own sandy coloured shar pei, Marmalade, who he had owned many years earlier. I remembered his enthusiasm for the breed and how they marched with the Chinese armies into battle. I placed the shar pei on the bedside cabinet next to the paw-waving cat and slipped into a long, deep sleep.

The day of the AGM dinner arrived and the Waldorf Astoria Hotel was a twenty minute walk from the Donghu so I decided against a cab in favour of stretching my legs. An hour later, as darkness descended, I was completely lost. Although it was the rush hour, there were few people in the back streets to ask directions and no taxis or main roads in sight. I showed the address written in Chinese characters to several people who shrugged their shoulders. In a silent avenue, I raised my hand to stop a Chinese man on his bicycle. Sitting in a basket attached to the handlebars was a small child holding a bouquet of flowers. I gave him the venue details and he nodded in recognition while pointing at the luggage rack above the rear mudguard. I understood that he wanted me to sit there. Dressed in the tuxedo, I perched myself on the metal rack, which was painfully uncomfortable. It took a little while to balance but within a few minutes the three of us were effortlessly moving through the alleyways with the wind in our hair. Father and daughter were singing, so what the hell, I joined in and hummed along. We glided diagonally over a busy main road in the pitch-black without lights before freewheeling downhill into the majestic entrance of the five-star hotel. The other delegates had arrived more gracefully in limousines and cabs. When I dismounted from the bicycle, I shook his hand with both of mine but he refused a payment of any kind. I was astonished by his reaction so I gave his lovable little daughter a kiss on the forehead and pushed a note into her petite hand. They rolled down the ramp singing and waving goodbye. It was a cherished experience. As I marched into reception, Olivia and her team were roaring with laughter as they had witnessed my arrival through the reflective glass.

The function room was a spectacular display of opulence with more than eighty decorative chandeliers. The tables were decked out with polished silverware and multi-coloured fresh flowers set on crisp white linen. My name plate was located on the premier one in front of the podium and whose point of difference was a deep red tablecloth. On a long thin stage, an eight-piece all woman Chinese folk band in long silk gowns of gold, silver and red sequins sat in an orderly row playing zithers of varying shapes and sizes.

Olivia whispered in my ear that Shu Zhu had requested my Chinese zodiac sign. 'Why would she want that information?' I asked.

'The zodiac is an important factor of our culture. It's influential in our decision making process and indicates an individual's personality traits.'

'Seriously? What sign am I?'

'You are a water dragon would you believe. Intelligent, friendly and relaxed.' She added, 'Both Shu and I are Tigers who are compatible with dragons. Here she comes.' Olivia stood up and I followed her lead.

'Pleased to meet you,' I shook her hand.

'Welcome to Shanghai,' she smiled and stared directly into my eyes causing me to blink. We took our seats and listened to the Chairman's introduction.

As the night progressed, Shu and I talked intermittently. She was an Anglophile with dual nationality who had attended Cambridge University and spoke faultless English. On her fortieth birthday, a few years earlier, she had become the managing partner of her father's company whose interests were in property development and toy manufacturing. The Zhu family originated from Bayan Nur close to the border with Mongolia and I could see the Mongolian influence in her facial features. I had the initial impression she was serious, strong, clever and ruthless.

As Olivia and I stood at the hotel entrance to bid her farewell, Shu placed her hand on my shoulder, 'Come to my office in Chengdu and we will discuss your toy business.'

When Shu departed in her limousine, Olivia sighed, 'Let's open a bottle of bubbly to celebrate and I can tell you all about our excursion at the weekend to the beautiful village of Tongli.'

'Our excursion?' I laughed, 'Are you coming with me?'

'If you wish? I will drive you there and show you around. We can meet my friend Wera who's an artist and lives in the village.'

'I gratefully accept and thank you. After the freneticism of the big city and all our hectic activities, a peaceful hamlet will be an oasis for us both.'

Olivia picked me up from the Donghu on Friday morning and we drove 200 miles to Tongli, a quiet settlement alongside the eastern shore of Lake Taihu, positioned amongst a labyrinth of river, lake, and canal systems. Tongli was first established in the Song Dynasty over ten centuries ago when it was known as Fu Tu, fertile land.

Stepping from the car into a rustic Tongli, I was instantly smitten by a special place preserved from a previous world. No manic crowds or beeping horns, simply birdsong and the gentle trickling of water. No diesel fumes or sweaty crowds, only an aroma of smouldering joss sticks fused with a rhubarb and custard perfumed scent from the pink honeysuckle. A serenity that was home to poets, painters and scholars who took their tea outside in charming narrow avenues paved with stone. The mahogany wooden houses built alongside the river with their temple-style flying eaves over carved and latticed windows, faced south onto compact, harmonious gardens which led down to the water's edge. Their roof overhangs were adorned by rows of brightly coloured lanterns made of red silk stretched over intricate bamboo frames with gold decorative tassels that waved gently in the warm breeze. There were forty-nine tiny ornate stone bridges in this quaint village, some of which were still standing after seven hundred and fifty years. This was the real China.

We toured the galleries and studied the various mediums used to create the diversity to be found in Chinese art. The bohemian residents of the village were also skilled in calligraphy, paper-cuttings and seals. Olivia's friend, Wera, an older, respected watercolour artist, gave me a series of paintings of Tongli, portraying spring, summer, autumn and winter.

We invited her to a restaurant as a thank you. A shallow wooden boat took us silently along the canal to Chen's fish café. It was next to Dubu, one of Tongli's oldest stone bridges, which translates to single step, only one metre wide and one and a half metres long. We sat in a herbaceous garden next to Dubu overlooking a confluence of rivers at sundown with the onset of creaking cicadas. The one-roomed eating house of blackened stone spread a miniature buffet over a rickety wooden table. Braised white abalone, thinly sliced and sprinkled with strips of dried seaweed were dribbled with anchovy oil and served in their mother of pearl shells.

Olivia placed her chopsticks on the rest, leant forward on her elbows, 'I've been thinking Miles. Your flight to London is not until next Thursday. Well, I have some spare time now the AGM is over and I don't want to leave this idyllic place, it gives vitamins to my heart.'

'Great idea, let's stay the whole week.'

We remained in this wondrous town. Wera and Olivia practised their tai chi in the early morning and late afternoon while I sat by the river. A group of friends called by each evening to play mahjong with handmade bone and bamboo tiles from an antique wooden case. Although I strived to understand the rules, the game involved a great deal of laughter, tension and surprises. On our last night, Wera prepared her poached speciality white fish from the lake topped with pureed ginger.

Eventually we dragged ourselves away from the tranquillity of Tongli and travelled back to Shanghai. Olivia took the motorway rather than the country roads when reality raised its ugly head. Overpowering diesel fumes, incessant honking and road rage returned to our daily life. At a service station, the toilet comprised of a wide wall where rows of men sat in squat positions reading newspapers, while their faeces dropped into a trough without running water. The smell was intense and my retching continued out into the car park. In the city, walking towards a busy intersection, I attempted to cross the road but Olivia dragged me back as thousands of silent mopeds flashed past my eyes.

'Remember! We cannot hear them now that petrol engines are banned and electric motors are the only ones allowed. You must look in all directions before crossing,' she said sternly.

A Buddhist monk in an orange robe bobbed up in front of me amidst the commotion and pressed a rosary into my palm. He made a hand gesture and melted back into the crowd.

'He gave you a blessing. They are Buddhist prayer beads made from rosewood and are lucky. You must keep them,' said Olivia.

On the day of my departure, Olivia and I took the Maglev Train from Shanghai Central to Pudong airport. The Maglev is a futuristic monorail system and within minutes of leaving the station the electronic speed indicator flipped higher and higher to nearly 250 miles per hour. The ride was silent as a dentist's waiting room and perfectly smooth. It felt as if we were stationary but the velocity was revealed by the picture postcard blur of a city suburb through the wide windows; or a sudden whoosh followed by mild buffeting as a Maglev travelled from the opposite direction.

In the terminal, Olivia looked sad. She wiped her eyes with the backs of her tiny hands and smiled through her tears, 'I will miss you,' she muttered.

'I'm forever indebted for all the things you have done for me. For your support and friendship during my time in Shanghai. It's been great fun to be with you on this journey. When you come to London, you can stay with me and I will be your guide.'

She smiled when I gave her the gift of an old manuscript, *Taoism and the teachings of Tao Te Ching*, which I had bought under Wera's guidance in Tongli.

'Tao Te Ching viewed simplicity, patience and compassion as the three greatest treasures which form a spiritual harmony within the individual,' I said.

'You've turned oriental,' she laughed.

I hugged her once again before disappearing through the check-in desk onto a China Airlines airbus. My flight home was routed through Europe, with a twenty-four hour stopover in Amsterdam where I took the metro into Nieuwmarkt. Sitting in the square watching a multitude of long-legged cyclists flow back and forth along the narrow pathways, I began to readjust to the everyday foibles of a chilly Europe. I emptied my hand luggage onto the table: a wooden shar pei dog, seasonal watercolours of Tongli, a set of rosewood prayer beads and a plastic paw-waving cat.

13 City of Giant Pandas

'Life is a series of natural and spontaneous changes. Don't resist them as that only creates sorrow. Let reality be reality. Let things flow naturally forward in whatever way they like.' Lao Tzu

Chengdu, China 2003

THE GIANT PANDA IS PERHAPS THE MOST POWERFUL SYMBOL IN THE world when it comes to species conservation and resonates a civic pride like no other in Chengdu – the City of Giant Pandas. This cuddly creature is a national treasure in China which endears people far and wide while panda diplomacy continues to forge friendships across the world.

The purpose of my visit to Chengdu, the capital of Sichuan Province in Southwest China, was to meet the toy manufacturer, Shu Zhu. I was introduced to her at the Waldorf Astoria Hotel in Shanghai with Olivia from the Shanghai Business Council the previous year when I attended Alfie's funeral.

In the airport terminal a chauffeur stood with a sign between his raised arms printed with my name. He drove to Shu's head office, a grey contemporary building with reflective windows situated in the financial district. Her boardroom was on the fortieth floor with towering views over Chengdu.

Shu strode into the room clutching a red moleskin notebook, 'There's always a grey cityscape in Chengdu – it's the pollution...not like the blue skies in Northumberland.'

'Have you been to the North East of England?' I replied.

'Yes, of course, I stayed in Bamburgh for several days a long time ago. Welcome to Chengdu,' she offered her hand and smiled, 'Take a seat, I believe you are fond of our green tea?'

'Yes please.'

She pressed a buzzer and an eager member of staff arrived with a teapot and bowls on a tray. As the pear-coloured liquid was being poured, her gaze studied my expression. I felt unnerved and shuffled about in the chair which seemed to amuse her.

'I'm often in the UK, my daughter, Qiaolian, goes to school at Cheltenham Ladies.'

'Now I understand why you have dual nationality.'

'Exactly Miles, I may look for a place in the Cotswolds to be close to Qiaolian. Perhaps you will help me find a home there?'

'Of course,' I nodded.

'Thank you,' her voice lowered an octave, 'now, you have quite a schedule. Roger, my PA, will go through your itinerary and take you to your hotel. I will see you later for dinner.'

She flicked through the pages of her organiser, 'Do you enjoy spicy food?'

'Yes I do.'

'Good, now where's Roger?'

A hesitant Roger peeked round the door.

'Come on in Roger!' She barked.

After a brief introduction, she left the room and Roger lightened up. He was an Englishman from Skipton in Yorkshire – a stringy man in his fifties with receding ginger-grey wiry hair – who came across as a down at heel lower middle management type struggling to keep on top of life.

'We have a homely expat café in Chengdu where we can talk. It's called the Bookworm and in walking distance from your hotel.'

'It sounds similar to Jenny's Bar in Shanghai,' I said as we left the office.

The Bookworm had an interesting range of English books on display relating to all things Chinese. There was also a bar with real ale and a restaurant which served fish and chips. The owners, Marien and Rikki, were a friendly Dutch couple who had lived in China for five years. We sat outside under a canopy amongst the oriental street life as the essence of hot chilli drifted from the noodle cart. Both the aroma and ambience reminded me of the French Quarter in Shanghai and my visit to the ancient village of Tongli – I made a pact with myself to visit the real China on this trip.

Rodger sat down with his coffee and pushed a pot of green tea over to me.

'How you can drink that slime is beyond me,' he sniggered.

'It ranges in quality from an Italian table wine up to a premier cru,' I said.

'Better you than me,' he smirked.

Roger explained that Shu intended to acquaint me with her business clique, in particular Mr Wu of the toy association who would appoint someone to liaise with the different factories on my behalf.

'Are you an owl or a lark?' He asked, 'Shu works late into the night and starts early in the morning. People who try to keep up with her normally burn out.'

'I'm a lark, but happy to work long hours.'

'Tomorrow I will allocate you an office and a translator,' he stood up to leave, 'Shu will pick you up at 7 p.m. tonight. Don't be late! She's insists upon punctuality.'

Roger was an unlikely PA to a Chinese oligarch but as he explained, all of his life he had this yearning to spend a few years living and working in China, in the same way as the average Chinese person. He had realised his dream and lived in a grubby one-room bedsit on the seventeenth floor of a dismal high-rise – huddled together with scores of other blocks which formed a depressing district of the city. His kitchen was an oil stove on a minute balcony and he was paid Chinese wages.

In the hotel at 6.59 p.m., the glass elevator descended gracefully into the imposing marble lobby and I could see Shu walking through the automatic front doors. As I emerged from the lift and greeted her, she looked at her wristwatch, 'You're late.' The clock in the foyer showed 7.02.p.m.

'That's because I'm a lark,' I smiled.

She chortled, linked my arm and we walked outside to her three black Mercedes.'

'How many of us are there tonight?' I asked out of curiosity.

'Just you and me. Do you have a problem?'

'Of course not but you have three cars.'

'They never know which one I travel in,' she smiled.

'I suppose you can afford the parking fees,' I joked. She guffawed and we got into the middle one.

The motorcade glided through the wide avenues over smooth tarmac and came to rest in front of a stand-alone restaurant, whose Chengdu speciality was the Sichuan hotpot, a crimson coloured spicy main course famous throughout Asia. The management were in awe of Shu's presence as we were shown to her table in front of the stage, where actors and musicians in flowing silk attire were performing a light opera. The pork chilli broth simmered in a cast-iron casserole sunk into the table from which we served ourselves. It was a fiery fare flavoured with jujube, a type of Chinese date and bright red goji berries to add sweetness.

'The hotpot is delicious but it's seriously hot,' I laughed.

'The heat comes from the Sichuan pepper which is the red-brown berry from the ash tree. It's one of the main ingredients of five-spice powder,' Shu said.

After several enjoyable hours in the restaurant, we drove to an older part of the city to visit a magical night market on Jinli Street. The traditional-style wooden structures had been fully restored to replicate the three kingdom period (220 BC – 280 BC). They were a mix of teahouses, temples and shops set amongst a network of canals and ornate water features bathed in a warm light. The shopkeepers displayed all manner of

Chinese arts and crafts including: bamboo teapots, locally produced lacquerware, flamboyantly colourful brocade and silk tapestries.

Although it was past midnight, Shu wanted to go for a massage in a period parlour above a teahouse. As we lay side by side on single beds, partially clothed, being pummelled by strong arms, she continued to chat. At 3 a.m., I was struggling to stay awake but she suggested yet another venue where we would take a breakfast of dim sum. My burn out was already underway.

'Shu, I need to sleep,' I pleaded, and she dropped me back at the hotel.

One of her drivers followed me in clutching a bag of gifts from the market. Anything I had shown an interest in, she had instructed her staff to buy.

At 8 a.m. prompt, I arrived at the clinical office tower with bloodshot eyes and forcefully wormed my way into the ugly scrum that crammed inside the lift. On the fortieth floor, I squeezed through the compressed crowd and popped out into the corridor. In the boardroom, Shu was bright and alert with a sharp wit in contrast to poor Rodger's demeanour which depicted a bumbling brow-beaten sidekick.

Rodger slinked through the offices with his baggy trousers at half-mast revealing odd socks and a crinkly shirt tail which hung over his backside.

'This is your office. Don't make a mess. Shu expects her associates to be neat and tidy. It represents harmony and balance in the workplace.' He talked with a sudden confidence as if he was in charge.

I sat behind the desk of my characterless glass box and Roger returned with the translator, 'Mei is also your PA and will report to you direct for the duration of your stay,' she curtsied when I shook her hand.

'Let me know if you need anything?' Roger snapped and disappeared up the corridor.

'Has he gone?' I whispered.

'Yes, I think so,' she stared at the floor.

Mei was a stylish girl with a pale complexion who wore a classical-style grey dress with a light blue lace overlay and her lengthy black hair was tightly braided.

'Mei, please close the door,' I looked into her eyes, 'I'm here for a few weeks and have no airs or graces. Feel free to be yourself, consider us as equals and please call me by my first name.' I picked up my bag, 'OK, fetch your files, we're going to the Bookworm.'

We sat in comfy sofas as Mei briefed me on the agenda. On Saturday afternoon I would meet with Shu's inner circle – she gave me the background to each individual – some of whom formed part of China's elite. The venue was her suite at the Chengdu football stadium during a crucial quarter-final match with Beijing.

Mei had studied English at university and secured a two year contract working for Shu to better understand the world of business. She was a single child whose mother was an author of children's books and her father, a commercial airline pilot.

Mei and I were received in royal style at the ground and given our own smartly attired waitress dressed in red and black, the colours of the club. She followed us around topping up the champagne flutes from a bottle of Nicholas Feuillatte or French sparkling water.

With help from Mei's fast translation techniques, I managed some interesting conversations with Shu's peer group: Mr Hu ran the giant panda research centres in Sichuan. Mr Wen, a property developer, owned most of Yalong Bay, a resort close to the city of Sanya on Hainan Island. Professor Deng was an economist with whom I shared my passion for green tea and whose knowledge on the subject was enthralling. Mr Wu, the President of the Toy Manufacturers Association, told me they were keen to develop joint venture initiatives with European companies. During the game, he claimed football was invented by the Chinese in the city of Luoyang in the year 1000.

Beijing won 3-2, which resulted in a rabble of angry Chengdu supporters blocking the exit. We watched the events unfold through the glass walls as chanting fans ripped off their football shirts and stamped on them with contorted expressions. First to challenge the mob were security personnel who launched an assault with long batons, followed by waves of police and then the military. It looked messy but they dispersed the enraged crowd and we were allowed to leave the stadium.

As we sat in the cab, I said to Mei, 'Please take Sunday as a rest break, everyone works seven days a week in China. The only holiday is Chinese New Year. Can you please drop me at the Bookworm on your way home?'

Mei placed a hand on my shoulder, 'I must talk to you tonight.'

'Why?' I asked impatiently.

'There are messages at the office from today's discussions that require urgent attention. I live near the Bookworm, if you agree, I will call by later?' She spoke nervously as if disturbing me.

'No problem Mei, that's fine, but as friends. You are not my translator or PA tonight, OK?'

'Of course, thank you,' her eyes smiled.

An elegant Mei arrived, dressed in a royal-blue kaftan. She looked older and more confident with her long ink-black hair straight down her back. I watched the eyes of the expats follow her as she strolled gracefully through the restaurant to the bar area. When she took a seat, Rikki appeared with two frothy cocktails.

'The blue lagoons are on the house and they match your outfit Mei. Enjoy.' He grinned and her olive cheeks flushed pink with embarrassment. Mei leant over and murmured in my ear that she was not a drinker.

I laughed, 'Well, give it a go, I'll take care of you if you fall over.'

She hurriedly talked about the outcome of our discussions at the stadium.

'Mr Wu has instructed his office to allocate a member of staff to source toy components on your behalf and Mr Wen's secretary has mailed an open invitation to Hainan Island. But the biggest surprise of all is Mr Hu who has organised a visit to the Panda Sanctuary. At 8 a.m. tomorrow, you will meet a giant panda called Bei Bei!' She cried.

'What a splendid result.'

'Did the invite include you Mei?'

'No, only one person each visit and its reserved in your name.'

'I will ask Shu to arrange another appointment in the near future.'

'That's kind, but I can see them in the park at any time.'

'Have you eaten?'

'No, not yet.'

I called out, 'Rikki, two fish and chips please and bring another round of blue lagoons, we are celebrating.' Mei looked mortified, making me roar with laughter.

By midnight, a packed Bookworm was singing along to the Irish folk band. Mei and I joined in, sitting side by side and moving to the music. Time and location evaporated from my frontal lobes, the blue lagoons were in full control.

'When we are ready to go, I will walk you back,' she said looking into my eyes with concern as the band played their final song of the night, *Seven Drunken Nights*.

'Come on, let's go,' I said.

We waved goodbye to the rowdy Irish contingent and made our way to the hotel. Mei stood in the foyer while I ordered her a cab.

She smiled, 'It's been a fun night and I will see you in the morning to meet Bei Bei.'

'Thank you for everything. You don't need to go tomorrow, stay at home with your family, I can manage on my own.'

She placed her finger on my lips, 'Shhh.... I want to,' she whispered before walking out of the door to the waiting taxi.

Sichuan province is home to more than thirty per cent of the world's panda population across seven nature reserves and nine parks located between the Qionglai and Jiajin mountains. The park in Chengdu includes a giant panda breeding and research base, which was our destination. Any form of personal contact with animals is rewarding, especially when we connect with our pets, so with this mindset in place, I was thrilled to have an opportunity to meet a giant panda.

At first light, Mei called from reception and I quickly threw on a t-shirt and jeans. The doors of the glass lift opened and an excited Mei ran over, 'What a beautiful day to see the pandas.'

At the park, I was issued with light protective clothing and informed that baby pandas had limited exposure to humans. If Bei Bei was distressed or even hesitant in any way, she would be taken away. She was nearly one year old and soon to be released into a conservation area where she would live in the wild.

The handler brought the giant panda into the room by trolley, she climbed onto the wooden bench and sat next to me chewing a piece of bamboo, held in left paw like a child with a lollipop. After a few minutes, Bei Bei swivelled around and looked into my eyes with curiosity. As she leaned against me, the handler quietly vacated the room and left us alone together.

She threw one leg over mine, placed her paw on my shoulder and pulled herself onto my lap while dropping bamboo debris all over my legs. She weighed about thirty kilos and felt so cuddly and furry. Her paws were wide and claws long. I could not resist kissing this delightful creature on the forehead through her deep black and white fur which exuded a pleasant light musky puppy aroma, unique to the giant panda. Bei Bei responded by delicately sniffing my nostrils and wiggling her small black fluffy ears. I was smitten.

'An experience to cherish for life,' Mei said. 'Come on, let's see her parents in the park and visit the red pandas.'

Bei Bei's father, a giant panda of considerable proportions lay on his back under a tree with his legs wide apart and his enormous belly covered in scraps of bamboo. The other pandas were spread over the sanctuary with the older ones sitting in the long grass and the youth hanging around in the trees. The skeletal frame of the panda is more arched than a black bear which accounts for their ability to climb effortlessly and sleep amongst the branches.

In contrast, the red panda is a completely different animal altogether in shape and size to that of the giant panda. In fact, it is more like a big raccoon with fur similar to a red fox. They have long red-brown bushy tails with black rings going all the way down to the tip.

On our way back into the city, I asked Mei, 'How far is Hainan Island from Chengdu?'

'My father flies there once a month and it takes three hours.'

'On my last trip to Shanghai, I visited the real China and believe Hainan may have that same oriental magic.'

'It's the second biggest island after Taiwan and known as our Hawaii.'

'With Mr Wen's invitation, I can route my flight home through Sanya on the south coast.'

'Dad tells me it's so relaxed down there and the Hainanese have a great sense of humour.'

During the weeks that followed, I held various seminars for Shu's Chinese business associates, including our new toy suppliers, to help develop their trading relationship with Europe. On my last day in Chengdu, Shu, Roger, Mei and I came together in the boardroom to close the file on my visit.

'Hope you've left your desk neat and tidy,' Roger quipped.

'I suggest we next meet in the Cotswolds and Mei will accompany me,' Shu smiled.

'Please agree Miles,' Mei spoke excitedly.

I put my finger on her lips, 'Shhh...I want to.'

Shu and I embraced, it was the beginning of a long friendship.

Hainan Island, China 2003

On the flight to Hainan Island I was upgraded to first class, the pilot welcomed me aboard by name and the red wine was served in a crystal glass. I laughed to myself and suspected Mei's father was responsible as a pilot with China Airlines. In the terminal a young man held up a sign, 'Mr Wen Welcome Mr Miles from Chengdu.' The air conditioned Mercedes purred along the water's edge to a five star hotel on Yalong Bay where I was allocated a suite with commanding views over the emerald sea.

Since leaving the UK, it was the first time I had seen a clear blue sky, felt warm sunshine on my skin and breathed in the salty sea air. A walk down to the beach was enough to rejuvenate my mind, body and soul. Although the luxury of being treated as a celebrity was fun and comfortable, sitting in front of the ocean with flocks of brown-headed gulls squawking overhead and groups of sandpipers scampering through the lapping water brought me gently back down to earth. It reminded me of what was important in life and how fulfilling it was to be amongst nature. The corporate world drained the soul but it had given me the opportunity to enjoy the beauty of a tropical island.

I thought to myself, 'I'm on my own with no distractions. A chance to reflect on the future.'

We had had offers to buy our toy company but I was too young to retire, however, I would consider random projects which took me to Latin America. An area of the world I yearned to return after my experience in El D.F., Mexico.

During a breakfast buffet of tropical fruit, the manager, Mr Guang, expressed his pleasure at having the honour of a special guest and friend of the owner, Mr Wen. He had left instruction that his private motor boat, Hńi Zhń (Sea Lord) and helmsman, Bo, were at my disposal.

A few days later, Bo and I sailed over the South China Sea to Monkey Island, a state protected sanctuary for macaque monkeys. We watched these fascinating primates display their splendid acrobatics in the dense forest. When we swam back to the boat, an ancient Chinese junk had anchored alongside. The twin black sails were made from canvass and stiffened with bamboo. Bo and I climbed aboard to be transported back to the fifteenth century. The polished dark wood interior with low ceilings had an aroma of mature timber and fusty leather. It was illuminated by two oil lamps and felt cosy. On deck, one of the crew used a camping stove to stir-fry noodles while two others sat cross-legged repairing a tear in the heavy sail.

The sailors spoke Hainanese, although a derivative of Mandarin, Bo struggled with the intonation. Similar to westerners learning Mandarin, the inflection was an important aspect of the spoken language and a slight variance could change the whole meaning of the sentence. Bo gave an example with the words, 'Mǎ mǔ,' which meant both mother-in-law and horse depending upon the pitch.

'This rule does not apply to me as my mother-in-law looks like a horse,' he joked.

Bo was remarkably tall for a Han Chinese whose career as a sea captain came to an abrupt end when he grounded a commercial vessel near Hong Kong.

One evening in Sanya, the coastal road was blocked by diversion signs so I decided to leave the taxi at this point and walk into town. I soon discovered the reason for the closure when I stumbled across a traditional Chinese opera being held on the beach. As I approached the venue, an official waved me through the aisles to a seat at the front. Under a starlit night, there were scores of singers, dancers and actors performing a colourful spectacle on a makeshift stage to an audience of around 800 people. It was a fusion of shamanistic ritual, martial arts and musical theatre with audience participation. The powerful harmonies were evocative of a past era and it made for an emotionally charged occasion.

After this unexpected delight, I ambled along the seashore through the pale blue luminescence in a state of retrospection to a fisherman's cabin steaming bullfrogs. In the clammy hut set among the palm trees, two frogs were placed side by side in a wicker basket with a spicy sauce of tamarind, ginger and garlic in a tin pot. I sat on the sand with a cold beer and ate the white meat which tasted similar to an overcooked chicken but with dangerously thin, sharp bones.

Hainan Island is regarded as one of the most stress-free places on earth. The Hainanese walk at a slower pace than anywhere else and react to life's challenges in a casual fashion. I found the relaxed atmosphere to be infectious. At sea, Bo asked me what day it was and I told him it could be Wednesday, while he was positive it was Thursday, but it turned out to be Friday.

Each night I found myself at the harbour among the local fishing community. Extended families and their friends clustered around sizzling seafood on glowing barbeques as circles of musicians played their zithers and lutes. I sat at the water's edge absorbing the ambience and listening to the oriental melodies in the sultry breeze.

Bo joined me for breakfast to explain that Sea Lord was decommissioned for its annual service. I offered to help and he agreed. We sailed it to the marina, took it out the water with a boat hoist, removed the barnacles from the hull and applied the anti-fouling paint. I was delighted to work alongside the local people. When we downed tools, a group of us went into Sanya for a few beers, not dissimilar to a night out in Newcastle. In the bar they taught me to ask the waitress for a round of drinks in Mandarin. As I strived with the intonation, they clutched their stomachs and shrieked with laughter. When we stumbled into an all-night noodle café, Bo and his wise friend Yang discussed their impending trip to the highlands within the Wuzhi Mountains. They were delivering machinery and invited me to join them. I accepted readily as it would be an excellent opportunity to visit the interior.

Before sleeping, I set the alarm for daybreak in readiness to sit on the balcony with a pot of green tea and watch the sunrise, serenaded by a crescendo of tropical birdsong. These colourful birds gave out an assortment of unrecognisable sounds like the deep-toned hoot of a Peruvian panpipe, the amplified flicking of playing cards or an intermittent screech. As the star-speckled darkness gave way to a magenta hue, the ascending blood-orange scattered rays of warm yellows and reds across the sleepy turquoise sea – I wanted to stay on Hainan Island forever.

A brown pickup bristling with engineering equipment stopped on the sea road. Bo and Yang were waving. I ran over to join them and we motored up country in-between tiered terraces of paddy fields before ascending the mountain and arriving in a small village of thatched huts made from a red coloured mud. The Li people were a minority ethnic group who spoke Hlai, a Sino-Tibetan language. They were an indigenous community who produced brocade – a rich woven fabric. The metal sections in the truck were pieces of loom, an apparatus to shuttle-weave their brightly coloured silks. Two women with strange facial tattoos like a spider's web gave us bowls of rice with what I thought were pieces of rough cut ginger but tasted medicinal.

'What are these brown bits, they're like tree bark?' I queried.

'I've no idea,' Bo replied, 'but they've stuck between my teeth.'

'Leigong root, it's a wild herb with many healthy properties,' said Yang through Bo's translation.

'Why do the older ladies have geometric patterns tattooed all over their faces?' I asked.

'Body tattoos were seen as a rite of passage into adulthood and made Li women less likely to be kidnapped as slaves but this custom ceased many years ago,' explained Yang.

As three young Li unloaded the loom, I walked through the village towards a group of older men sitting outside a hut playing one and two metre long bamboo nose flutes called kǒuxiāos. Neither Yang nor Bo knew why they played the instrument through their nose but they were apparently practising for a festival.

The women wore long colourful tight-fitting dresses and an embroidered handkerchief draped over their head. Their long black hair was knotted at the back of the neck in a ballet bun and held together with a bone. The men dressed in red or orange striped, armless and buttonless waistcoats. As we were about to leave the village a pretty Li girl with a sunshine smile ran over and gave us each a sticky rice sweet in a green leaf.

It was sundown when we arrived at Yang's yacht moored along the coast next to a pearl farm, 100 miles north of Sanya. His friend, Jian, joined us to play mahjong and over bowls of spicy noodles, Yang described the courtship rituals of the Li people.

'When the daughter reaches the age of sixteen, she leaves the family home to live alone in a hut and is free to date young men. She may like someone enough to ask them to stay the night at her boudoir. Once the relationship is consummated, the parents of the young man meet with the girl's family to formally propose and donate a gift of betel leaves. The wedding is a musical theatre of love songs, wine and a hog roast. It's a colourful occasion over several days.'

Early the next morning I left the snoring crew and wandered over to the pearl farm. Beautiful displays of gold, pink, silver and peach coloured pearls in triangular heaps were spread over the wooden benches. I bought a silk bag filled with twenty of each type for £12.

On my last day on Hainan Island, I sat on the balcony and listened to the jungle dawn chorus before Bo and Yang took me to the airport for my flight via Shanghai to London. At the immigration gate, Bo gave me a book entitled 'learn yourself mandarin in three weeks' and Yang pushed a miniature zither into my hand. We would stay in a Li village as guests of a wedding festival during my next visit to Hainan. Unbeknown to both of them, I had organised a celebratory feast at the bull frog cabin and Bo would be notified on his return to Sea Lord.

Yang gave me a warm hug and spoke through his kind eyes, 'Huā yǒu chóng kāi rì, rén wú zài shào nián,' Bo translated, 'Flowers may bloom again but a person never has the chance to be young again so don't waste your time.'

It was my time to change direction, and my next destination would be Latin America.

14 State of Jalisco

'Happiness is a journey, not a destination, work like you don't need money, love like you've never been hurt and dance like no one's looking.' GAUTAMA BUDDHA

Guadalajara, Tlaquepaque and Ajijic, Mexico 2004

THERE IS A FAMOUS MARIACHI SONG, *GUADALAJARA, GUADALAJARA, Guadalajara* which describes Guadalajara as the most romantic city in Latin America...my destination in Mexico by way of Puerto Vallarta on the Pacific Coast. On the aircraft steps a fragrance of guava spread through the humidity. Its strong, sweet, floral scent personified Mexico and delivered a resurgence of memories from my first experience of Latin America six years earlier in Mexico City during a riot. A recollection which triggered an adrenaline rush which placed my sensory perception on full alert.

Having worked in Mexico during my time in the toy industry, a Danish cooperative hired me to obtain a supply of an edible cactus. Having attended a food supplement exhibition in Los Angeles, I spent several days at the coast writing up my notes before catching a flight to Guadalajara, 400 miles to the east, in which I had planned to take up six months temporary residency for this project.

The Licenciado Gustavo Diaz Ordaz airport in Puerto Vallarta is named after a Mexican President from the 1960s whose authoritarian rule resulted in the shooting of numerous unarmed student protesters, known as the

Tlatelolco massacre. I was reading my pocket guide to the state of Jalisco when a member of staff returned my ticket.

'Sorry, sir, this is not your departure point.'

'But Puerto Vallarta has only one airport?' I queried.

'There is another but it's a private airfield. Give this address to the desk opposite and they will assist. Enjoy your day, sir.'

At transportation, an attendant who appeared more European than Mexican, studied the note.

'I will call them to confirm your flight.' She placed the phone back on the rest and smiled. 'It's on time and cab number seven will take you to the airfield.'

'Where are you from if you don't mind me asking?'

'I'm a Tapatia.'

'What's that?'

'It's a name given to a girl from Guadalajara and for a boy, Tapatio.'

'Interesting. Thank you for your help.'

The cab drove around in circles before locating a track which led to the airstrip. The terminal was a wooden hut with a wobbly table as the check-in desk next a set of bathroom scales and their entire facilities comprised of one self-service fridge. A scruffy boy wearing a New York Red Bulls baseball cap told me to weigh myself together with the luggage. He scribbled something on the ticket and I was ready to board. Three Mexican Indians and an overweight Colombian were also on the flight making a total of five passengers.

The aircraft taxied from a corner of a field to the hut – it was a Cessna 209 flown by Aero Litoral. We boarded the ageing single-engine turboprop up a stepladder into the narrow tube. The big man was instructed to sit on one side and the rest of us sat opposite to balance out the weight.

The plane took some time to leave the ground. It groaned and rattled for the next two hours up and over the Sierra Madre Mountain before landing in a meadow thirty kilometres outside Guadalajara. The Indians celebrated our arrival by clapping their hands as the whirring vibration slowed to a stop in front of a wooden shed smaller again to the one in Puerto Vallarta. When I descended the short ladder the climate was notably more comfortable, drier and much less humid than the coast.

Guadalajara is the capital of the state of Jalisco and is regarded as the cultural centre of the country. Geographically it consists of 220 miles of coastline alongside the Pacific Ocean where tropical evergreen forests on the seaboard slowly transform into temperate oaks and firs across the mountainous areas of the Sierra Madre Sur. These cordilleras surround an expansive fertile plateau where Guadalajara is located, 2,000 metres above sea level, 200 miles from the sea and next to the single largest stretch of fresh water in Mexico, Lake Chapala. The sub-tropical climate produces a vast array of fruit and vegetables, including avocados, sweet limes, cacti and mangos. The avenues of the city are bordered with tiger-orange hedging, gigantic fragrant jasmine bushes and the deep red of the royal poinciana trees. It is Mexico's second biggest metropolis comprising of three separate cities – downtown Guadalajara, Zapopan and Tlaquepaque.

I decided to rent a house in Tlaquepaque, pronounced Tla-keh-pah-keh, which translates from Nahuatl native Indian, the ancient language of the Aztecs, to 'The best of everything.' It was one of the most vibrant and bohemian areas of the conurbation. While I searched for a permanent home, my first few weeks were in the Quinta Don Jose boutique hotel. Their delightful Mexican courtyard garden was enclosed by terracotta tiled walls smothered in flowering vines where pretty humming birds fed on the sweet jasmine nectar. With its graceful trellised arcades, hand-carved stone pillars and water fountains, the rich textures of wood, stone, and ceramic gave it that certain depth of distinction which epitomised Latin serenity. It was my tranquil oasis in an otherwise frantic city, where I could relax each night on the patio in the rosewood and leather chairs.

On my first working day, I visited a commercial cactus plantation to understand how the vegetable was grown and harvested. The Mexican government had introduced me to the Nopal Cactus Growers Association, NCGA, who in turn arranged for me to be picked up at 8 a.m. by the owner of a local cactus farm. Abel, a short ranchero with a big hat, blocked the entrance to the hotel with his enormous, jacked up, eight litre pickup covered in red dust. It was a struggle to climb aboard this monstrosity. The engine rumbled and growled as we motored out of the city towards the mountains, Los Altos de Jalisco, and his ranch.

Abel spoke slowly in Spanish to give me a detailed description of the Nopal cactus.

'It's an edible vegetable eaten raw in salads or used to thicken stews, has the consistency and taste of a green bean and is an integral part of Mexican cuisine. Inside the cactus pad, there's a sticky soluble fibre surrounded by an insoluble fibrous structure which holds it securely to the stem as it grows in size and weight. This combination of roughage is the key element of the food supplement, which is sold as a digestive aid.'

As we ascended the massif, the roads turned into cobbled tracks and in some places were centimetres away from vertical drops to the valleys below. The hacienda at the ranch was a single story whitewashed building with a red pantile roof and slept forty people. At the rear of the property, there was a deep fishing lake stocked with bighead carp which led through to a corral with a dozen well-muscled horses from the Azteca breed. Abel and his wife Nena had two sons and five daughters, all of whom worked in the family business.

The cacti were laid out in neat rows one to two metres in height. When the pads reached a specific size, similar in dimension to a side plate, they were harvested by hand using a thick protective glove. A wide flat bladed machete removed the stronger spines before the pads were carefully stacked and interwoven like a dry stone wall. They formed a cylindrical tower about two metres high. Both ends were protected with a muslin cloth and secured with rope in preparation for transit.

We gathered a bucket of guamúchiles from short thorny trees which surrounded the plantation. These vegetables were exclusive to Jalisco and resembled an oversized haricot bean. On removing the green outer shell and black seed, the white bean was eaten raw. They were an acquired taste due to their bitterness and were renowned to cause excessive wind but nevertheless, I found them moreish and ate handfuls much to the amusement of the children.

On the patio, Nena prepared a typical ranchero lunch of carne asada, thinly sliced steak grilled on a barbeque made from half an oil drum, served with Mexican sauce, cactus strips and corn tortillas. The ubiquitous Mexican sauce is a blend of: tomato, onion, chilli and coriander, the same colours as the national flag, red white and green. Abel crushed the ingredients to a paste with a mortar in a heavy pestle called a molcajete hewn from a silvery grey volcanic rock, in this case, shaped as a pig.

Nena described the preparation of cactus as being tortuous, 'Although the big spikes are taken away during harvesting, the tiny hair-like spines remain and during preparation they fly in the air. I remember years ago when one stuck in my eyeball and it took forever to pull it out with pincers.'

Over lunch, Abel worked his way through the best part of a bottle of tequila and on the return journey gibbered incessantly, unconcerned by our close proximity to the sheer drops. On one exceptionally sharp incline, the truck jolted sideways causing his hat to slip over his nose which temporarily blinded him as we zigzagged perilously close to the edge. His sobered up after this incident and when we reached the open road, he invited me to the next NCGA conference soon to be held in Guadalajara. An opportunity to meet their Chairman, Don Juan Santos, who happened to own the adjacent ranch.

My new home would not be ready until the following week so I took time out to explore the city. Nena had suggested a visit to the oldest market in Guadalajara, famed for its special five – a drink made from: celery, parsley, pineapple, cucumber and cactus, flavoured with coriander and lime juice. It opened every day at dawn and sold fresh and cooked produce.

The market was located in Santa Teresita, a vibrant district of downtown Guadalajara. I arrived during the early morning rush hour when the entrance was choked with handcart traffic jams. Once inside, the hubbub reverberated around the domed building as the sellers bellowed out their daily deals. Traders stood proudly in front of their beautifully presented wares as if it was a fruit and vegetable fashion show. Neat rows of luscious green avocados, polished red tomatoes and glossy purple aubergines stood beside moulded heaps of cloves, cumin and garlic. Obelisk-shaped mounds of cherry red chillies in wide wicker baskets stood to attention flanked by slabs of chocolate brown mole pastes. The tropical perfume of guava with its green skin and reddish-pink flesh combined with the essence of roasting chillies and baking corn cakes epitomised Mexico.

The juice bar was located in the middle of this hustle and bustle and an ideal spot to view all the activity while drinking the dark green gooey special five. I sat on a wooden stool beneath an enormous display of coriander and watched the tortilla makers at work, amazed by their speed and dexterity. I learned that a typical tortilla contained eight portions of maize flour and two of wheat. A little water was added before a lump of dough was squished into a round ball and flattened into a tortilla with a hand press. A brief stint in a hot, dry pan where they were flipped twice then stacked in a muslin cloth and sold by the kilo. The corn tortilla prevalent in south and central Mexico was much tastier than the plain flour version which predominated in the north.

Rows of fish heads stared vacantly from a wall of crushed ice next to a Mexican Indian selling chicharron, wafer thin sheets of crispy pork skin. They resembled rigid tea towels protruding from a square wicker basket and served with a dollop of Mexican sauce. Further down the aisle, an old woman in a yellow dress sat cross-legged on the floor with an oven glove in one hand and a scalpel in the other. She used the sharp device to delicately remove the spines from a tuna morada, a prickly pear fruit, similar in shape to a sea urchin. It made a delectable sweet purple drink. There were other prickly pear varieties to that of the tuna morada. The pitaya for instance, coloured crimson, bright orange, red or white grew on an inedible cactus tree with tall stems. The farmers used a four metre pole with a tiny net to harvest these exquisite fruits available for three months of the year from April to June.

On my way to the metro, groups of mariachi congregated on Mariachi Corner, a cobbled square where the genre originated. These talented musicians were immaculately dressed in their charro outfits and sombreros. Restaurants hired these bands to entertain their customers or individuals paid them to perform a romantic serenade for their partner.

A few days later, I visited the factory which processed the cactus into capsules. The cactus pads were washed in a grapefruit solution, sliced into thin strips and dried in a hot oven then ground to a fine powder and sterilized by steam. The powder was encapsulated into 500mg vegetable gelatine capsules. The first shipment to Denmark subject to their approval, was scheduled to leave in two months. All that was left for me to do was to source a significantly larger volume of cactus pads.

The following Sunday I visited Tonalá, a rustic district on the edge of the city and close to Lake Chapala, which was famous for its handicrafts. Rows of single story bungalows with family-run workshops displayed their wares on market stalls in front of their homes. These talented families designed and made their own ceramics, papier mâché figures and furniture from palm, pine and rosewood. There were also artisan collectives who specialised in terracotta pottery, coloured glass and wrought iron sculptures. I bought various decorations for my new house and as was the norm in Mexico, I hired the household goods such as the kitchen appliances, tables and sofa.

Later in the day I drove to Ajijic, pronounced ah-ee-ee-heek, a pretty hamlet alongside Lake Chapala which inspires a thriving community of artists and sculptors. Picturesque cobbled streets weave their way through quaint town houses, art galleries and boutiques painted pink, orange and powder blue down to the lake, 625 square miles of clear water. A stress-free Shangri-La with one of the best climates in the world which attracts retirees from Latin America and to some extent, the USA.

La Nueva Posada Hotel in Ajijic became a weekend retreat and a second home whose beauty embodied colonial Mexico. The sandstone staircase with its smooth balustrade and ornate newels swept alongside the elegant stone-mullioned arched windows as it ascended to the first floor. In the corridors, diamond-shaped brick-red tiles were illuminated by the apricot glow of bronze lamps set back into arched recesses. In the bedroom, wrought iron glazed doors opened onto a balcony with views across the water. The king-sized bed was made of polished rosewood with rounded finials and its claw-feet gripped the terracotta flooring. Fine watercolours of the lake by local artists were spread over the tangerine walls.

Their restaurant on the terrace was popular with the locals who dined al fresco on fish from the lake. The menu of the day was grilled whitebait dusted with red chilli and a hint of lime juice followed by carp or tilapia, pan fried or steamed, and a sorbet made from walnut, guava or cajeta, a caramelised goat's milk. The patio, which was home to a pair of scarlet macaws, extended into a well-manicured garden leading down to the water's edge and the border of Jalisco state. On the other side of the lake was the indigenous state of Michoacán, a Nahuatl Indian name meaning, 'Possessor of fish.'

During the week that followed, I moved into the townhouse in Tlaquepaque and took delivery of the furniture to include a full-sized papier mâché statue of Don Quixote astride his stallion with his compadre, Sancho Panza on a donkey. I unpacked an assortment of coloured glass ornaments, a terracotta water filter and a string of ceramic fruits in bright colours completed the décor. In my new home, numerous tradesmen arrived on the avenue in their vans, tri-scooters and handcarts. They would announce their arrival by yelling into a megaphone. 'Aaaguaaa,' the water salesman, 'El gaaaz,' butane gas and 'El paaan,' the baker. Hugo sold camotes, sweet potato in syrup, whose self-made signature tune was the most hideous. When they appeared together, the entire street became an unbearable chorus of loud hailers and screeching music.

An invitation arrived by courier from the NCGA to attend their annual meeting at the Abastos Market – a wholesale fruit and vegetable market in downtown Guadalajara. The cactus conference was held in a suite of first floor offices above a pineapple warehouse. I was welcomed by their president, Don Juan Santos, a distinguished Mexican ranchero known for being firm but fair. The significance of the 'Don' normally reserved for royalty was a mark of esteem for this community leader. He was a dumpy, well-coiffured, silver-haired, middle-aged gentleman who introduced me to each member of the elected committee. There were over 10,000 cactus farms in Mexico most of which were run by family cooperatives. Don Juan's brother, Antonio, spoke English and would be my point of contact to assist with the procurement of cactus products. Antonio talked in a slow, deep drawl and had a zany sense of humour. An athletic man in his early forties whose main occupation was as a politician and the cactus activity related to his family business. He invited me to the rodeo in the Arena Stadium at the weekend.

On our way to the rodeo, Antonio had an appointment beforehand to play tennis at his gym, situated in the bowels of an old colonial style building next to the San Juan leather market in downtown Guadalajara. He described the day this building miraculously survived a blast which had shaken the city two years earlier when thieves siphoned off gas from the mains supply, causing several huge explosions, killing over 250 people and destroying five miles of streets.

Antonio played a strange form of tennis – a local hybrid similar to pelota using a sturdy badminton racket and a lethal projectile resembling an oversized golf ball. I watched from a wooden bench above a squash court encased by a fine mesh cage. The players wore no protection and the game was fiercely competitive.

During the opening ceremony at the stadium, the participants in charro (cowboy) and charra (cowgirl) outfits paraded into the arena on horseback, accompanied by a twelve-piece mariachi band. The first task for the cowboys was to demonstrate their control of the horse with commands, followed by rope work and lassoing at speed to bring down a calf or catch a wild horse. They also mounted a bull bareback and attempted to remain seated until it stopped bucking. Points were given for the many skills needed to perform all of these tasks. The final event was a display of horsemanship by the cowgirls, who were also immensely talented as they rode side-saddle in beautiful multi-coloured hand-embroidered dresses while they exhibited a variety of precision riding techniques.

After the show we visited Antonio's favourite pozole restaurant where he told me all about his eight children, four brothers and six sisters. Their business was a family collective which comprised of a 50,000 acre ranch where they grew: mangos, nopal cactus, sweet limes, avocados and blue agave to make tequila. They also owned apple orchards on the US border, a banana plantation in Colima and a commercial portfolio in the Abastos Market, all of which were managed by members of the Santos ménage. Their father, Don Pedro, an orphan, began his working life at the age of fourteen selling bananas and built up an empire with the sole intention of sustaining the household. Profits from the enterprise were reinvested. No one within the family of seventy people possessed considerable wealth but each member had healthcare and a job.

Steaming bowls of pozole arrived at the table, a native dish enjoyed throughout Mexico and in essence, an aromatic meat stew. Kilos of especially large, dried white corn kernels, mirasol chilli peppers with a shoulder of pork or sometimes a pig's head and trotters were simmered together for twelve hours. A substantial meal with a strong but delicious corn flavour decorated by sliced avocado, diced onion and bunches of coriander.

Antonio was a straightforward character so I took the opportunity and asked him some probing questions about the cartels and safety in general, a subject matter most Mexicans would rather not discuss.

'A great deal depends on the level of control a cartel has acquired. In areas where they dominate and all the various corrupt politicians and police are in line, there's less danger to law-abiding citizens. When their activities are disrupted by turf wars for instance, there's more opportunity for criminals to freelance, which in turn, lowers public security. Guadalajara is still a great deal safer than other Mexican cities such as Nuevo Laredo in the north or Morelia to the south. Statistically it's more secure than many US cities but I warn you to be especially wary of the police.'

Two years later, a new government headed by Felipe Calderón would declare war on drugs and initiate a large scale deployment of federal troops against the cartels, resulting in a colossal loss of life.

There were several individuals in the restaurant with blond hair, light-coloured skin and blue eyes who Antonio pointed out were from Tepatitlan, a town in the Sierra Madre known for its concentration of Mexican Caucasians

– a throwback from their European ancestry. In general, people from Jalisco had a wider variation of complexions and hair colour to that of other areas of Mexico.

Antonio invited me to a fiesta at their ranch in the tiny mountain village of El Escalón when family and friends celebrated the end of the mango season. The party happened to coincide with a religious festival to honour Mary, the Virgin of Guadalupe, held at the church in the square opposite their hacienda.

Driving back to Tlaquepaque, most major roundabouts in the downtown area were ornamented with huge, impressive metal sculptures of horses, abstract shapes and water features. These intersections were connecting points in a grid of broad avenues which criss-crossed the city. Hurdling up and down these thoroughfares were umpteen trucks laden with blue agave husks. These enormous pineapple shaped hearts weighed in at thirty-five to seventy kilos and were destined for a multitude of distilleries. The state of Jalisco produced eighty per cent of the tequila in Mexico.

At sundown we met Antonio's Jewish friend, Alfonso, at a trendy cocktail bar in the plaza. He suggested I travel with him to the ranch for the mango celebration. We would stay over and use the opportunity to go walking in the mountains, something not considered a pastime in Mexico. Out of curiosity, I asked him how Jewish people faired in a predominantly Catholic society.

'I have homes in both Guadalajara and Puerto Vallarta and never experienced the slightest element of antisemitism.'

During the week, a message from Denmark requested I secure a reliable source of cactus powder in bulk. They gave me a contact in Puebla, a city to the south of Mexico. I called into Antonio's office to check their credentials and he confirmed that the company was part of the NCGA, a bigger operation than most, run by a well-known figure in the industry called Guillermo. After which, Antonio took me on a tour of the Abastos Market.

The mighty Mexican juggernauts with their double trailers up to fifteen metres in length thundered in and out of the Abastos Market twenty-four hours a day. Mostly owned by the driver who kept his colourful second home pristine and personalised by dramatic airbrushing, gleaming chrome and an abundance of accessories. The fruit and vegetable warehouses were laid out in wide boulevards to accommodate these monster trucks. The depots were two or three stories high with commercial lifts to transport the fruit into temperature controlled dry rooms where a variety of techniques were used to slow down the ripening process.

El Escalón, Mexico 2004

AT THE WEEKEND, ALFONSO DROVE OUT OF TOWN ON THE SAME road that Abel had travelled until we branched off towards a more remote location higher up the mountain. As we ascended Los Altos de Jalisco, the road reached a precipitous point where the onward route disappeared from view. The pickup crept to the edge and slid down a near vertical incline into a sharp bend which entered El Escalón. The village had the notion of being a stationary cloud in the sky with panoramic views over the massif and lush valleys below.

After Don Pedro acquired the land, he built the road, installed a sewage system, a water supply and brought the electricity from afar. He then constructed: the ranch, a church, the village square, a general store and a variety of mud and straw houses for the farmhands. The Santos hacienda was an immense two storey building painted white and topped by a red pantile roof. It slept eighty people and was built around a courtyard with a shallow swimming pool for the toddlers surrounded by alcoves and barbeques. Up to twenty pickups could be parked on the forecourt behind the huge metal doors which recessed into an arched entrance and sealed the entire structure from intruders.

Antonio welcomed Alfonso and I by introducing us to everyone as his compadres although it was difficult to digest all the names belonging to all the faces. I sensed a strong family unit and felt honoured to be part of their celebration. My bedroom was an annex on a flat roof next to a vertical drop with a far-reaching outlook over the mountainscape.

Outside the room, I watched the activities in the village fanned by a welcome breeze whose sweet fragrance was perfumed by yellow honeysuckle clinging to the hacienda. The plaza teemed with cowboys in their celebratory white Stetsons and polished cowboy boots. Cowgirls attired in embroidered dresses and their children as little rancheros who wore the same mini-outfits. An aging ranchero stood behind a trestle table and sold terracotta pots of chilled margaritas and a lopsided two metre high framework of fireworks took centre stage.

Antonio fell into his hammock followed by a few of his offsprings while Alfonso appeared with a tray of margaritas. Alfonso pointed towards a tree, stretching out from the mountainside, and a fork in the branches where Don Pedro used to sit and view his estate. He had been well respected in Jalisco before he tragically passed away in a traffic accident, a few years earlier, while bringing a water truck up the mountain. I wanted to go there and experience his private moment. His widow, Mama Jolis, was now head of the family. A warm and caring individual with a stoical inner strength who dedicated her life to others. She had given birth to fourteen children and brought up five orphans.

'Mama Jolis remembers the birthdays and anniversaries of all seventy-two family members,' said Alfonso.

We were joined by the sons, Don Juan of the NCGA and his younger brother Pedro, a short stout man with a forceful personality who ran the Santos ranch. Victor, the youngest and tallest, arrived soon after with his musical mentor and compadre, Pablo Mendes; Victor managed the warehouses but his lifelong passion for singing Mexican ballads took pole position.

Pablo was a cultural icon in Mexico and famous throughout Latin America. A singer, songwriter, actor and musician with a long list of achievements that included fifty albums and thirty films. He was a distinguished figure but a cowboy at heart, known as the King of Ranchero who lived on the adjacent ranch. Antonio mentioned that Victor and Pablo enjoy jamming sessions late into the night at these celebrations.

As the light faded, a sinister navy-blue pickup with six policemen standing by their rifles drove onto the square. In the past, party revellers would shoot into the air during fiestas but a recent law stated possession of a gun or any part of a weapon without authorisation carried an automatic one year jail sentence. Victor told me the story of when Don Pedro had been hit in the backside by a ricocheting bullet and it had taken four hours to drive him to the nearest doctor.

Fireworks marked the grand finale to the religious festival. When they set fire to the rickety display, rockets whistled perilously close to the crowd. It was a miracle that everyone escaped unscathed. As the Catherine Wheels fizzled to a stop over 100 people filtered from the plaza into the hacienda for the mango party.

The Santos mangos were small but had the enviable reputation of being the best tasting fruit in Jalisco. Every year they hired the same squad of professional mango-pickers. They were native Indians who scaled the twenty metre trees to harvest the crop one by one. A long extendable pole with a tiny net was used to collect the ripe fruit identified by their first flush of red.

Pedro dragged a wicker basket heaped with ready to eat mangos into the courtyard. Deemed the king of fruits, these green, yellow and cherry red beauties were at their best. With a potato peeler, I delicately shaved the skin and released an exotic perfume as the luscious juice ran down my arm. Oval-shaped and apple-sized with the rich pulpy texture of an overripe plum, they were succulent, sweet, tropical and silky.

Brightly coloured piñatas in the shape of donkeys and fish hung from the ceiling as excited children thrashed at them with sticks to dislodge the gifts and sweets inside which rained down and scattered over the floor.

As the night progressed, Victor and Pablo entertained the party with their distinctly classical style of Mexican music and had all of us singing along until the early hours. Before we retired, Pedro warned me not to forget to check my boots in the morning, just in case a scorpion or deadly beetle had crawled inside.

At sunrise, the view from my room through the shimmering heat haze over the subtropical forest below was inspirational and I remembered to check my footwear for uninvited guests. We convened around the pool as Antonio's sisters, Nena, Marita and Güerita with her daughter Rosa cooked chilaquiles. The Mexican equivalent of an English breakfast made from fragments of lightly fried tortilla dipped in a red chilli and tomato sauce with two fried eggs, diced red onion, refried beans and avocados. In Mexico, you were never served one egg, always two.

Alfonso, Antonio, Carlos his oldest son, Pedro and I prepared ourselves to walk around the summit and visit Pablo in his ranch. We set off in single file through the green vegetation in-between cascading rivulets, up and down tapered footpaths which followed the contours of the mountain. On a vertiginous ledge we came face to face with a family of raccoons who erected their long tails to use as rudders when scampering downhill over the rough scree. The pathway suddenly opened out onto a windswept plateau, referred to as La Mesa, which formed part of the ranch. It was planted with rows of the blue agave interspersed with wild cactus.

The entrance to Pablo's ranch was manned by four armed guards, located in a sentry box next to an electronic gate and attached to a high metal fence which surrounded the hacienda. Pablo welcomed us to his home and insisted that we stay for lunch – most of his family were visiting relatives in the USA. In his creative hideaway where he composed, a glass wall had sublime views over the mountain peaks. The others were covered in gold awards, silver discs and signed photos of famous people, including Frank Sinatra. On the patio, pure cool water was available from a terracotta urn and black beers protruded from an ice bucket. Pablo's chef had prepared his favourite, huitlacoche, a speciality dish made with blue and black fungus from the ears of corn. In some parts of the world it is regarded as an agricultural disease, in Mexico, it was a delicacy. The fungus, sautéed in butter had a sort of earthy or truffle flavour and was served alongside tamales, a dough steamed in corn husks and filled with spicy chicken. A platter of calabaza enmielada, a baked pumpkin with honey was brought to the terrace, a popular sweet in Mexico.

Pablo had recently been the subject of a failed kidnapping attempt which accounted for the security. Two years after our visit, a criminal gang would abduct Pablo junior and glue his severed index finger to the ransom demand. By the time the cash had been gathered, a second finger arrived in the post fastened to the reminder. It would cost Pablo over a million dollars to have his son released by the gang and Pablo junior would have to re-learn to play the guitar with just two fingers and one thumb. Pablo senior was forced to come out of retirement and go on tour to plug the financial gap.

As we were leaving, Pablo said, 'Because you appreciate good food, I recommend you pay a visit to my favourite eating house in Tlaquepaque.'

'What's it called?' I asked.

'The Restaurant with No Name.'

'How do I find it?'

'You will,' he roared, 'When you visit, tell the owner, Juan José, you are a friend of my family.'

We walked back through the agave plantation and down into El Escalón where the families were packed into a convoy of pickups, facing forward like carefully stacked garden gnomes. The motorcade drove up the steep hill and returned to their homes in the city. In the early days, before Don Pedro finished building the road, they used to leave their trucks at the base of the mountain and it took a whole day to reach the ranch on horseback. To secure the children to the ponies, three of them were wrapped together in a poncho and the strongest one held the reins. I imagined the entire family aboard a string of horses snaking up the narrow path which clung to the mountainside.

Antonio, Güerita, Teresita, Rosa and I were the only ones remaining in the huge hacienda. Rosa prepared quesadillas with some leftovers from the party. Antonio fell asleep in his hammock while Teresita and Rosa went to their rooms to read. Güerita and I sat in front of a terracotta chimenea as the flames flickered in the dark. She was a polished, worldly and stylish lady. Her light skin, fair hair and kind, honey-coloured eyes stood out as being different from the rest of the family. She laughed readily and exuded a warmth from her heart.

Antonio told me that Güerita was her father's favourite daughter. At the age of fifteen, he taught her to drive their enormous trailers and had been given special dispensation from the Mexican government to take them onto the highway. In this machismo world of Latin America, it was unusual to consider a female climb up into a cab and get behind the wheel of one of these juggernauts. She can reverse a double trailer into a loading bay and park it on a peso was Antonio's description her truck driving skills.

Güerita and I continued to talk throughout the night. She married a socialite from Guadalajara and had one daughter, but the marriage failed when Rosa was a baby and for the past fourteen years Güerita remained single. She spoke English without an American accent even though she learned the language at a university in Colorado and was also fluent in Italian and Portuguese. As a teenager she toured Europe, the

UK and Israel with her parents and had been the only sibling to travel overseas. She was a successful interior designer and watercolour artist with a passion for photography.

The orange-gold mountain peaks were the first sign of dawn breaking as Güerita took me by the hand and we walked through the rustling mango trees in the warm breeze, up a lofty pathway to her secret hideaway. A clear pool set back into a wooded copse with views over the green valley below and where she had spent many an hour of her happy childhood. We shared mangos and dangled our bare feet in the cool water, our laughter echoed around the mountain chamber. In the far distance, we could hear Antonio's faint voice from the ranch below, so our time was up. As I helped Güerita clamber down over the rocks, she fell into my arms and her musky aroma intoxicated my thoughts. I invited her to The Restaurant with No Name and she accepted.

Güerita and Teresita left for the city and I stayed with Antonio and Rosa to help lock up. Antonio guessed I was attracted to Güerita and wanted the best for his sister. He patiently explained that many prominent men, including well-known celebrities, had tried to date her without success, nevertheless he was still supportive. I invited him and his wife Teresita to join us at The Restaurant with No Name as a thank you for their hospitality.

On the return journey we visited Antonio's brother-in-law, Juan José, married to his sister Violeta. He ran a chilli farm and grew seventy varieties in poly tunnels. We pulled into his smallholding and switched off the engine. All we could hear was snoring coming from a bench seat under a poinciana tree where Juan José was lying flat out taking his daily siesta. He sleepily made us some coffee and his pet marmoset, Raoul, sat on my knee chewing pieces of pineapple and occasionally standing up to sniff my lips.

'You must have eaten mangos earlier as they're Raoul's favourite,' Rosa laughed.

'Next time, I will bring him some ripe mangos,' I grinned.

Rosa was a mature girl for her teenage years with sparkling hazel eyes and a quick wit. She had a propensity for languages and spoke both English and French in addition to her native Spanish. Rosa had a wonderful sense of humour and a passion for the arts, film and travel. At her young age she had already visited Colombia, Canada, Italy and the Caribbean. *En route* to Guadalajara, she told me some interesting facts about the cinema in Mexico.

'Whenever I have free time, I love to escape and watch a movie at the cinema. The VIP section is only a few peso's more but the wide reclining leather armchairs have a table either side and there's an extensive menu with waitress service. My cousin likes the sushi and Irish coffee but my favourite is the mixed popcorn bucket which is split into four sections: caramel, butter, chilli and natural.'

'It sounds like air conditioned luxury, you must take me there one day?'

'You're welcome anytime.'

At home in Tlaquepaque, an instruction had arrived from Denmark for me to attend the natural health exhibition in Tokyo at the end of the month and my flights tickets had been despatched by FedEx. Alfonso had given me the contact number of The Restaurant with No Name and I made the reservation for the following Friday. Antonio, Teresita, Güerita and I would meet beforehand at El Parián, a cluster of restaurants surrounding a central bandstand in the main square of Tlaquepaque.

I sat with a coffee in El Parián and an elegant Güerita emerged from the crowd. Her tumbling waves of golden hair framed her kind-hearted amber eyes and warm smile.

'It's nice to see you again,' she spoke softly.

'You're so beautiful,' I stammered.

'Don't forget us,' drawled Antonio tugging at my sleeve.

'Welcome to Tlaquepaque,' I laughed and we made our way to the restaurant.

The owner, Juan José, gave us a royal greeting, especially

Güerita who was the queen. Our table was outside on the terrace in a traditional Mexican courtyard among wandering peacocks. He explained that El Restaurante sin Nombre had no menu either but he questioned our preferences and brought a magnificent variety of dishes in buffet style, laid out in the same colourways as the Mexican flag – green, white and red. There were stuffed pasilla peppers with tomatillo, a green tomato unique to Mexico, jalapeno guacamole and avocado cream. In the middle, white goat's cheese enchiladas with a mango infused jicama salad, a type of yam. On the end, red chipotle shrimp burritos and a spicy halibut ceviche on a bed of quinoa.

Although the restaurant was famous for its steak, Antonio was the only one who ordered meat. As a peacock sauntered by, it suddenly turned its attention our way and with lightning precision snatched his sirloin, threw its head back and swallowed it in one go. Güerita, Teresita and I laughed until the tears rolled down our cheeks. The stolen fillet was replaced along with a bottle of tequila, compliments of the house, after which, Antonio suggested we go to El Parián and listen to the mariachi playing on the bandstand.

Güerita and I danced to *Qué Bonito Amor*, what a beautiful love. With her so close, an emotional energy charged through my body like an electromagnetic field. An uncanny serenity quickly followed such as the stillness between lightning and thunder. Our eyes flowed into each other – we came together through a wordless bond, a mute understanding, an undeclared unity – a pair of spiritual birds on the wing. We were in love.

As the music faded and the evening came to an end, I whispered into Güerita's ear, 'You are my half-orange.' At home, I threw my jacket over the statue of Don Quixote and slept on the sofa with a smile on my face.

STATE OF JALISCO

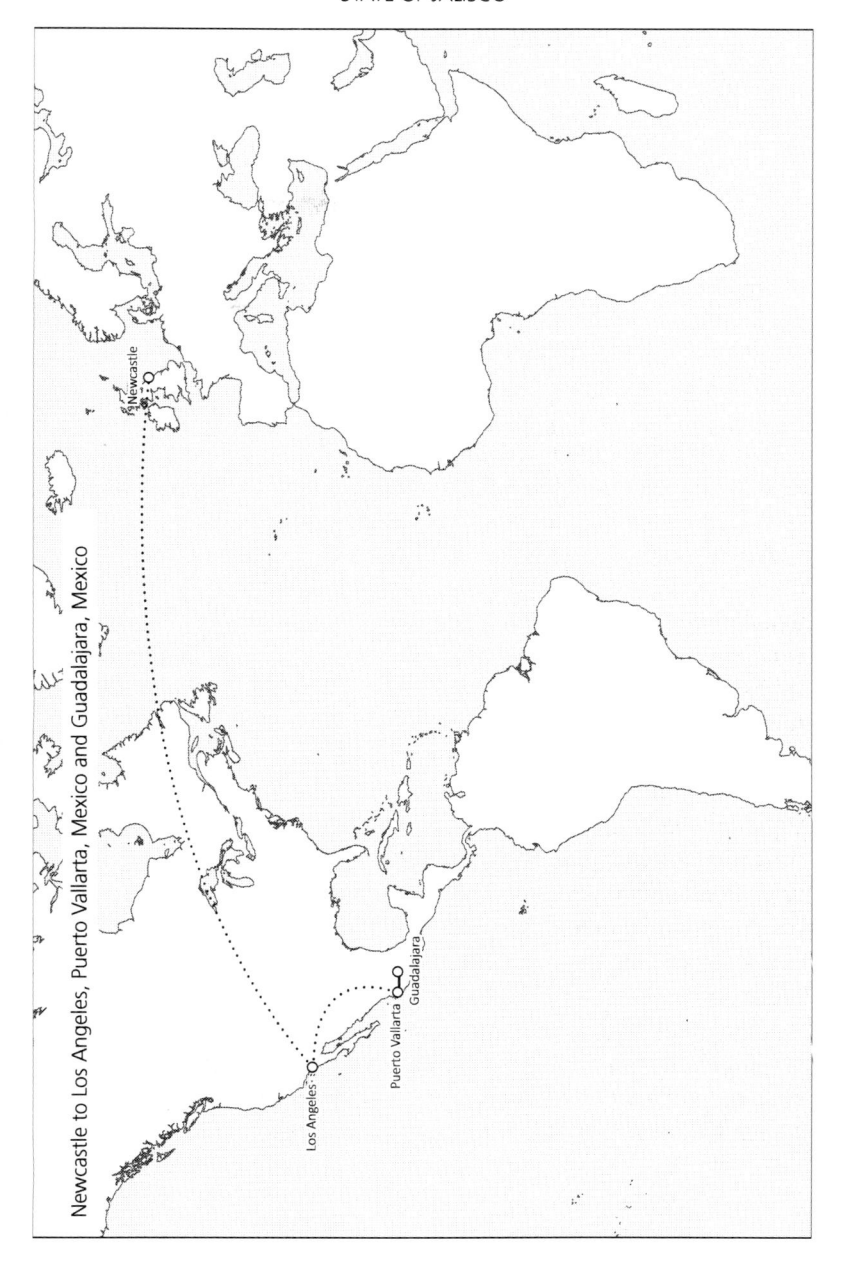

Newcastle to Los Angeles, Puerto Vallarta, Mexico and Guadalajara, Mexico

15 Neon Cities

'Do not take life too seriously. You will never get out of it alive.'
ELBERT HUBBARD, AMERICAN PHILOSOPHER

Tokyo, Japan 2005

TOKYO IS THE LARGEST CITY METROPOLIS IN THE WORLD, HOME TO more than forty million people, with a colossal GDP of one trillion pounds sterling. Gerrysan met me at Narita airport and we took a bullet train into the city. His home was a single room on the second floor above a dentist in downtown Shibuya. The sofa converted into a futon at night and the bathroom was a plastic pod with a base footprint of one square metre.

Emerging onto the street, we plunged into swarms of people flowing through a network of elevated footpath bridges which criss-crossed the roads below and connected skyscrapers at varying levels. These sky-high pavements were often carpeted with a black rubber matting to absorb sound. Yellow metro trains on monorails ran between these towering buildings alongside noiseless aircraft descending gracefully. It was a neon lit cityscape of overwhelming proportions.

The Danes had appointed a Japanese distributor by the name of Yocho & Co, whose British director, Gerry Sanford, was known to his colleagues as Gerrysan. His company had a facility in the Tokyo suburbs where they processed organic matter into powders, tablets and tinctures. My brief was to introduce the Mexican cactus powder to their clients at the organic expo, held annually at the Tokyo Big Sight Exhibition Centre.

My accommodation was a capsule hotel in Shinjuku with shared facilities, including a sauna, changing room and lockers. I used a short ladder to slide feet first into the two metre square cylindrical bedroom. It had a miniature TV fixed to the ceiling and a flimsy blind for privacy. The compact space was relatively comfortable but the snoring from drunken Japanese businessmen played havoc with my sleep pattern. The next day, I moved to a motel on the same street. My room had no windows and it contained a round bed with a variety of vibration settings. When Gerrysan arrived, he pointed out I had mistakenly relocated to a love hotel, normally hired by the hour.

Gerrysan wanted to create a team spirit among his exhibition staff and had booked a table that evening in a restaurant in Memory Lane, Shinjuku. A district famous for its yakitori, skewers of chicken grilled over charcoal. The gang included Kyoko, his Japanese chairman who was a stone-faced, mature individual with little or no conversation. Two translators, one of which was Tamico, a serious minded student studying chemistry. Then there was Lulana, a tri-lingual Spanish speaker whose father was Brazilian and mother Japanese. Her main occupation was as a showgirl at a well-known entertainment venue in Yokohama. Last but not least was Gerrysan, a chemist with a passion for the natural health industry. He was a thickset expat from Croydon in his mid-forties who had lived in Japan for twelve years and developed a reasonable understanding of the language.

The yakitoris were served on individual trays with cucumber salad, plain rice and a glass of Sapporo beer. We left the restaurant and walked under the endless clusters of gaudy neon signs and flickering screens until we reached a karaoke parlour in an upmarket area close to the Ginza. They allocated a particular room with a glass floor on which three pink sofas formed a semi-circle around a small stage painted lime green. Saffron yellow paint was spread over the walls with built-in disco lights, booming sound system and an enormous TV screen. When the song menus arrived, Kyoko warbled *Let It Be* by The Beatles which sounded more like the mating call of a rook. Lulana performed *The Girl from Ipanema* in the most provocative way and had us all transfixed whereas Tamico tastefully crooned a sweet Japanese ballad. Gerrysan and I screeched together, *These Boots Are Made for Walkin* by Nancy Sinatra and I could see the anguish in everyone's eyes. On the way back to the love hotel at 3 a.m., the streets were still teeming with people and the neon signs continued to flash in this non-stop twenty-four hour metropolis.

After a restless night's sleep on the vibrating bed, I was relieved to move into an aparthotel centrally located behind the metro station in Shibuya. This was a type of hotel that provided self-catering apartments instead of rooms. My flat was on the second floor of a six story block and serviced twice a week. I had the luxury of windows, a modern kitchen and a hi-tech bathroom. Attached to the lavatory was a digital control system to heat the toilet seat, with three settings: lukewarm, comfortable or hot. There was also a bidet device which operated a rotating pop out brush and spray.

The exhibition got underway and as we approached the subway, Gerrysan took his daily chlorella. He chewed these algae tablets instead of swallowing them with water and as a result, his lips, teeth and tongue were stained a bright green. We did not want to mention it right away but once aboard the packed metro, instead of being crushed, an empty space appeared all around us which gave the game away. It took him hours to remove the colouring from his mouth.

Gerrysan had a love of salsa dancing which he enthusiastically described as hot and spicy. It stemmed from his time in New York listening to Columbian, Cuban and Afro-Caribbean music in the bars and clubs. As a result, his weekly dance lesson was non-negotiable, so Lulana, Tamico and I decided to visit their favourite nigiri sushi bar. We sat on stools in front of a long narrow table and selected our dishes from a conveyor belt which served sliced raw tuna, shrimp, eel, squid or octopus over a moulded ball of rice. We dipped these delicacies into soy sauce with a dab of wasabi, a hot Japanese mustard, washed down with cups of Sencha, light organic green tea. Afterwards, we visited the pastry shop next door for ningyoyaki, a sweet cake infused with a red bean sauce elegantly presented in the shape of a dove.

Lulana was a single child whose father, Artur, began his working life as a poor maize farmer in rural Brazil. When he visited Japan on a trade mission he fell in love with Maiko, a Japanese professor of music, and had remained in Tokyo ever since. Tamico also lived with her parents and brother in a ground floor apartment. She described their garden as being small enough to fit into a briefcase and her father cut the grass with a pair of nail scissors. I assumed she meant a window box.

Throughout Japan, there are over five millions vending machines in shopping streets, up alleys and in residential areas. They sell everything from bras to live crabs. I noted: toys, umbrellas, gloves, ties and all manner of foodstuff, mashed potato, boiled eggs and bananas. Tamico knew of several Tokyoite students who lived from these machines. They bought their meals, drinks and clothes and rarely cooked or entered a store.

Early on Sunday morning, I breakfasted on sushi from a vending machine and was dive-bombed by a group of aggressive black birds which resembled ravens but with longer dark-grey beaks. The Japanese referred to them, as 'jungle crows.' Their hideous squawking, which was much deeper and more resonant than a crow, made for a spooky and surreal scenario in a big city. There were thousands of them, akin to flocks of oversized starlings, fanned out above the skyscrapers. They reminded me of the starlings that congregated on buildings in Newcastle upon Tyne during twilight hours and the delightful atmospheric sound of their chattering.

Travelling by subway in Tokyo at peak times was not for the faint-hearted. One weekday morning, the metro arrived in the station and the doors slid open but it was full. The uniformed rail guards in white gloves used a type of wide brush to squeeze everyone on the platform into the crammed carriages. For the next five minutes I suffered from acute claustrophobia, unable to move or breath, until the next station, where I ejected myself and happily waited in a cafe until the rush hour had passed.

On the last day of the show we met a new client from South Korea who was a distributor of fruit juice in Asia. They were sourcing a supply of tuna morada, the fruit which grows on the cactus plant and makes a sweet purple drink. The company was represented by Hwon, a wizened square-jawed executive director and Joon his PA, a younger more studious type. They both spoke good English and invited us to a shabu-shabu restaurant in a nightclub district called Roppongi, where they served raw food to cook at the table. Joon demonstrated how to blanch the vegetables in boiling water and cook the meat on a hot plate. The fixed price deal included all we could eat and drink in three hours of which Hwon and Joon took full advantage but we could not match their ability to imbibe.

'Historically, there's always been a drinking culture in Korea. We believe that alcohol helps us get closer to others. Did you know our consumption is the highest in the world?' said Hwon proudly.

'Yes I've heard,' said Gerrysan, 'And by a big margin.'

After the shabu-shabu grand prix we visited a whisky boutique on the fourteenth floor of a high street tower block. A private club cocooned in maroon chintz with a hushed ambience. Hwon and Joon were whisky connoisseurs who deliberated and argued the merits of individual malts from a display of 200 of the worlds' finest. We sat on cinema seats in a row cradling our glass of twelve year old Hibiki and watched a Charlie Chaplin movie. At the end of the evening, they invited us to visit their distribution facility in Seoul.

Lulana gave us tickets to a musical in which she would appear as a dancer on the stage at a theatre in Yokohama. On Saturday night, Artur, her father, Gerrysan, Tamico and I caught the train from Tokyo. Artur was a slightly built septuagenarian with a big personality, similar to his daughter, who spoke some English and good Spanish.

'In Brazil, the three most important things in life begin with the carnival, followed by family and then religion,' Artur grinned, 'Everyone saves a few reals each week for the big party.'

The theatrical production was a spectacular display of glittering sequins and towering plumes of outspread peacock feathers, supported by the unmistakeable rhythm of samba beating out from a twelve-piece band. During the interval, Lulana visited our table, elevated to over two metres tall with her colourful headwear, high heels, feathery quill and body-hugging outfit. Gerrysan was wide-eyed and speechless, Artur, very proud, while I whistled and Tamico clapped her hands.

After the extravaganza, Artur invited us to a churrasco restaurant to sample a typical Brazilian barbeque. The table mats were illustrated with an image of a cow indicating the different cuts of meat: sirloin, flank, tenderloin, fillet and rib. Each of the five types were represented by their own specific bow-tied waiter. Sizeable chunks of meat on a roasting skewer were carved at the table and regular visits by the waiters could be stopped or started by flipping a disc. The quality of the food was exceptional and the restaurant high end. Artur fell fast asleep on the return journey from Yokohama and we had difficulty waking him in Tokyo until Lulana threw water over his face. There followed a burst of Portuguese expletives from a furious Artur.

Early on Sunday morning, I was shocked and saddened to hear the news from England that my travel companion and long-term friend Swinko had died suddenly from an aneurysm. He was in his early 50s. Swinko and I worked together in the Australian bush during the 1970s and we travelled through the Soviet Union to the Far East in 1981. Swinko featured in the chapters, *Western Australia, Through the Iron Curtain and Quezon City*. With several weeks to wait before our visit to South Korea, I made a decision on the spot to retrace the steps Swinko and I had taken twenty-four years earlier when we fished in the fast-flowing rivers which fed into Lake Chubetsu on the island of Hokkaido.

Hokkaido, Japan 2005

IN 1981, THE JAPANESE WERE AN INWARDLY THINKING SOCIETY WHO would stop and stare at most foreigners. Swinko and I had been regarded with intense curiosity and referred to as, 'gaijins,' men from outside country. By 2005, it had blossomed into a cosmopolitan metropolis with millions of foreign nationals who visited or lived in Japan.

Instead of the older style locomotive that took five hours to reach Sendai from Tokyo, the brand new high-speed bullet train shot its way between the cities in a comfortable 100 minutes. From Sendai, I took a swish coach for the smooth ride up to the northern tip of Japan's main island of Honshu. At the port of Aomori, I boarded a ferry for the two hour sailing to Hakodate on the southernmost tip of Hokkaido.

After booking into a waterside hotel at the port in Hakodate, I strolled around the town looking for the backstreet restaurant where Swinko and I had first tried natto – fermented soy beans. I remembered the overpowering stench which reminded me of smelly socks, and its revolting slimy consistency. Not only did I find the café but I sat at the same table. The place had not changed whatsoever. *Mr Tambourine Man* by Bob Dylan was playing on the radio, a favourite of Swinko's. I could sense his presence and even hear him singing along. He had been a close friend and I experienced a feeling of emptiness and loss.

The cook, Tomo, emerged from the kitchen to take the order and a lovely woman called Kameyo sitting on the table opposite translated as I told the story of our visit in the 1980s. Fortunately the natto was not available and Tomo brought a plate of sushi instead. Kameyo joined me and we chatted about Japanese food while she described her favourite dish.

'I love my funazushi.'

'Is it a carp?'

'Yes, it's a freshwater crucian carp which is caught in large volumes during the rainy season and fermentation is a way in which to preserve the meat.'

'Are they fermented for a long period?'

'We cover the gutted fish with rice and allow it to decompose from one to three years. It's a speciality available for three months of the year.'

Early the next day I took the train around Ichiura Bay and across the island to Sapporo on the east coast, Japan's fourth largest city. From the water's edge close to Ishikariwanshin harbour, I could see the outline of the Russian mainland on the horizon. A couple on the train suggested a visit to the beer museum at the Sapporo brewery, neither of which had existed on Hokkaido in 1981. After sampling a range of roasted malt reserve ales made especially for the museum, I staggered through the city streets to my hotel raiding the vending machines along the way.

From Sapporo, I hired a car and drove towards the Daisetsuzan National Park and Lake Chubetsu. The summer forests of broad-leaved trees hugged the rivers of clear water which cascaded down from the wild mountains. In the country village of Higashikawa close to the lake, I discovered the pension that Swinko and I had stayed but the new owners spoke no English. In exactly the same way as we did in 1981, I removed my shoes at the front door and replaced them with a pair of cream-coloured slippers. Inside the bedroom, a white bathrobe was neatly folded and positioned at the base of a rolled futon. The interior walls were sliding panels of translucent paper in a bamboo frame which diffused the light and reflected shadows to give it that distinct essence of Japan.

A silver-haired lady in a cerise kimono of shiny silk performed a choreographed ritual of preparing matcha, a powdered green tea. She placed a porcelain teapot next to a chawan bowl on a wide but low table of red pine and delicately poured the exquisite lime-green liquid. The mindful nature of chanoyu, the Japanese tea ceremony, made it a calming experience. She slid open the dividing door and departed silently. The room took on a church-like stillness bathed in a warm glow from a paper lantern. I sat cross-legged on a zabutan, a thin pillow placed on the rush matting, and focused on the present moment. This ancient art, derived from Buddhism, was still popular in modern day Japan.

The hiking store in the village furnished me with a pair of sturdy boots and a local map of the surrounding walks. For the next week I toured the area on foot, visiting the lake and mountains. The route led me through forests of ash, golden birch and abundant coniferous varieties. From the riverbank, climbing wild roses of red and yellow with splashes of lavender made way to colourful carpets of alpine plants on the steeper slopes.

The pathways were clearly marked and occasionally I came across a notice pinned to a wooden post with a cartoon image of an angry bear, with the date and time it was spotted. I found the presence of bears unsettling, considering I spent most of the day alone. Fortunately, there were no brown bears in sight, just the odd fly fisherman on the lake or next to the river. Their most interesting catch was the cherry salmon, known as masu, a wild species with dark red and green stripes. I remembered how Swinko had been keen to land one but we only caught rainbow trout. I was hoping to see the elusive and cute sika deer but instead I was rewarded with the chattering sound of pikas and the odd one that flashed over the trail. These tiny mammals resembled guinea pigs without a tail, have reddish-brown fur and are akin to hares.

On my way back to Tokyo I reflected on the changes in Japan since 1981. I recalled it as being expensive but after years of stagflation it had become much cheaper. I also noticed that the rising sun imagery, a symbol of an imperialistic past, had been removed from product packaging and advertisements. Gerrysan met me from the train at Shinjuku station and the following day we boarded a two hour flight to South Korea.

Seoul, South Korea 2005

SEOUL IS THE FOURTEENTH LARGEST CITY ON THE PLANET, A futuristic high-tech capital located in the far north of the country; home to half the population of South Korea and thirty miles from the North Korean border. Modern skyscrapers dominate the metropolis above ground and below is the world's biggest underground shopping mall.

On our first day in Seoul it was hot and sticky outside but comfortably cool in the air conditioned boardroom on the seventy-third floor. Chilled drinks made from the prickly pear cactus fruit were served and the dark purple liquid was delicious, sweet and refreshing. Throughout the day we discussed the finite detail of the contract and a deal was signed to supply the Mexican produce in bulk. To celebrate our agreement, we expected another whisky drinking session, but as Hwon and Joon were accompanied by their chairman, Wook, a teetotaller, we drank tea during the evening. The following night, Wook took us to a musical in the Seoul Arts Centre played on kitchen utensils, which was both unusual and entertaining.

Our plan was to stay in Seoul for ten days before I travelled back to Mexico and Gerrysan to Japan. After the meetings, we swapped the four-star hotel which they had so kindly provided to a more authentic inn and teahouse in Insa-dong. This district was close to the narrow alleys of Bukchon Hanok, a preserved hamlet of the Joseon dynasty dating from the fourteenth century. We were delighted to discover it was still a working village as opposed to a museum.

The hanok was a traditional Korean home from this period. A carefully considered piece of architecture, as well as being an environmentally sound structure, even by today's standards. They were built to face south for the best use of light, with their backs to the mountain to shield them from the strong winds and provide ventilation. The walls were made of straw and earth, whereas wood was used for the internal structure of the rafters, doors, pillars and windows. Clay pantiles or thatch covered the roof. Original Korean paper, which is a tough semi-opaque fibrous material, was glued to the panels of the sliding doors and windows. What was also unusual was the masonry flooring, under which horizontal smoke passages were installed against a vertical chimney. The floor was covered with clay, topped with Korean paper and polished with bean oil to make it waterproof. The fire heated the house and the floor, which was used for both dining and sleeping on, making it necessary to remove one's shoes at the door and keep the area clean – a tradition that still exists in modern day Korea.

Late at night in Bukchon Hanok we ate in a backstreet café where the only food available was a hot chilli soup served in an immense bowl. As I ladled the contents into my mouth, two eyeballs suddenly bobbed up to the surface simultaneously as if a live animal was staring up at me through the liquid. Gerrysan was partial to eyeballs so I threw them into his dish.

Most restaurants hosted the spicy Korean barbeque, where each diner is their own chef by cooking the food at the table, but the national staple of the Korean cuisine is the renowned kimchi. A seasoned and fermented cabbage which accompanies almost every meal to the extent that each person averages twenty kilos of kimchi a year. In the pension we met an English speaking woman who told us her own recipe for kimchi.

'Smooth out layers of napa cabbage leaves and smear each one with a spicy fish sauce, pureed garlic, ginger and red pepper before adding salted shrimp. Leave multiple tiers of the coated cabbage to ferment for three days, after which, roll the leaves carefully into sausage shapes. It should smell pungent and taste sour.'

It was an acquired flavour which I preferred to avoid at breakfast. When we left Seoul and were airborne, Gerrysan leant over and whispered, 'Thank God the smell of kimchi has finally left my nostrils.' Two minutes later the whole aircraft filled with that familiar fermented smell of microwaved kimchi.

Gerrysan had hosted our venture into Asia and in return we would help Yocho & Co introduce their speciality range of health supplements and niche superfoods to Mexico. They included camu camu, a tiny red berry known for its high vitamin C content, wild crafted from the Peruvian rainforest and Chlorella, a green algae loaded with chlorophyll grown on manmade lakes in Taiwan. We planned our next meeting for two months hence in Puebla, Mexico where I would connect Gerrysan to a contact within their natural health industry.

From Tokyo, my destination city in Mexico was Puerto Vallarta to visit Alfonso, the Jewish friend of Antonio Santos, who I travelled with to the mango party at El Escalón in the chapter 'State of Jalisco'. After which, I would make my way back to my temporary home in Tlaquepaque, Guadalajara from where I had departed earlier to visit Japan.

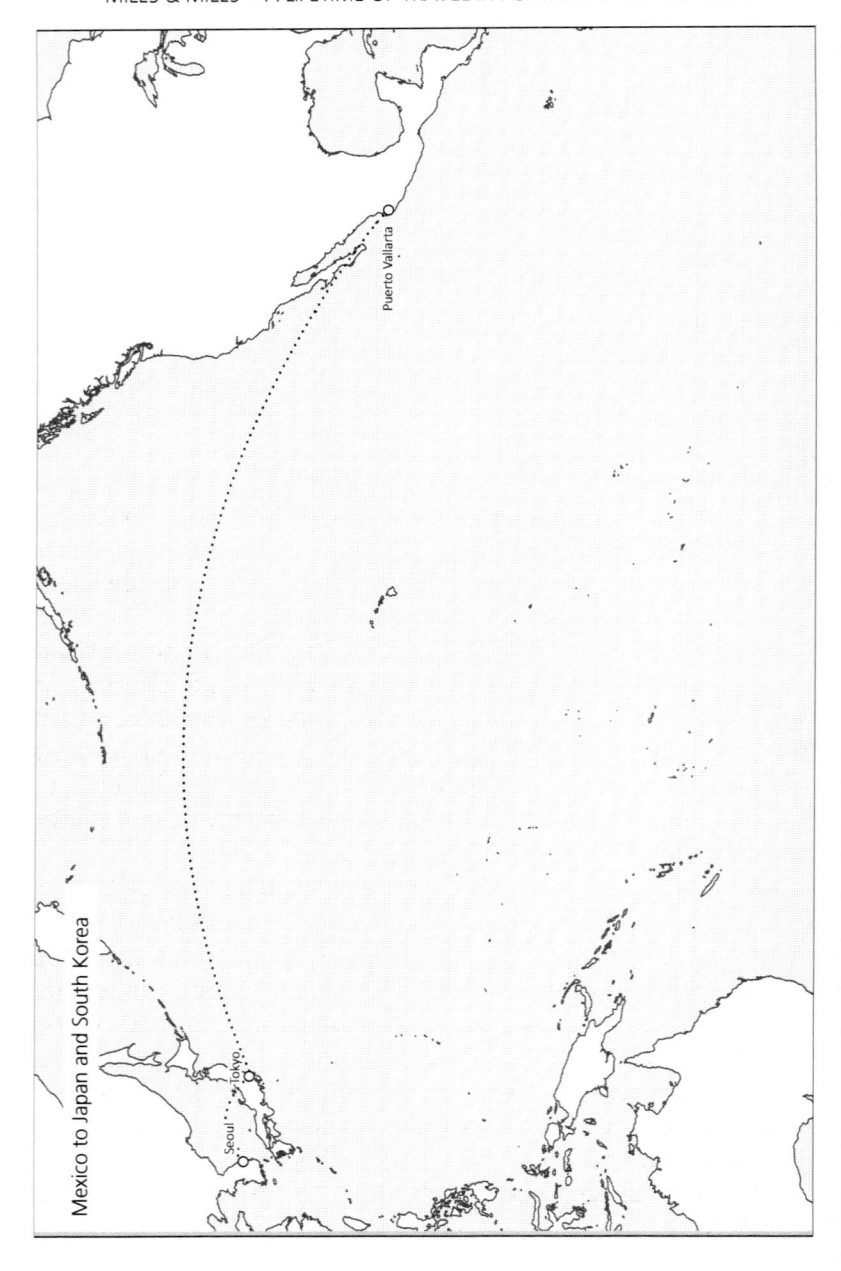

MILES & MILES ~ A LIFETIME OF TRAVEL IN ASIA AND LATIN AMERICA

Mexico to Japan and South Korea

16 Viva Mexico

'For me, love is the most important force. It moves the universe.'
LAURA ESQUIVEL, MEXICAN NOVELIST

Puerto Vallarta 2005

LA CIUDAD MÁS AMIGABLE DEL MUNDO, THE FRIENDLIEST CITY IN the world read the message over passport control. I arrived exhausted but exhilarated to Puerto Vallarta on the western seaboard of Mexico after my trip to the *Neon Cities* of Japan and South Korea.

Alfonso met me at the airport and we drove to his roundhouse on the beach where we would meet Antonio Santos the following day. Alfonso's circular home, coloured matt terracotta, was attached to a terrace with an oval swimming pool shaded by a domed thatch. His property overlooked the magnificent Bay of Banderas which forms part of the pacific coastline of Jalisco.

The Bay is famous as a calving ground for thousands of humpback whales, fifteen metres long and weighing in at thirty ton. The humidity at the coast is uncomfortable even in winter but it was the warm water which attracted the whales during the breeding season. These magnificent animals could be seen with other species like the sperm, blue and orca. The Bay teemed with all manner of marine life: tuna, snapper, marlin and sailfish. There were designated areas for sea turtle conservation and local fishermen adhered to the strict laws imposed by the Mexican government to protect the different species.

Puerto Vallarta was notorious during the 1960s as a playground for the rich and famous. Frank Sinatra and his rat pack regularly sailed from California to the Bay. It was also the location in which the romance between Elizabeth Taylor and Richard Burton had flourished during the filming of *The Night of The Iguana* directed by John Huston.

The promenade leading from Alfonso's home around the Bay and into the town was lined with contemporary sculptures interspersed with market stalls selling handicrafts. In the historic centre of Puerto Vallarta there were whitewashed colonnades with red pantile roofs around a cobblestone square. In the corner sat the elaborately decorated church of Nuestra Senora de Guadalupe.

From the plaza, a spider's web of narrow curving streets with art galleries, boutiques and jewellery design studios led down to the marketplace. In an open workshop, a sculptor hand-carved marine creatures from the Bay and I bought a family of dolphins made of rosewood for Güerita when Alfonso told me they were her favourite.

Alfonso had a passion for horses which he stabled at the opposite end of the Bay and where he introduced me to Loco, a grey mare from the Azteca breed. She peered with contempt and crushed me against the stable door much to Alfonso's amusement.

'She loves you,' he chortled.

The following morning Antonio arrived from Guadalajara and Alfonso saddled up Blanco, a magnificent white steed, Hombre, a smaller chestnut-and-white beast and Loco. We trotted by the water's edge and into the jungle before they galloped ahead while Loco and I ambled along in their wake. The ride covered miles of bridleways under the cooling canopies of the lush rainforest. Once we returned to the seashore, Loco stopped abruptly and refused to go any further. She turned her head several times in a vain attempt to communicate, when unexpectedly, she reared up and tipped me from the saddle over her tail onto the beach.

The towering animal continued to fall backwards and as I scrambled out of the way she crashed down with a glancing blow which buried me into the sand. Loco stood up and regained her composure but I was injured and could not move.

Antonio and Alfonso galloped up the shoreline, secured Loco and called for help. A dilapidated pickup driven by a local farmer came to the rescue. They hoisted my painful body onto the back of the truck for the bumpy ride to hospital. From the bed, I looked up at a red-faced doctor with a burning cigarette hanging from lip who appeared to be slightly drunk. The shutters were banging in the wind and dust was blowing in my face.

'I'm in agony,' I groaned.

The medic untied a worn leather case and pulled out a large syringe, filled it from a phial and pushed the needle into my buttocks. Within a few minutes the pain had gone but there was severe bruising all down my right side from the armpit to above the knee.

'What do we do now?' I asked the doctor.

'Señor Meeles has to wait for three or four hours. If you pees blood, we have a problem as your internal organs maybe damaged, if you don't pees blood you're free to go.' The ash from his cigarette dropped onto the pillow.

Fortunately I was fine, black-and-blue and embarrassed but extremely lucky. That same evening, we three amigos painted the town red. Next morning I opened the patio doors and came face-to-face with an alligator on the breakfast table. It turned out to be a man-sized iguana lizard but it made me jump with fright and was a painful reminder of the injury and reaffirmed my decision to stay away from horses.

We took our morning coffee on the terrace as a family of violet crowned hummingbirds fed from the flower nectar of a rose bush. Antonio and I thanked our friend Alfonso for his hospitality and made preparations for our journey to Tlaquepaque. As we drove out of town, Antonio talked of an incident which had taken place before they built the highway when the only way to Guadalajara from Puerto Vallarta was by mountain tracks, often frequented by bandits.

'My wife Teresita and Carlos, our first child, were with me in the car when we broke down in a remote area on a tight bend. As I looked under the hood, a group of bandits appeared on horseback from either direction. There was no escape and I believed that our lives were over. The bandits dismounted and pushed the car downhill into a village. Their wives gave us food while two men fixed an electrical fault. They told me to allow 1,000 miles before the part would need replaced. I could not believe our luck and furthermore, 1,250 miles later, when we were motoring into Dallas, the car broke down again with the exact same problem.'

Our drive to Guadalajara took six hours, leaving me two days to prepare for my trip to Puebla. As I would not see Güerita until the following month, I left the rosewood dolphin sculpture with Antonio.

At Guadalajara International airport, while I was waiting by the Air Mexicana departure gate, I observed the pilot making a sign of the cross before boarding the tatty-looking Douglas DC-3. When the aircraft manoeuvred on the tarmac in readiness to take-off for the two hour flight to Puebla, I tried to secure the seat belt but it was broken and lay limply on my lap. I swiftly moved to another seat which had the exact same problem but by this time we were hurtling down the runway. As soon as we were airborne, a young girl sitting alongside handed me her baby while she prepared arroz roco, red rice with tortilla and avocado. The little boy wiggled his feet and gurgled. It was the first time I had held a human baby. A giant panda, numerous monkeys, puppies and kittens had been in my arms but never a human. I returned the little one and she gave me my supper.

Puebla 2005

It was dusk when the grandiloquent skyline of golden cathedral domes emerged through the setting sun. The aircraft descended with a tremorless glide into Puebla, known as the City of Angels, and which claims to have a domed church for every day of the year. The historic centre is listed by UNESCO as a World Heritage Site and covers more than 5,000 buildings from the architectural style of Renaissance, Baroque and Classical. Snowy mountain peaks and volcanos surround Puebla, one of which is Popocatepetl, Mexico's most active volcano, a restless giant in a group of twenty spread over a juncture of three tectonic plates. It is the fourth largest city in Mexico and the capital of Puebla State, 100 miles to the south of Mexico City.

Outside the airport terminal, one clapped-out taxi was parked in the rank and the driver looked to be sitting on the floor due to the ruptured suspension. Inside, he cradled a pet lizard and I asked for the main square, el zocalo. A cobweb of cracks were spread over his filthy windscreen which made it virtually impossible to navigate through the jerky headlights coming towards us. The wheel bearings gave out an awkward hum and every undulation in the road caused it to thump, bang or crunch.

At the hotel, I picked up two messages. Gerrysan from Japan was arriving later and Guillermo, our cactus contact, would pick us up at 9am the next day. In the meantime I wandered into the zocalo and visited a studio which displayed Talavera ceramics, sometimes referred to as Majolica, made from a fine clay found only in Puebla. The industry had been introduced by the Spanish during the colonial era in the sixteenth century and was famed for its wonderfully detailed handcrafted designs. I bought a beautiful vase for Güerita.

Gerrysan appeared with a grin and shook my hand, 'Have you found the nearest salsa club yet?'

'I was hoping Guillermo would steer us to a safer place than the one we escaped from in San Francisco,' I laughed.

It was good to see Gerrysan again, whose passion for Latin dancing had taken us to so many seedy bars all over the world. There was always a great atmosphere when the dance communities came together and shared their passion. What gave salsa its life was not only the various techniques used with foot patterns or shoulder shimmies but the spontaneity and rhythm of the Afro-Cuban music. A silver-haired Mexican overheard our conversation and wrote down the address of a well-known Cuban venue by the name of El Gato Caliente, the Hot Cat. Gerrysan and I agreed we would visit after the business was concluded.

'This is your first time in Mexico and mine to Puebla so let's try the famous mixiote, pronounced meeshoteh. It's a local speciality,' I said.

Rafa's was recommended as the best place for mixiote and close to the zocalo. I translated from the menu, 'Mutton on the bone is marinated with ancho peppers, guajillo chillies and herbs for twenty-four hours. Carrots, potatoes, cubes of cactus, cinnamon, orange juice and a secret ingredient are added to the meat. The mix is wrapped in avocado leaves for flavour and outer layers of maguey fronds are used to secure them into parcels which are slow-baked in a wood-fired oven.'

Once we peeled open the fronds and leaves, the powerful aroma aroused and stimulated our senses. The honeyed mutton exuded a torrent of pungent caramelized flavours with a slight tangy balsamic edge. It was an astounding dish and kept Gerrysan quiet for a prolonged period.

The next morning, Guillermo arrived several hours late in a brand new red pickup and wearing an immaculate white Stetson. He was a smallish, dark-skinned man in his thirties with shiny black hair, slicked back Elvis Presley style, which accentuated his prominent gold teeth. He wore a cheeky smile but I detected a serious businessman behind the joviality. He spoke good English and had been brought up by an affluent middle class family who were farm-owning rancheros. After university in New York, he had returned to Puebla to work in the family firm and had recently taken over from his father's role as chief executive.

Gerrysan and I clambered aboard his pride and joy to visit their cactus farm and factory on the edge of town where they processed numerous herbs and plants into powders and liquids. Their operation had the capacity to supply the volumes needed with the consistent quality required by our clients in both the Far East and Europe. When our meeting came to an end, Guillermo was anxious to entertain. At 3 p.m. precisely, he tapped his gold Rolex and insisted it was time for lunch. He planned to introduce us to mole, pronounced molay, a national dish with its roots in Puebla.

Mole is a unique sauce normally prepared for special celebrations. It originates from the pre-Colombian era, prior to the Spanish arrival in the 1500s. Nahuatl Indian speakers call it 'molli,' which translates as 'concoction,' and also defines its Mesoamerican origin. The rich paste is produced in a range of colours: green, red, sienna, mahogany and even black. The classic version from Puebla is called mole poblano and is a thick, dark red chocolate-tinged sauce which has between thirty and seventy ingredients, including peanuts, almonds, cinnamon, chillies and cloves. The process of making mole is complex, time-consuming and labour intensive but nothing tastes quite like the rich, sweet and savoury, spicy Christmas cake paste. Its distinctive and refined aroma, once tasted, is always remembered.

Because of the elaborate preparations Mexicans usually buy it ready made from specialist mole shops or the thousands of private households who have their own recipe passed down through the generations. The homemade version is a national cottage industry where individuals make a batch to sell on to family and friends. Once refrigerated, it keeps for six months.

Guillermo, Gerrysan and I visited a local mole store where two metre high pyramids of the rich opulent paste stood solidly in wide, brightly coloured plastic buckets. The sumptuous, pungent odour discharging from the many varieties was somewhat heady but helped to understand the definitive and distinct flavour of mole. It was not surprising that Mexicans openly crave it. I bought a kilo of seven different kinds to take back to Guadalajara for Güerita's family.

My first experience of mole had been in Mexico City. The sauce was jet black with a runny consistency poured over a pork chop. It looked unappetizing and tasted mass-produced. Since then, I have tried many recipes from private sources or local mole makers and have developed my own taste for this special flavour. In the same way as the Mexicans, I also yearned for mole from time to time but had yet to sample the famed poblano. Guillermo took us to a restaurant whose chef created their own dark red version served with chicken, red rice and avocado on terracotta plates. This was an original recipe from Puebla which accentuated the key elements of the paste and was a true representation of the dish – poblano became my favourite mole.

Lunch turned into a machismo event with copious jugs of beer followed by shots of tequila. Guillermo then ordered a bottle of the hard stuff, Mescal, made from the heart of the maguey plant. I sipped at the powerful liquor but it made my eyes squint and tasted of raw alcohol laced with diesel. Guillermo and Gerrysan finished the bottle after which Guillermo cautiously climbed into his pickup and drove us to Porky's, a gentleman's club. How he managed to drive was beyond me, although he did go at a snail's pace and sat bolt upright with his eyes fixed to the windscreen.

The air-conditioned lap dancing nightclub must have been wallpapered in silver foil, with matching tables, bar and dance floor. It was like standing inside an enormous ice-cold biscuit tin. No sooner had we sat down when a towering, well-proportioned, partially clad female of African descent straddled me with her muscular thighs as if mounting a horse. She pushed her designer breasts into my face and gyrated. I wished that I had drank more of the Mescal.

We left the club well after midnight and walked back through the zocalo to the hotel. Gerrysan insisted on eating anything and everything from the late night street vendors. The following morning, he was ill, lying on his back holding his bloated belly. I phoned Guillermo and he kindly arranged for a doctor to visit. The medic diagnosed his condition as being curable but Gerrysan was positive he was dying.

'Take this liquid three time a day, stay in bed for the next twenty-four hours and you will be fine.'

Guillermo and I put the final touches to the supply contract for the Korean client to include the specification of the prickly pear cactus fruit concentrate. By this time, I decided to write up my notes while watching Tin Tan on the television, a Mexican comedian who was famous for his off the cuff remarks. He had made an undeniable impression during the Mexican golden era of movie making in the 1940s and 1950s. I enjoyed the *Chavo del Ocho* series, which was adored throughout Latin America. The housemaid told me she could hear moaning coming from one room and laughter from the next.

The following morning Gerrysan's stomach had deflated to its normal rotund shape and he was ready to visit the El Gato Caliente on our final night in Puebla. The cab driver was not keen on taking us to the district where the venue was located due to its violent reputation. When we arrived at the club, the dingy entrance was patrolled by five stocky men in black overcoats with pump action shotguns by their sides. The guys with the guns allowed us through the double doors and dark flock curtains into a reception area where there were four more security guards in dark suits with exposed handguns and ear pieces. It gave the impression of an event hosting a cartel conference rather than a place of entertainment.

Inside the club, there was a fun and vibrant ambience, the dance floor was buzzing and the Afro-Cuban musicians pumped out a rhythm with a physical and emotional intensity. Gerrysan melted into the throng doing his salsa thing and I made my way to the bar area. Cocktails were on offer but they lacked alcohol, so I complained to the waiter. A few minutes later, a small mature hard faced woman with gnarled hands turned up and, having introduced herself as Betina, proceeded to take several sips from my glass.

'I'm so sorry, please accept two complimentary drinks on the house,' she smiled.

'Thank you Betina.'

'It's quite rare for gringos to visit my club. What are you doing here?'

'I'm British, not American. We're visiting a supplier and my business partner is partial to salsa dancing.'

'An English gentleman, Wow! That's a first,' she laughed, 'I'm not Mexican either, I'm originally from Brazil.'

She took my hand, 'Come with me, lets' dance.'

'My salsa skills are minimal to say the least,' I pleaded.

'Follow my lead.'

She dragged me onto the dance floor and as my style morphed from a frolic into a pogo, she gave up and we returned to the table.

While Gerrysan continued to pirouette with pretty Mexican girls, Betina told me her life story. She had defended herself by shooting dead an armed criminal in Porto Alegre, Brazil, for which she had been locked up for life in 1983. There followed three years of incarceration before she escaped and had broken both wrists when she dropped out of a cell window. Her disfigured hands were a reminder of that horrendous experience. She became the sole owner of El Gato Caliente when her Cuban husband passed away as a result of cancer in 2002.

When the band stopped playing, they rearranged the set for a single performer. Betina stood up and stroked my arm, 'For you,' and leapt onto the stage to sing *Aquanile*, with a passionate, sensual energy which could only come from a Latina soul. She returned to the table with a look of contentment.

'You're a professional, that was beautiful,' I said.

'You're so kind. I had a successful singing career in Brazil when I was younger,' she said happily.

'Will you ever sell the club and leave Mexico?'

'Because of my past, I would have to travel on a fake passport but my dream is to live in Costa Rica one day and perhaps run a small bar on the beach. It's safe there and the people are friendly. It's a natural paradise.' Her eyes saddened and her lower lip quivered.

Gerrysan arrived at the table glistening with sweat.

'You are a talented performer,' he remarked.

'Thank you...two English gentlemen in one night.' Betina's smile returned.

'Good lord it's after 2am, we must go,' Gerrysan wheezed.

'In a few hours he's returning to Tokyo and I leave for Guadalajara,' I said.

'I must take care of your transport back to the city. It's dangerous in this area after dark,' she said.

'I will invite you for mole when I'm next in Puebla. We appreciate your warm hospitality. It's been a wonderful to meet you and I will always think of Betina when I hear the song, *Aquanile*.' I hugged her.

When the doors of the black sedan closed with a clunk, the tiny stature of Betina waving enthusiastically appeared as a lost soul stood among the tall men in dark coats.

'You're unusually quiet,' Gerrysan laughed and pushed my shoulder.

'I can't help feel for Betina, she's a fallen angel in a cruel world,' I frowned.

At the airport, Gerrysan's flight left on time but I had a few hours to wait. In the departure lounge, I heard a recurring message being broadcast over the tannoy but could not make out the exact wording. 'Concurso mercantile,' meaning bankruptcy. A representative of the airline confirmed the bad news that the service was cancelled and there were no alternatives.

The Silver Cities and Michoacán 2005

TRAINS ARE A RARE FORM OF TRAVEL IN MEXICO BUT THE BUS network is extensive, efficient and cheap. The private motorways are pristine with a small amount of traffic but car hire was a risky option for a lone foreigner. I decided to make my way overland by bus from Puebla to Guadalajara and take the opportunity to visit several romantic cities on the way. Furthermore, the route ran through the magical indigenous state of Michoacán within the heartland of Mexico.

Bus journeys in Mexico had varying levels of comfort. The cheapest by far was the American style school bus with open windows referred to as the chicken carrier, el pollero, often gaily coloured and always full. The scale gravitated from the rickety up to the finest in the super executive – a luxurious and secure coach with air conditioning, food and drink served by an attendant, a TV screen every three rows and a toilet at the rear. It carried a maximum of fourteen passengers in wide leather reclining seats.

The sleek super executive took three hours to reach my first stopover, Cuernavaca, in the state of Morelos. I checked into a seedy motel near the bus station and bought a few tacos from a street seller. I ate them sitting cross-legged on an old iron hospital bed and watched Tin Tan on a small fuzzy black and white portable TV.

The next day, I booked an overnight bus to Guanajuato, a Silver City. These silver-mining cities produced two thirds of the world's silver during the colonial period which also included: San Miguel de Allende, Querétaro, San Luis Potosí and Zacatecas which lie to the northwest of Mexico City in the mountains of the Sierra Madre Occidental.

As the coach did not leave until midnight, it gave me enough time to walk down to the Palace of Cortes, situated in the centre of Cuernavaca. The Palace had been the sixteenth century home of Hernan Cortes, the Spanish Conquistador who had overthrown the Aztec empire. One of the oldest civil structures from that period with the added bonus of murals painted by Diego Rivera, regarded as one of the most influential Mexican artists of the twentieth century. Rivera's work depicted the lives and struggles of the Mexican working class. He had created his own style, known as Mexicanidad, which gave rise to the movement of the same name and focused on indigenous heritage and culture. He was also known for his stormy relationship with Frida Kahlo whose role within Mexicanidad was displayed through her use of Aztec objects. The Palace was all mine, I was the sole visitor surrounded by Diego Rivera's enormous historical narratives portraying the Mexican War of Independence of 1821. A chapter which finally brought justice to a people long oppressed by foreign powers.

The following morning the coach began its descent into Guanajuato, capital of the state with the same name. The view from the high pass was a spectacular display of tangerine, strawberry and lilac coloured sandstone buildings clinging to the mountainside. We wound our way down the steep incline into the city's underground bus station. I walked through the dark tunnels and up the steep cobblestoned alleyways to its heart where I found a room in the charming Hotel San Diego next door to the magnificent Juarez Theatre.

In the hacienda style four storey hotel, my balcony overlooked what was probably Mexico's finest theatre and possibly the most outstanding structure within a city of many fine buildings. The façade of Juarez Theatre was neoclassical in style with wide stone steps which led up to a majestic entrance supported by twelve stone pillars that mirrored the Pantheon of Rome. On each of the eight stone plinths were bronze statues depicting the Muses of Greek mythology. An old world charm inside was given further prominence by the wrought iron lampposts in the foyer. There was a profusion of polished wood, stained glass and velvety red and gold furnishings, including an idiosyncratic art nouveau smoking room.

My second balcony had a bird's eye view over the zocalo which was triangular in shape and positioned alongside the Union Garden, a small park surrounded by manicured, box-cut laurel trees. This foliage gave shade to young lovers as they strolled hand in hand while listening to the mariachi music playing in the square...my mind drifted to Güerita.

'Maybe one day we will visit the Hotel San Diego and stay in this very room,' I thought to myself.

As it was only two hours away from Guanajuato and in the direction of Michoacán state, I visited San Miguel de Allende, also a Silver City. A cultured place with a baroque style of architecture, thriving arts scene and a tourist hotspot inhabited by American expats. At the bus station, I ate a hot corn on the cob smeared with red chilli butter and returned to the street seller for another. I spent the rest of the day wandering around pretty cobbled avenues filled with lavender-coloured blossom of the jacaranda trees. Various art galleries and workshops were set amongst the well preserved colonial buildings coloured apricot, ruby red and Persian blue. The magnificent gothic façade of the Parroquia de San Miguel Arcangel church was constructed from terracotta sandstone and dominated the zocalo. After dark, it was illuminated by a spectrum of mauves and warm yellows which gravitated up the building to a brightly-lit cross on a pink spire.

That evening the super executive left for Morelia, the state capital of Michoacán, where I transferred to a local bus for Lake Patzcuaro. In the early morning sunlight, the mist lingered on the silvery-blue water of the lake surrounded by dark green mountains as the fishermen in wooden boats cast their butterfly nets. I waited on the jetty for the first ferry of the day which took thirty minutes to sail over to the tiny island village of Janitzio.

Janitzio is home to the indigenous Purépecha who were never conquered by the Aztec Empire and is known as the epicentre of the Day of the Dead, Dia de los Muertos. This celebration takes place during March when deceased loved ones return to the land of the living. The people of Michoacán consider death as a continuation of life and each year they make an abundance of handicrafts for the festival. These items range from skeleton dolls in hand-made dresses to plastic skulls as ashtrays, mugs and lanterns. The island is also noted for its Indian woven textiles, lacquered wood boxes and basketry made of reeds from the lake. A subdued market sold these wares under the arches of colonial buildings with their wrought iron balconies and whitewashed walls which contrasted to the terracotta coloured doors and windows frames. The colour combination that personified Michoacán.

Mexicans in general viewed the state of Michoacán as a foreign country, which I totally empathised with, as the architecture and overall feel was unlike anywhere else I had visited in Latin America, including Mexico.

In the Hotel Patzcuaro, I was the only guest and advised not to go out after dark. A chunky handmade blanket of coloured patchwork was draped over an antique bedstead in the fusty bedroom. Outside my door, the internal balcony overlooked a creepy foyer with a wooden floor painted black as thunder. It was barely illuminated by dark candles flickering in hidden recesses, a setting which typified Michoacán and its pre-Hispanic traditions. The next day a local bus took me to Uruapan, Michoacán's second city, where I boarded a super executive coach for Guadalajara.

Guadalajara 2005

IN TLAQUEPAQUE, I CALLED ANTONIO TO DISCOVER GÜERITA WAS still in Paris staying at the Raffles Le Royal Monceau Hotel. She would be arriving in Guadalajara a few days before I left for Europe. What was I to do?

I called her hotel in Paris.

'Hola Güerita.'

'Quien es?'

'Meeles de Guadalajara.'

'You're turning into a Tapatio,' she laughed, 'Thank you for the beautiful dolphin sculpture from Puerto Vallarta.'

'Are you available Friday?'

'Of course but you have to choose the venue.'

'La Nueva Posada Hotel in Ajijic.'

'What a lovely idea, I went there with my father on my fourteenth birthday and they served whitebait from the lake.'

'I will make the reservation.'

'Thank you Miles, I look forward, kisses.'

I called the hotel to book two rooms and chose a table in the restaurant next to the scarlet macaws.

Güerita and I arrived in Ajijic at the same time as if the spiritual birds on the wing had landed simultaneously. Our eyes smiled and we reunited like an old pair of slippers, it felt comfortable and homely. We meandered down to the lakeside chattering about art, travel, animals and the important things in life like love and laughter.

In the evening, Güerita wore a classic black dress as she walked into the restaurant all heads turned towards this refined lady. We were beaming. Even the parrots were swaying back and forth on their perch. For a moment we both stopped talking. I gazed into her soft golden eyes, our arms reached out and the moment her elegant fingers wrapped around mine, the big red parrot squawked, 'Watcha baby.' We laughed and the parrots cackled.

From the balcony we stared at the moon's reflection on the lake before she lowered her eyelids, squeezed my hand and retired into her room. I attempted to sleep and repeatedly stood under a cold shower hoping to cool down without success. When I did eventually drop off, a screeching 'cock-a-doodle-doo' woke me up a few hours later. Drowsily, I stepped onto the balcony at sunrise and Güerita appeared with a smile.

'Good morning mi amor,' she ran her finger lightly down my cheek and kissed me softly as the orange-red orb peeked over the horizon.

Over the weekend, we found ourselves relaxing in the courtyard bars and quaint cafes having spontaneous discussions with local people. In the galleries, we discovered the quality of the local artists to be exceptional and particularly admired Ernesto Velazquez who worked from a studio next to the lake. His immense watercolours radiated vibrancy and somehow captured the essence of Ajijic.

On our final morning, during coffee at the same table next to the macaws, I wanted to smooth away any uncertainty.

'I will see you soon, very soon.' I spoke from the heart to reassure us both. 'In New York, Memphis, Guadalajara or Newcastle, wherever you are, I will be there.'

We agreed to call each other every other day, until we met again. The minute she left, I felt myself descending into an emotional turmoil but took control and made my way to reception to check out.

The manageress smiled, 'Where's your partner?'

'She's gone to Memphis.'

'You're a lovely couple.'

'Thank you.'

'The account is settled but don't forget the painting.'

She gave me a metre long tube with a handwritten message, 'For our home one day, te quiero, Güerita xx.'

Rolled up inside was an original watercolour of a traditional fishing boat with white sails on Lake Chapala by E. Velazquez whose stunning image had been my favourite.

Now that the cactus project in Mexico had come to an end, I travelled back to England as Güerita began her assignment in Memphis. From the office in Newcastle, I worked with the Danes and continued to manage shipments of cactus powder and prickly pear concentrate. We liaised with Abel, Antonio and Guillermo to effect deliveries from Mexico to South Korea and Japan. Güerita and I kept to our promise.

Occasionally on sunny days, I would collect my fishing gear and meet Geordie at the marina. A stocky, bearded and red-faced skipper whose boat, Northern Soul, took us on the

North Sea to catch cod near the Farne Islands off the coast of Northumberland. At dawn, we chugged out of Seahouses harbour and onto the smooth rolling swell. Dazzling rays of sunlight sparkled over the steely blue water. A gentle south-westerly wind followed us to our first fishing mark between the silhouette of Bamburgh Castle and the characteristic red and white stripes of Longstone lighthouse. Busy puffins skipped over the water with their colourful stripy beaks stuffed full of silvery sand eels. Large blubbery grey seals with docile eyes and pointed whiskers lay stretched out, sunning themselves on windswept rocks. Geordie cut the diesel engine and as it spluttered to a silence my mobile rang out.

'Hola Miles, how are you today?' said Güerita.

'Hola mi amor, I'm feeling great now that I hear your voice. Are you in New York?'

'Yes my darling, I arrived not long ago. The assignment will be finished in seven days.'

'I want to take you somewhere special at the weekend. Can you manage a month's leave?'

'Why not? Rosa is at an English school in Vancouver until December.'

When she hung up I was in another world until Geordie grunted, 'You've got a fish on man, put that bloody phone away and stop talkin' shite, its' wor first cod of the day man for Christ's sake!'

Clusters of crying seagulls hovered noisily overhead as we glided through the harbour entrance. Geordie edged Northern Soul into a mooring alongside bright blue, red and yellow fishing vessels neatly stacked in rows along the harbour wall.

'Geordie!' I yelled above the noise of the rattling and rasping motor, 'Keep all the fish, I'm in a hurry.'

'Are ee mad or what, ya daft bugga? Cheers son!' He shouted as I ran up the slipway.

By midnight, I booked a flight to New York and our two tickets from New York to San José in Costa Rica known in Latin America as Pura Vida. My life was ready to be transformed...

VIVA MEXICO

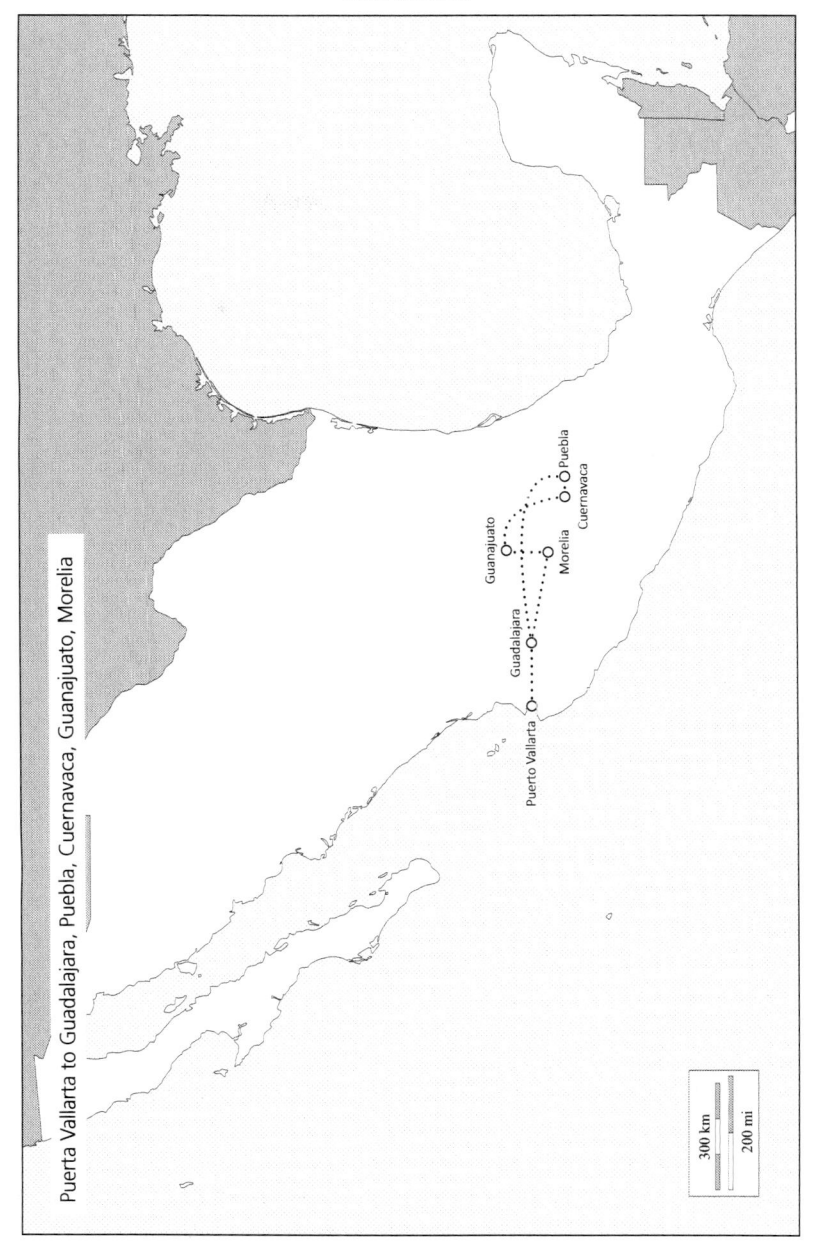

Puerta Vallarta to Guadalajara, Puebla, Cuernavaca, Guanajuato, Morelia

17 Pura Vida

'And if travel is like love, it is, in the end, mostly because it's a heightened state of awareness, in which we are mindful, receptive, undimmed by familiarity and ready to be transformed. That is why the best trips, like the best love affairs, never really end.' Pico Iyer

New York City 2006

Geordie would give me a lift to Newcastle Airport. I sat in the garden waiting for his arrival and gazed at the panoramic blue skies of Northumberland that stretched out to the end of the world. The cool March easterly howled through the budding lime trees. A delicate soufflé of cumuli diffused the sunlight and threw brilliant beams at clusters of daffodils – neon yellow daubs on lush green fields – splashes of egg yolk under square-cut hedgerows. Dark rooks transported beakfuls of dry twigs to a kaahing chorus of feverish nest building. The farmers' dog barked and a crowded rookery exploded like dust from a thrashed pillow. An English springtime was a delightful time of year and a rosy harbinger of an impending summer.

Geordie's red MG Midget with the hood down appeared at the front gate, his white-bearded silhouette protruding from the vehicle. We drove through the winding country lanes to the drop off point outside the terminal, he wished me luck, 'Watch wat ya deein in them foreign places mind and gie hor one for me,' he laughed.

Seven relaxing hours later, the aircraft approached New York City and circled the twinkling golden skyline several times before landing. At the transportation desk in JFK airport, I ordered a cab into the core of the Big Apple, Manhattan.

'Berkeley Hotel at the top of 7th,' I said to the driver.

Güerita would complete her assignment the following day and by the end of the week we would be in Costa Rica. Our suite on the second floor had views over Central Park and opposite to Carnegie's Deli where I took brunch at a window seat. An endless stream of canary yellow cabs glided down the avenue over smooth tarmac in-between alternating shadows cast by the lofty skyscrapers. A sandwich of corned beef on rye was served as a family-sized flank of meat cut into slabs and stacked neatly between two slices of rye bread with a lone gherkin on the side.

In preparation for Güerita's arrival, a mariachi four-piece dressed in red and grey charro outfits would perform her favourite song *Qué Bonito Amor* as she entered the hotel foyer. A florist in Little Italy arranged for fifty red velvet roses to be delivered fresh in the morning and a reservation was made at Morello's – a quintessential bistro in Greenwich Village known for its mix of classic and contemporary with a rustic twist.

The following day the concierge called, 'Ms Robledo Santos has arrived, sir.' In the foyer I gave the musicians their cue and appeared through the band brandishing her bouquet of flowers. Güerita looked shocked as she threw her arms around me and laughed through her tears. The mariachi continued singing in the elevator alongside the waiter clutching our silver ice bucket of Dom Pérignon. The suite door closed behind us with a 'Do Not Disturb' sign and pop went the champagne. Eventually, we emerged arm in arm with shy smiles and made it to Morello's albeit a day late.

In Greenwich Village we strolled down Bleecker Street for some night air and stopped to listen to the rich, melodic sound of the blues filtering through a hidden entrance onto the sidewalk. I peeked inside and raised an eyebrow but Güerita looked unsure. The darkened venue was full of

New Yorkers being entertained by a celebrated singer on a small stage when, as I was about to close the door, the music suddenly stopped.

'Hey yo honkies!' Her voice echoed around the chamber.

'Us?' I said quizzically.

'Yeah, yo honey, get yer ass right down here,' she bellowed.

The crowd opened up a passageway and we walked through the cavernous room to the two empty barstools in front of Sweet Georgia Brown. Unknown outside New York, the locals called her 'The Queen of the Village' and 'The last of the Red Hot Blues Mamas' who would at a later date steal the show from B.B. King at the Montreux Jazz Festival. After a memorable night, we skipped up 7th Avenue through flurries of snowflakes.

The next morning, the hotel was invaded by hundreds of pugs and their owners who were attending a dog show. In the lifts and corridors these charismatic little creatures stared up into our eyes with their comical, inquisitive short-muzzled faces. They were often given aristocratic names like: Ophelia, Kipling, Granville or Milton. I remember Winston, a pug owned by my cousin whose other pets were two Alsatians but Winston was firmly in charge and he ruled the household.

During our last night in New York, we walked through Central Park to a floodlit open-air ice rink and watched the dark bulky figures in furry flap-hats sail across the white frost. It reminded us of an L.S. Lowry painting, a twentieth century English artist known for his 'matchstick men' imagery of human figures. On the pathway, fast-moving rollerbladers clad in vivid Lycra with matching helmets whooshed by as we made our way to the Russian Tea Rooms on 57th Street.

Founded by members of the Russian Imperial Ballet in 1927 this legendry club and restaurant, near to Carnegie Hall and the Metropolitan Tower, was a regular meeting place for New York's elite. Located inside a typical NYC brownstone building whose narrow frontage was squeezed between two skyscrapers. It was a special event to dine in their opulent

Bear Lounge with its tapestry style wood flooring under spectacular chandeliers.

We sat on luxurious cherry-red soft leather bench seats in a horseshoe shaped booth next to a golden samovar. Chilled Stolichnaya vodka was served neat in crystal goblets on a silver tray with pickled cucumber. Our table was surrounded by mirrored walls which reflected the scarlet and amber lighting. In front, a full-sized glass sculpture of a juggling bear took centre stage. We feasted on their celebrated red borscht; beef, braised in a short-rib broth with bright red pickled beetroot and sour cream. Güerita and I discussed the contrast between her lifestyle in Guadalajara and time spent at university in Denver.

'How did you find Colorado by comparison to Jalisco?'

'The American culture is different way of life. Activities are prearranged by appointment and there's less opportunity for spontaneity which is at the heart of a Latino lifestyle. Most people in the USA do their food shopping at out-of-town malls whereas we buy our produce from local markets.'

'During my time in Mexico, I noticed friends were treated as family members.'

'Yes, that's right, friends are family. Our home is an open door. People arrive unannounced at any time of day and are always made to feel welcome. Each morning we prepare food for these visits.'

'Do you remember a different Mexico from your childhood?'

'Oh yes, during the school holidays my parents sent us to Aunt Angelita and Uncle Rafael's farm. When I think back, there was no running water or electricity and it was like living in the nineteenth century,' she enthused.

'Where was their farmhouse?'

'La Sienaga, an isolated settlement deep inside Los Altos de Jalisco.'

'How long did it take your Dad to drive from Guadalajara?'

'After two hours the road narrowed into a bridle path,' she smiled, 'We left the trucks and travelled on horseback. It took a full day to climb up and over the mountain to the river below and through the mango forest to their remote valley. The farmhouse was close to a waterfall and surrounded by sweet lime trees. It was built from blocks of mud held together with grass. The roof was tiled with clay and the open windows were covered with mosquito nets. Inside the kitchen, the work surface was a mud bench with a wood fire underneath. There was a round metal plate over the flames where various items were cooked at the same time: a pot of black coffee with cane molasses sugar, a pan of red beans and a casserole dish of rice with milk and cinnamon. They all surrounded the tortillas in the middle,' she laughed.

'Incredible, I can visualise it. My grandparents in Northumberland had an outside toilet with no running water and a neat wad of newspaper squares threaded through string. There were electric lights in two rooms. The cast-iron range kept the terraced cottage warm and baked the food. The fruit scones from the hot plate were delicious.'

'I'll make those for you one day, with cinnamon. In La Sienaga, portable oil lamps lit the house and the mud walls and terracotta floors kept us cool. We bathed ourselves in the river using salvia, a leaf which frothed up like soap. The plunge pool under the waterfall was a social venue for the older girls who pummelled the laundry on smooth rocks while boys would gather round hoping to find a partner. They also helped us carry the cantáros, the water-filled terracotta urns, back to the house,' she gave an embarrassed smile.

I laughed, 'Once a week on a Sunday night my grandmother would scrub my body as I sat in a portable tin bath in front of a coal fire and she used the soapy water to wash the kitchen floor. In the half-light we would play monopoly or grandad would show me how to make a catapult.'

She gushed, 'We had so much fun playing games on the patio under the shade of a willow tree, even my uncle and aunt joined in.'

'My grandparents died together on the same night. They were in their late eighties,' I said.

'That's so sad, they must have been in love and couldn't live without each other. My uncle was ninety-eight when he passed away and my auntie died soon after from a broken heart at ninety-two. I loved them,' her eyes moistened.

We left the cosiness of the Russian Tea Rooms and stepped out into the freezing black night with a sharp intake of breath. Güerita held my arm as we braced ourselves against the icy headwind and walked along the frosty sidewalks up West 57th Street and down 7th Avenue through swirls of snow. We tumbled out of the darkness into the brightly lit lobby with happy red faces.

Huddled together under the duvet in our queen bed with the curtains open, we stared out at the glowing, gleaming and glittering night lights of a Manhattan luminescence. After a few minutes, I watched Güerita's eyes drowse into a peaceful slumber.

Costa Rica 2006

IN SIX SWIFT HOURS WE WERE TRANSPORTED FROM THE COLD northern climes of New York City to the warm sunshine of Costa Rica and their attractive capital, San José. Close to Sabana Park, referred to as the lungs of the city, we stayed overnight in a thatched pension and swapped the coats and scarves for t-shirts and shorts. The tropical dawn chorus was our alarm call. We hired a jeep and bought a map before leaving San José and motoring up country without a plan.

When we stopped for breakfast at a wooden café in a deserted ramshackle village, there were wild monkeys loitering on street corners. A happy old woman brought us coffee onto the veranda in tin pots as the spider monkeys came a step closer. They were light brown or red and black with white chin whiskers and used their tails as a fifth hand to manoeuvre through the trees.

'Please don't give any food to the monkeys. It makes them fat and lazy,' said the happy woman, 'Normally they travel up to ten miles a day picking fruit and nuts.'

A group of young men with glistening skin and carrying machetes appeared from nowhere. Güerita instantly connected with them in their native Spanish and together we studied the map. Costa Ricans were fond of Mexicans and especially those from Guadalajara, the birthplace of mariachi, so we felt welcome. With the benefit of their local knowledge we would visit the volcanic district to the northwest, followed by the coffee plantations nearby and then make our way down to the pacific coast.

Costa Rica is not a huge country, about twice the size of Scotland with twelve climatic zones which vary from hot and humid dense jungle to cold and frosty cloud forests. In the north, it is bordered by Nicaragua and to the south by Panama, the Caribbean Sea is to the east and the Pacific Ocean to the west. It became one of the greenest nation states on earth when the government abolished the armed forces in 1948 and declared most of the country a national park. There is a strong emphasis on education and English is spoken extensively, especially on the coast and in the larger cities. It has a reputation as one of the safest places in Latin America. The Costa Ricans refer to themselves as 'Ticos' and to their homeland as 'Pura Vida' or 'Pure Life.' It is a pacifist society with more teachers than policemen and has followed a path of peace in an area of the world notorious for its violence.

We travelled inland through the rain forests to the state of Alajuela known as the land of mangos and home to the most active volcano in the world, El Arenal. We soon realised why a four wheel-drive truck was essential as we cautiously climbed the narrow potholed road, hewn into the vertical mountainside, up to the base of El Arenal. There we discovered rivers of hot clear water which flowed down from the volcano into the dense vegetation. In the forest we spotted the long vibrant coloured beaks of wild toucans, the bright reds and yellows of macaws in flight and several smaller ruby-red birds with black wings called scarlet tanagers.

On our way down the mountain, we drove round a tight bend and braked abruptly where the road had fallen away. It left barely enough space to edge the truck across but with no room for error. We stood staring at the vertical drop into the valley below when Enrique, a forest ranger, pulled up behind and offered to assist. He instructed us to walk to the other side of the landslip and direct him forward; he kept the doors ajar to jump free in case they toppled over the bluff. Both vehicles scraped the mountainside as he moved each one, inch by inch, to safety. It enabled us to resume our journey but darkness descended as if someone had switched off the lights. It was too dangerous to continue in the pitch-black so Enrique took us to a family home tucked away up a bumpy trail belonging to Isabel and Alonso, a retired couple who occasionally let their spare room to eco-travellers and where we stayed overnight.

On their wooden terrace Isabel cooked casado, a typical Costa Rican dish of black beans, rice and crispy plantains; a vegetable-banana fried in butter while they are still green. These plantains tasted more like sweet potato than a banana. As we dined, a flock of parakeets landed on my shoulders. I froze, thinking they would take chunks out of my ears, until Alonso introduced them as Rodrigo, Julio and Ana. They were his pets and lived in the garden. While Isabel and Güerita did the washing-up, Alonso placed a bottle of guaro on the table – strong clear liquor distilled from sugar cane – a sweet tasting drink that trickled fire.

'You must visit Marino Las Baulas,' said Alonso.

'What is it?' I asked.

'A national park where you will see more animals and birds than the whole of South America,' Alonso said proudly.

'Costa Rica must be the only country in the world with no armed forces? I queried.

'The state do employ some private militia for certain duties including the patrolling of the Nicaraguan border, which helps reduce the flow of illegal immigrants entering the country.'

'Are they fleeing an unstable environment for a better life?'

'No doubt in some cases but we do not want these people. Many have criminal backgrounds and cause trouble in our country,' he poured more guaro, 'Those who survive the perilous journey make for a district in downtown San José which we call, 'Little Managua,' after the capital of Nicaragua.'

'I believe there was only one per cent difference between the two parties during the general election?' I enquired.

'Yes, the voters were split down the middle and Óscar Arias Sánchez was confirmed as our new president as of yesterday. He's an old hand at the job and has a Noble Peace Laureate from his previous tenure during the Central American Crisis of the 80s.'

Alonso dribbled the last of the guaro into my glass and soon after we retired to a basic wooden hut in their garden with fly screens for windows and a whirring table fan. We lay on the thin rubber mattress and tuned in to the tropical soundscape of the forest at night while watching the silhouettes of bats zig-zag across the full moon.

In the early morning, Güerita was the most relaxed I had ever seen her, smiling and chatting as she helped Isabel prepare breakfast in their tiny kitchen. The family of curious parakeets joined us on the terrace where we enjoyed poached duck eggs and red beans with local coffee.

After leaving Isabel and Alonso's home, we descended to the valley below and started to ascend once again but this time the mountain was much higher. We drove up and up through a dense cumulus with our main beam and fog lights blaring and popped out onto a clear sunny plateau where we discovered a biodiverse forest next to a coffee plantation. The moisture from the low passing clouds drip fed the ecosystem that produced the fine coffee and supported a bewildering array of animals, birds and plants.

In the tiny mountaintop village of Santa Elena, we hired a cosy room in a wooden lodge with commanding views over the now wispy cumuli. The cloud forest below hung either side of a vertiginous gorge with a frothy opal-green river threading through the middle.

Outside our cabin, the air carried a fragrance of pork roasting over coffee wood and the sound of the crackling embers lured us to a nearby café. Shots of guaro were served with the tender, juicy and smoky meat on a bed of rice with black beans and fried plantains.

At sunrise we walked through the mist over a hillock and amongst the shrub-like trees of a coffee plantation. Their shiny red berries hung in clusters beneath the evergreen leaves. Something rustling in the foliage turned out to be a family of Baird tapirs who crossed our path. The oldest male was much bigger than a pig, close to 200 kilos. Their impressive nose is a prehensile snout equivalent to a miniature elephant's trunk. One of the younger tapirs wandered towards us stopping only a metre away; she rooted around in the twigs, occasionally raising her head and twitching her nostrils before ambling back to the group. They were not afraid of humans.

A few days later on the mountain descent, Güerita spotted more tapirs scrambling out of a lake. As we got closer, the animals were much smaller than a tapir, almost fifty kilos in weight. They were in fact capybaras in a pack of twenty. Alonso had described these animals as the largest rodents in the world which resembled a colossal guinea pig that barked like a dog. I took a photograph of a young capybara with what I thought was a kingfisher standing on its back, but once enlarged the bird proved to be a motmot – the national bird of Costa Rica identified by its bright turquoise tail feather.

Driving along the Pacific Ocean through leafy lanes on the Nicoya Peninsular, known as the Gold Coast, we tumbled to a stop in the middle of a quiet village next to Brasilito Bay. As the engine noise faded and the dust settled, we gave each other a knowing look and made a decision to stay for a while. Something in that late afternoon appealed to our sixth sense and told us Brasilito was a special place. A fisherman directed us to a decrepit wooden house hotel next to a beautiful white beach made from millions of tiny sea shells. The owner, Otto, was a balding German with a flabby pot belly who continually mopped his forehead with a filthy grey handkerchief. Our room was a garden shed with a ceiling fan, but its location, on that exceptional beach overlooking the sea, was superb. The weekly rental amounted to a fistful of colons so it was cheap, wild, peaceful and safe. We welcomed it as our temporary home.

Within a couple of days we had integrated into the small community of Brasilito Ticos. I helped Mauricio on his open boat line-fishing in Brasilito Bay for Corvina (Sea Bass), Pargo Rojo (Red Snapper) and Dorado (Mahi Mahi) while Güerita painted seascapes in an open studio with Martha and Emmanuel, an affable Tico couple who were wildlife artists.

Otto asked us to switch off the light or close the shutters at night as the glow disorientated the leatherback turtles. In the moonlight through our bedroom window we watched these creatures paddle up the beach. At dawn their flippers worked hard to propel them back down over the sea shells into the water. They were much bigger than I imagined. Emmanuel told us leatherbacks are usually between 300 and 500 kilos but official records show these turtles to weigh up to 1,000 kilos.

There was such an abundance of fruit varieties in Costa Rica and each day we drank pure juice from the green coconuts, guavas or papayas. One morning a neighbour left a basket of zapotes on our veranda. They reminded me of a large green avocado but with a bright orange-red flesh that tasted of a velvety molasses.

'The Mexican version is called sapote with a black skin and pulp which is very sweet,' said Güerita.

On Juan Santamaria day, a public holiday, everyone in the village was invited to a commemoration which honoured a Costa Rican soldier. Juan Santamaria was a national hero from the nineteenth century who made a decisive contribution in the war with Nicaragua and lost his life in the process. At sunset, the salty aroma of barbequed fish permeated the warm humid breeze. The inhabitants gathered on long communal tables illuminated by pools of orange glow from hanging oil lanterns. Many of the villagers brought their own special dish to make up the buffet. Our table had a peppery Corvina ceviche, black bean soup, empanadas, chayote (a type of green squash) and tapa dulce, a sweet made from raw cane sugar.

The fiesta was in full swing when a ragtag army of around 100 men with rifles strapped over their chests marched into town. They were led by a giant of a man wearing a pirate's black beard and crowned by a shiny shaven head. The column of soldiers stopped to attention next to our party and Otto invited their commander, Santiago, to join us. Santiago barked a deep resonant instruction to his platoon who promptly disappeared into the darkness. Otto introduced him as the general whose private army was responsible for preventing illegal immigrants making it through the jungle from Nicaragua into Costa Rica. He sat next to me and hung his hairy arm around my neck exuding a strong odour of sweat, guaro and cannabis.

'You are the slimmest American I have ever met.' He talked through his bushy facial hair.

The party resumed its previous ambience as Santiago and I engaged in conversation.

'That's because I'm English,' I chortled, 'If you don't mind me asking, how do you stop illegal immigrants walking through a forest? Do you have roadblocks?'

He spat out his beer and roared with laughter. He told the party my question and they cheered.

'We shoot them!' he guffawed.

I felt a bit silly. He described the border as being 200 miles of dense jungle which the government hired his militia to patrol. As the night progressed Santiago became more sozzled, stripping off his shirt to the waist to show the ladies his nine bullet wounds.

'Must be his party trick,' chuckled Otto.

'I'm surprised it's only nine, he's an easy target,' I laughed.

In the early hours, when the fiesta had petered out, I walked up to the far end of Brasilito Bay with Santiago. His men were asleep on the sand apart from a hard core drinking guaro around the smouldering cinders of a camp fire. Santiago told me initially, he had worked for the government in land management and changed to a new career in security. He had spent time in Colombia where he trained in jungle warfare. His brother Eduardo was a magazine editor for the National Theatre and lived in San José. Santiago scrawled Eduardo's number on a cigarette paper and gave it to me should I need a local contact. We chatted continuously throughout the night about all aspects of life in Latin America. At first light, I stood up precariously after having had too much of everything and shook his hand before staggering back to the hut, careful not to wake Güerita. She was curled up in a ball and fast asleep. I crawled under the sheet and held her in my arms. The next day Santiago and his men had vanished.

We continued to live in the village as if we were Brasilito Ticos and used it as a base from which to explore the west coast. We visited the white sands of Conchal beach and the Nicoya Peninsula to the south, careful to avoid the muddy river banks which were home to the long and wide docile looking crocodiles that slithered in and out of the water. When they moved rapidly and without warning, it was unnerving. In the Marino Las Baulas National Park we took an image of a miniature anteater feeding on a huge anthill surrounded by mauve, pink and blue orchids.

Mauricio had a passion for these flowers, 'There are over 1400 different species of orchid in Costa Rica.' He possessed a wall of books on the subject.

Güerita has a fear of rats and I vividly remember an instance in Mexico when we came across two large rodents in the food cupboard. She flew out the door and kept on running, returning home with a pest control squad armed with adhesive squares which they placed on the kitchen floor. After an evening out, we returned to find two big rats stuck firmly to the glue and staring up at us. We spent the night at her sisters. When an agouti, which has the appearance of a gigantic rat, ran past her feet, she jumped up into the air with a squeal so loud that several people rushed out from their houses in a state of alarm.

For our friends in Brasilito, Güerita prepared a Costa Rican banquet with clams, crab, shrimp, squid and gallo pinto. She added in some Mexican chipotle to spice up a local recipe. Round the table, the conversational chatter suddenly died when Otto took an urgent call. The volcano, El Arenal, had erupted in the same park where we spent the afternoon next to the clear rivers and three gardeners had lost their lives. The area was now covered in molten magma.

Güerita sent a postcard earlier with an image of the volcano to her family so we made contact to put their minds at rest. Once online, there were urgent messages from my business in the UK. Otto's computer and internet connection were virtually non-existent. The only way in which to deal with the matter was to travel back to San José, stay in the Radisson Hotel and use their business facilities. In the meantime the Newcastle office would send the documents for signature. In my absence, Martha and Emmanuel suggested Güerita join them to tour the art galleries in Liberia, a town twenty miles from Brasilito.

The alarm woke me at 5am. Güerita was already up, had cooked an English breakfast and prepared my hand luggage.

'Take care on these crazy roads my love,' she gave me a blessing.

San José is situated on a plateau 1,000 metres above sea level in the Central Valley region of the country with the Talamanca Mountains to the south. It took five hours to drive from Brasilito on rough roads and muddy tracks to the capital.

I manoeuvred the now filthy jeep through the colonial streets of the city to the hotel and for the first time became aware of the sophistication and elegance of San José.

The time difference with England was in my favour so I got straight to work. By late evening, exhausted but happy, most of the communications were up to date. The following day, I had a lengthy conference call with the office and FedEx collected the signed documents.

Otto and Mauricio had given me a shopping list of marine engine parts and machine tools not available outside the main city but the hotel staff were unsure of the correct stockists. A solution sprang to mind and I contacted Santiago's brother, Eduardo.

'Hello Eduardo, my name is Miles from England. I met your brother in Brasilito, I hope you don't mind me calling with a request?'

'Hola Miles, it would be a pleasure to assist. Santiago told me all about you. How can I help?'

'I'm in San José for a few days and there are some specialist items to take back to Brasilito but I have no idea where to find them.'

'Come to my office in the morning at 10am. We'll meet in the Theatre Café which faces the Plaza de la Cultura. Take a red cab as they are registered cooperatives and are the cheapest. Ask the driver to take you to El Teatro Nacional.'

The following morning a red taxi took me to the National Theatre, a treasured historic building reputedly modelled on the Paris Opéra and the finest in San José. As I waited by the entrance to the café, a tall distinguished raven-haired man with candid green eyes and a walrus moustache strode towards me, 'Hola Miles, I'm Eduardo, mucho gusto,' he shook my hand.

'Thank you for your time and help, Ticos are kind people like your brother.'

'Santiago is a little crazy,' he said. 'One day, he could easily lose his life doing that dangerous job on the border. I try and get him to quit before the worst happens but he won't listen to reason.'

'I can understand your concern, especially since he's been shot nine times.'

'He didn't do that party trick in Brasilito, did he?'

I nodded and we both laughed.

'Come on, I will show you round the building. We have some remedial work going on so it will be brief.'

From the marble lobby, we toured the exquisitely decorated interior with its lavish furnishings. There were many breathtaking murals and paintings especially one which captured the essence of Costa Rican rural life, harvesting coffee and bananas, called *Alegoria al Café y al Banano* by an Italian artist, J. Vila. This gigantic painting of vibrant colours was a tremendous feature of the theatre but as Eduardo pointed out, 'The image is technically incorrect as it depicts a coffee plantation next to the sea when coffee actually grows at a much higher altitude,' he toyed with the tips of his moustache.

'The other anomaly is the plantation worker clutching a bunch of bananas as if it was a baby when the correct technique is to hoist it onto your shoulder.'

'Why the obvious mistakes?'

'An Italian artist who never visited Costa Rica.'

We continued to talk as we strolled into his office. He gave his assistant Jolanda the shopping list and asked her to drive to the different stores and buy each item. I handed her the cash. Eduardo had certain deadlines to meet and I had one last call to make so we agreed to reconvene at the hotel later and dine at a restaurant in the city.

I concluded the Skype discussion by early evening and planned to travel back to Brasilito in the morning. Reception handed me a heavy box which Jolanda had delivered earlier and it contained everything requested by Otto and Mauricio. They would be delighted.

In the Central Market, I bought two bottles of Cacique guaro for Eduardo and his assistant, some touristy type gifts for Martha and Emmanuel and a colourful hand-crocheted poncho for Güerita. Eduardo stood next to the fountain when I arrived back in the lobby. He reminded me of an intrepid traveller with his wide-brimmed Panama hat, wine-red smoking jacket and well-groomed walrus moustache.

'Jolanda did a great job, thank you very much.'

'It was my pleasure.'

We took a red cab to the Black Pearl, a trendy cocktail bar in a contemporary structure made from bamboo with sweeping night-time views over the city.

Eduardo ordered two Jaguar Coladas. 'What are these?' I grinned.

'They make the best JCs in town. Its guaro, passion fruit and coconut cream.'

Eduardo continued to select the various cocktails on offer and my head began to swim. We left the Black Pearl and took a taxi across the city to an Argentinian steakhouse in a splendid octagonal shaped building, painted an olive green. The fillet was gaucho grilled over a wood fire and I pencilled into my notebook, 'One of the best steaks in the Americas.'

During Santiago's military training in Colombia, Eduardo had visited him in Cartagena, a colourful colonial city next to the Caribbean Sea. When Santiago collected him from the airport, Eduardo noticed he was walking awkwardly. It transpired he had a handgun shoved into his trousers at the base of his back, one strapped to both of his lower legs, more under his armpits and another in his pocket.

'I know it's dangerous in this country but not quite WW3!' Eduardo had said to Santiago.

We laughed at the thought of Santiago unloading his weapons at bedtime, snoring away next to heaps of handguns with more jutting out from underneath the pillow. During the same trip, Eduardo had met his Colombian girlfriend at a museum in Cartagena and now Pilar was the love of his life.

'She's on a modelling assignment in Brazil for two weeks,' he said proudly.

My eyes were drawn to the blunt ends of Eduardo's walrus which had turned a mustard yellow from the consumption. He leaned forward as if to tell me a secret.

'There's a famous Tico saying,' he raised one eyebrow and slurred through his lip weasel, 'A man can only be a man, if a woman is a woman.'

I understood the underlying message from this Latin American paradox.

We had our final few beers in a quaint jazz café where we met some of Eduardo's friends, Lucia and her partner Mateo who managed a veterinary practise in Cartago. On the tiny dancefloor, Eduardo made us all laugh with a Fred Astaire routine in the style of a man being tasered. After the live music died away, I dipped into my bag and handed Eduardo the two gifts of Cacique guaro. I declined Mateo's offer to open one of the bottles right away. Eduardo and Pilar would visit us in Mexico or England. After the hugging and handshaking, I fell into a red cab back to the hotel. Walking to my room, the corridors swayed from side to side like the aisles of a cross channel ferry during a winter storm.

In the early hours, standing in front of the toilet in my comatose state, I suddenly panicked when a large brown gooey insect burrowed into my cheek. I slapped it away violently but on further inspection found it to be an After Eight chocolate mint the chambermaid had left on the pillow. I woke up to a trail of clothes from the door to the bed, the crisp white bedsheet had a chocolate-peppermint-streak running down the middle and my head was throbbing. At the breakfast buffet, I drank coffee after coffee before loading the jeep and gingerly driving out of the city.

At Santa Cruz, a pretty rural town on the way to Brasilito, I refuelled and drank yet more coffee. Sitting outside the café on their terrace, a family of cute capuchin monkeys were chasing each other through the trees. They were endearing creatures with cheeky white furry faces crowned by a black fluffy cap.

I pulled up outside Otto's as the sun was setting. Güerita ran out to greet me with a flying cuddle, 'Come with me, I have something special for you.' She looked radiant. On the veranda, a romantic buffet was laid out for two in the centre of which flickered a candle, shaped as an angel. She told me all about her exciting trip to Liberia and the art galleries.

Güerita talked enthusiastically, 'The Ticos call Liberia the white city because it has scores of whitewashed buildings clad with purple bougainvillea and pink magnolias. It's where the Costa Rican cowboy culture originates, known as the Sabanero. Rancheros ride around the streets on horseback and the wooden shops have raised sidewalks made from timber in the same way as Texas. It was like being in a western movie.'

In the galleries, she was inspired by the spirit of Tico art and read a passage from the local magazine, 'The intrinsic way in which local artists embody the exotic colours that define our tropical paradise with a freedom to express the vibrant sense of joy that flows through the Costa Rican lifestyle.'

'Their imagery is adorable, did you select a favourite artist?' I asked.

'I loved so many but if I had to pick one, it would be Francisco Amighetti for his wide variety of artistic styles.'

'Is he a Tico?'

'He's a local artist of Italian descent whose work epitomises Tico art.'

'Let's choose a painting by Francisco to take home.'

'Yes please.'

The next morning, Güerita told me of an eye-catching bird on the palm tree outside our front door making a sound like a whimpering dog. We managed to take photographs of this wondrous creature whose striking plumage was made up of azure blue with a ruby red breast and brilliantly green incredibly long tail feathers. Martha recognised the bird from the image as a resplendent quetzal – the most beautiful bird in all of the America's – whose feathers were regarded as treasure by the Aztecs with a value exceeding that of gold.

'They roost inside holes in trees made by the woodpeckers and their favourite food is a type of miniature avocado,' said Martha.

Otto and Mauricio were delighted with their tools and spare parts. They thought I would never be able to find everything. Otto refused to accept our final week's rent and Mauricio gave us a box of shrimps and a bottle of homemade guaro.

The village became active as everyone prepared for an impending storm. Otto asked for urgent help to secure the building with ratchet straps criss-crossed over the roof and tied onto four concrete blocks. All the loose items were removed from outside to inside: tables and chairs, barbeques and bicycles.

The wind started to gather strength to gale force and beyond. It became more terrifying as the menacing coal-black skies bore down on us and rotated like screws going into wood. The tempestuous sea transformed into an angry myriad of white crests. The darkness released rain with volleys of hailstone-gunfire which lashed the wooden structure with relentless energy. Strobic flashes of white lightening floodlit the night for a millisecond before resonant cracks thundered overhead and the building shuddered. At one point, the howling gale lifted the corner of the hut but the ratchet straps creaked and groaned in defiance. Outside our window, towering palm trees were bent over with their fronds reaching out like a girl blow-drying her long hair.

Güerita and I held each other tight under the bed sheet listening to the crashing, splashing, banging and clanging. I whispered in her ear, 'I love you with all the smiles and tears of my life.' Her golden eyes appeared and reappeared in the blue beams of flickering luminosity streaking from the violent night sky. 'Of course mi cariño, you are my half orange.'

The End

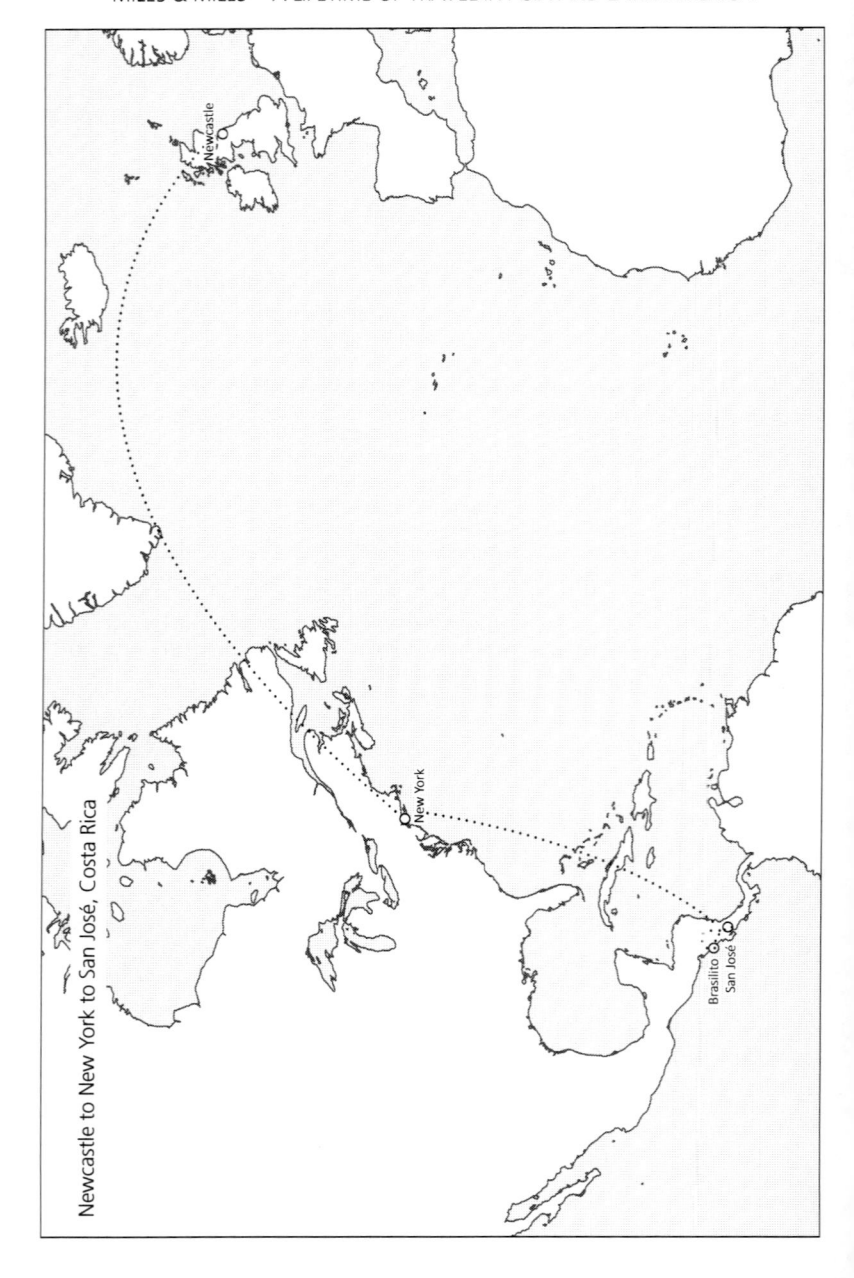

MILES & MILES ~ A LIFETIME OF TRAVEL IN ASIA AND LATIN AMERICA

Newcastle to New York to San José, Costa Rica

Printed in Great Britain
by Amazon